The COURT *of* APPEALS *of* INDIANA

★ ★ ★ ★ ★ ★ ★ ★ ★ ★ ★ ★ ★ ★ ★ ★ ★ ★ ★

The COURT *of* APPEALS *of* INDIANA

Edited by LINDA C. GUGIN *and* JAMES E. ST. CLAIR

Published by the Indiana Historical Society Press
in cooperation with the Court of Appeals of Indiana
Indianapolis 2022

Printed in the United States of America

This book is a publication of the
Indiana Historical Society Press
Eugene and Marilyn Glick Indiana History Center
450 West Ohio Street
Indianapolis, Indiana 46202-3269 USA
www.indianahistory.org
Telephone orders 1-317-234-0020
Online orders @ http://shop.indianahistory.org

The paper in this publication meets the minimum requirements of American National Standard for Information Sciences—Permanence of Paper for Printed Library Materials, ANSI Z39. 48–1984

Library of Congress Cataloging-in-Publication Data

Names: Gugin, Linda C., editor. | St. Clair, James E., editor.
Title: The Court of Appeals of Indiana / edited by Linda C. Gugin and James E. St. Clair.
Description: Indianapolis : Published by the Indiana Historical Society Press in cooperation with the Court of Appeals of Indiana, 2022. | Includes bibliographical references and index.
Identifiers: LCCN 2021017941 (print) | LCCN 2021017942 (ebook) | ISBN 9780871954602 (hardback) | ISBN 9780871954619 (epub)
Subjects: LCSH: Judges–Indiana–Biography. | Indiana. Court of Appeals–History.
Classification: LCC KF354.I56 C68 2022 (print) | LCC KF354.I56 (ebook) | DDC 347.772/0334–dc23
LC record available at https://lccn.loc.gov/2021017941
LC ebook record available at https://lccn.loc.gov/2021017942

Table of Contents

Acknowledgments

When we were asked to be coeditors of this book on the Court of Appeals of Indiana, we were happy to oblige. We saw it as an opportunity to write a companion book for the volume *Justices of the Indiana Supreme Court*, published by the Indiana Historical Society Press in 2010. The two courts are intertwined in many ways. The Court of Appeals has been a stepping-stone for many justices who have served on the Supreme Court. In fact, nine members of the Supreme Court we profiled in the *Justices* book had been judges on the Court of Appeals. The jurisdictions of the two courts have been inextricably intertwined. As the history of the Court of Appeals, outlined in the Milestone section of this book, reveals, changes made to reduce the caseload of the Supreme Court have resulted in the expansion of the jurisdiction of the Court of Appeals. And of course, decisions of the Court of Appeals, if appealable, will be heard by the U.S. Supreme Court. Those decisions will result in a reaffirmation or overturning of the decisions. The connections between these two courts will be evident throughout this book.

We believe this book will make an important contribution to Indiana legal history and the history of the state in general. It is written not only for lawyers and judges but also for the general public. We hope that the biographical essays of the 120 men and women judges who have served on the Court of Appeals will inform readers not only about legal matters but also about the people who contributed to the development of the Court of Appeals over its 130-year history.

The book has been in the making since early 2018, when we met with Judge Ted Najam, the main promoter of the project for the Court of Appeals; Ray E. Boomhower and Kathleen Breen, editors at the IHS Press; Amy Lamb, Vice President Marketing and Sales; and Elizabeth R. Osborn, the project director. We owe a debt of gratitude to many people who helped us along the way.

First, we are indebted to all of our contributors for their excellent scholarly work. We asked a lot of these very busy people who are mostly judges, lawyers, law clerks, court administrators and staff, university professors, and high school teachers, and we are grateful they were willing to take on the assignment. We were fortunate to reconnect with many authors who contributed to our previous works. We trust you know who you are.

Osborn, the project director, had a large responsibility for getting this work off the ground. She provided essential service in helping to organize the project and in recruiting many of the essay authors. Her connections to judges and staff at the Court of Appeals was a big benefit in this regard. She was also a sounding board for us as we encountered issues and questions along the way.

Larry Morris, Court Administrator for the Court of Appeals, provided invaluable help in answering factual questions we had about Court history, practices, and policies. Larry was our "go to" person on the Court and we appreciate how willingly he gave of his time and knowledge to help us with the myriad of questions that we had.

We also owe a debt to Brigette Adams, Secretary for the School of Social Sciences at Indiana University Southeast, who typed and revised many lists of authors and contributors for us. She never tired of our requests to prepare a list or redo something. She did this on her own time and without remuneration. Her work spared us a lot of time that we would have spent on these tasks.

Finally, our heartfelt thanks go to the wonderful staff at the IHS Press. These include Boomhower and Breen, who helped even after she retired. We cannot imagine tackling a book of this magnitude without the support and guidance of these two editors. We appreciate how they addressed all our needs and queries with such good grace, humor, and patience, as well as their expert eye that caught mistakes that we made in our editing duties. We expect they will be happy when our endless emails stop showing up in their Inbox.

Linda C. Gugin
James E. St. Clair

Milestones in the History of the Court of Appeals of Indiana

The Indiana Constitution of 1816, the nineteenth state's first constitution, created a state Supreme Court and Circuit Courts at the county level. There was no mention of an intermediate appellate court. Over time, as the population of the state grew, manufacturing increased, and changes in transportation facilitated movement from rural to urban areas, the state outgrew the 1816 constitution, prompting calls for a constitutional convention to propose a new constitution. The convention, held from 1850 to 1851, produced the Indiana Constitution of 1851. This document laid the groundwork for the eventual establishment of an intermediate court of appeals by the Indiana General Assembly.

In 1891 the legislature created a temporary intermediate court of appeals, known as the Appellate Court of Indiana. Seventy-nine years later, in 1970, the Appellate Court finally gained the status of a constitutional court. In 1971 the official title Court of Appeals of Indiana was adopted. Since 1991 the Court has been comprised of five districts, each with three judges. A chief judge presides over the entire court, while each district has a presiding judge.

I. The Court of Appeals Existence as a Statutory Court (1816–1970) June 29, 1816—The state's first constitution created one Supreme Court with three judges* and seven circuit courts but made no mention of an intermediate appellate court.

November 1, 1851—Indiana's new constitution vested judicial power in a Supreme Court and in Circuit Courts and in "such inferior courts the General Assembly may establish." The number of Supreme Court judges was to be no fewer than three, but no more than five; again, no provision for an intermediate appellate court.

1870 to 1881—The number of Supreme Court judges was expanded by two during this period. To lessen the caseload on the Supreme Court, a Supreme Court Commission was created in 1881 with five commissioners appointed for terms of two years, later extended to another two years.

1881—Voters approved a constitutional amendment that granted the legislature the power to establish "other" courts deemed necessary, rather than the more restrictive language referring to "inferior courts."

1885 to 1889—The terms of Supreme Court Commissioners expired but an attempt to revive a commission by the legislature was ruled unconstitutional by the Indiana Supreme Court.

1891—A burgeoning caseload confronted the Supreme Court. In response, the legislature created a temporary second appellate court consisting of five judges, one from each of the five districts represented on the Supreme Court. The new court, called the Appellate Court of Indiana, was granted final jurisdiction in such minor matters as cases for recovery of less than $1,000, appeals from justices of the peace, and appeals of misdemeanors, making it a court of last resort for these types of cases. The court was to exist for only six years, at which time pending cases would be handled by the Supreme Court.

1893—After two years the Supreme Court was still overloaded with appeals, which led the state legislature to broaden the jurisdiction of the new appellate court, increasing a disputed monetary amount to $3,500 from $1,000 and granting the court the exclusive jurisdiction of appeals from circuit, superior, and criminal courts.

1897 to 1901—The life of the Appellate Court of Indiana was extended for an additional four years before the court was finally made permanent and was given an additional judge. The court's role shifted from a court of last resort in specific cases to an intermediate appellate court designated as the Appellate Court of Indiana, Divisions Number One and Two. Limits were also placed on cases directly appealable to the Supreme Court.

1903 to 1913—This period was marked by several changes to the jurisdictions of the Appellate Court of Indiana and the Supreme Court, expanding, for example, the types of cases directly appealable to the Supreme Court. An attempt to give the intermediate appellate court final jurisdiction in specified cases was struck down by the Indiana Supreme Court as unconstitutional.

1929—The Appellate Court was granted temporary jurisdiction for a two-year period by the legislature to decide appeals of misdemeanor convictions where the penalty was not death or imprisonment. After that period all pending criminal appeals would go to the Supreme Court.

II. The Court of Appeals becomes a Constitutional Court (1970 and beyond)

1950s to 1970—Advocates for judicial reform began lobbying in the 1950s to address what many considered to be undue partisanship in judicial decisions and the instability caused by frequent turnover on the courts. The Indiana General Assembly responded to these concerns with an amendment to the Judicial Article of the state constitution that substantially reformed both appellate courts—the Supreme Court and the Court of Appeals.

1970—The amendment, approved by the voters in 1970, brought about the following changes:

- Made the Appellate Court of Indiana a constitutional court that is now known as the Court of Appeals of Indiana, a title adopted for the Court in 1971.
- Replaced partisan elections for justices of the Supreme Court as well as judges of the Court of Appeals with a merit-based system coupled with gubernatorial appointment. The initial appointment is for two years.
- Established nonpartisan retention elections in which voters decide whether to remove or retain a member of the bench
- Provided that judges who are retained serve for ten more years, with no limit on the number of terms served.
- Required that the three geographic districts represented on the Court would consist of three judges each, bringing the total number of judges to nine. Judges in these districts are elected by the voters in those districts.

1978—The Indiana General Assembly created a fourth at-large district covering the entire state. This brought the number of judges to twelve. Judges in this district face a statewide retention election.

1978—Vivian Sue Shields became the first woman appointed to the Court of Appeals on July 1, 1978.

1988—A constitutional amendment known as Proposition Two was passed in response to the growing number of criminal appeals clogging the docket of the Supreme Court. Proposition Two provided that only sentences of fifty years or more for a single offense would go directly to the Supreme Court, diverting cases with lesser sentences to the Court of Appeals.

1989—The general assembly authorized the creation of the Senior Judge Program, which permits retired judges to hear cases to reduce the caseload of the regular judges of the Court of Appeals and trial courts. All Senior Judges are certified by the Indiana Judicial Nominating Commission.

1991—On January 1, 1991, Robert Rucker became the first African American appointed to the Court of Appeals.

1991—Proposition Two, passed in 1988, created a significant increase in the appeals heard by the Court of Appeals. In response, the legislature created a fifth at-large district adding three more judges to the Court of Appeals, bringing the total number of judges to fifteen.

1993—The legislature passed a law requiring all appellate judges to retire by the age of seventy-five.

1998—The Court of Appeals began using random, rotating panels to decide cases. Before then, cases were assigned strictly by county of geographical origin and all panels were "pure," meaning that a case initiated in each county was assigned to the judges in the district in which the county was located. Since 1998 geographical origin has played no role in determining which judges are assigned to a case and the composition of the panels rotates several times per year and is random.

2001—In the early 1970s the Court of Appeals began the practice of conducting oral arguments at remote sites. That practice was not widespread and amounted to just a few oral arguments per year. However, in 2001, in conjunction with its centennial celebration, the Court converted that practice into a program called "Appeals on Wheels." In the first year the Court conducted thirteen such arguments. The program later expanded to include arguments at such venues as law schools, colleges and universities, high schools, and county courts.

2001—Voters approved a constitutional amendment that affected the jurisdiction of both the Supreme Court and the Court of Appeals. The amendment provided that any appeals for cases imposing a sentence of death go directly to the Supreme Court. All other appeals in criminal cases follow the same route as civil cases and go first to the Court of Appeals. Today, under the Indiana Rules of Procedure, the Supreme Court also has exclusive jurisdiction in cases in which a sentence of life imprisonment is imposed.

2008—The appointment of Elaine B. Brown to the Court of Appeals on May 5, 2008, made the Fifth District the first district comprised of all females. The other two judges were Margaret Robb and Nancy H. Vaidik.

2015—The Indiana Supreme Court initiated a statewide project for electronic filing, or e-filing, of documents relating to appeals. It was first implemented in Hamilton County in 2015 and culminated in 2019 when all ninety-two counties were e-filing. This dramatically changed the way the Court of Appeals conducts its business, making it more efficient and economical.

* Members of the Indiana Supreme Court were called judges until the passage of the Judicial Reform Act in 1970, when the titles were changed to justices.

For those interested in a more detailed analysis of the history of the Court of Appeals up through 1997, the authors recommend, Robert H. Staton and Gina M. Hicklin, "The History of the Court of Appeals of Indiana," Indiana Law Review *30, no.1 (1997): 203–31. This article is also posted on the website for the Court of Appeals of Indiana (in.gov/judiciary/appeals/2338.htm).*

INDIANA SUPREME COURT

JAMES B. BLACK

March 12, 1891–January 1, 1893; January 1, 1897–January 1, 1907

ROGER HARDIG

James B. Black, who lived during one of the most transformative times of Western Civilization, served in the Union army during the Civil War as a young man and died during the Great War that was supposed to end all wars.

In his service to Indiana and to the practice of law, Black played a key role in the creation, direction, and scope of the Appellate Court of Indiana, which he achieved through a combination of sound legal training and savvy political involvement.

Born in Morristown, New Jersey, on July 21, 1838, Black moved with his family to Indiana at an early age when his father set roots as minister of the Methodist Episcopal Church in Wabash. As a young man, Black took a job as a schoolteacher so that he could afford a college education. He first enrolled at DePauw University and then transferred to Indiana University, a move that would forever change his life.

On April 14, 1861, Black and other students attended a campus rally led by Mary Maxwell of Bloomington to recruit soldiers for the Union army. Three days later, 191 students set out with Captain James R. Kelley's student company to preserve the Union. Black served with bravery and honor for the entirety of the conflict and was mustered out after the war at the rank of colonel and remained involved in the Grand Army of the Republic for the rest of his life.

Black's earliest documented legal training was as a wartime judge advocate. After the Civil War, he moved to Indianapolis, read law under Benjamin Harrison, and was admitted to the bar in 1866. For the next two years, Black formed a legal partnership with Judge Byron K. Elliott, a distinguished jurist who later served twelve years on the Indiana Supreme Court. In 1868 Black was elected to succeed Harrison as Supreme Court Reporter. In that position he quickly gained a reputation for solid research and a clear ability to "present the substance of the decisions with the comprehensiveness and perspicuity consistent with necessary and desirable brevity."

Black served as reporter of the court until 1872 and then resumed his private law practice. From 1879 to 1882 he taught law courses and was a key figure in arguably the first law school in Indianapolis, the Central Indiana Law School, which was the dream of his partner, Elliott. In addition to Elliott, Black served on faculty with Charles P. Jacobs, and various guest lecturers. The school was successful but after Elliott was elected to the Supreme Court and Black was appointed to the Supreme Court Commission in 1882, the school dissolved.

The Supreme Court Commission was created in 1881 as a temporary solution to address a massive backlog of cases. The combination of talents and strong connections made Black a natural choice to sit on this bench. To ensure that its authority was not usurped, the Indiana Supreme Court could accept, reject, or modify the opinions written by the commission. While this did help streamline work, the Supreme Court still had the judicial responsibility to render the actual decision of the case. The five judges who comprised this commission were paid a salary equal to a supreme court judge and were given terms of two years because the legislature was advised that the court was two years behind in its work. However, the mission and purpose to relieve the court failed. The next five years were marked by a combination of bitter partisan debate and fear by the Supreme Court of encroachment on its power, the backlog became insurmountable.

A second appeals court was created in 1891 with Black and four others appointed by Governor Alvin P. Hovey. Black, elected by his colleagues as the first chief judge, distinguished himself as a fair and decisive leader. Beginning in early 1895, Black presided as a special judge in a trial over the contested will of prominent Richmond, Indiana, businessman James L. Morrisson, whose heirs squabbled over his estate of more than $600,000. The trial, which lasted four months, was also notable for the nearly $100,000 in fees paid to attorneys in the case.

Black, who served on the court until 1907, died in Indianapolis on December 11, 1916.

Selected Bibliography

Black, James B. *A Digest of the Decisions of the Supreme Court of Indiana,* 1889.
Dunn, Jacob Piatt, Jr. *Greater Indianapolis.* Chicago: Lewis Publishing Company, 1910.
In Memoriam, James B. Black. To the Chief Judge and Members of the Appellate Court Of Indiana: John C. McNutt, J. G. Ibach, Frederick S. Caldwell, pp. xxxiv, xxxv.
Indianapolis Journal, June 12, 1895.
Indianapolis Star, April 15, 1911.
Sievers, Harry J. *Benjamin Harrison: Hoosier Statesman.* Newton, CT: American Political Biography Press, 1996.
Staton, Robert H., and Gina M. *Hicklin*. "The History of the Court of Appeals of Indiana." *Indiana Law Review* 30, no. 1 (1997).

INDIANA SUPREME COURT

JEPTHA D. NEW

March 12, 1891–July 9, 1892

RYAN T. SCHWIER

Jeptha Dudley New joined the Appellate Court of Indiana at a time of intense political strife in Indiana. With a shifting and uncertain electorate, both major parties fought bitterly for control over state and federal offices. At the front line of these partisan battles stood Indiana courts, with judges playing an active—although not always neutral—role as arbiters of the law. Throughout his professional career, New stood above the fray, garnering support from both political camps in his rise to the appellate bench.

Born November 28, 1830, New came of age in Jennings County, Indiana, working as a young man in his father's cabinet shop. He studied theology at Vernon Seminary, later departing for Bethany College in West Virginia. After graduating in 1850, he returned home, teaching school for several years while studying law in Indianapolis. In 1857 he started a private practice in Vernon and began a family with his wife, Sallie Butler.

Together they raised three children—Mary, Willard, and Burt—the second of whom succeeded his father on the appellate bench.

After two years as district prosecuting attorney, New became judge of the common pleas court for Bartholomew, Jackson, Jennings, and Lawrence Counties in 1864. His political acumen eventually propelled him to Congress. A loyal Democrat, he served two nonconsecutive terms as U.S. Representative, from 1875 to 1877 and again from 1879 to 1881, serving on the Judiciary Committee and chairing a commission investigating the disputed 1876 presidential election. He also advocated, albeit unsuccessfully, for settling Hoosier claims stemming from Morgan's Raid—the destructive 1863 invasion of Confederate forces in southern Indiana.

In 1889, following a six-year term as circuit court judge, New was named as one of five Indiana Supreme Court commissioners. His tenure in office, however, never materialized. The general assembly had created a similar commission eight years earlier, designed to "aid and assist" the Court with its growing backlog of pending cases. That commission expired in 1885. But when the appellate case docket expanded yet again, Democrats resurrected the commission, exploiting the opportunity to exercise its influence over the bench in retaliation for judicial losses in the previous election. To accomplish this, the 1889 measure vested the appointment power in the legislature rather than the Supreme Court.

While Republicans attacked the law as unconstitutional, their protests failed. With Democrats fully in control of the general assembly, the legislation passed by a comfortable margin, taking effect over the veto of Republican governor Alvin P. Hovey. Still, the governor refused to issue the commissions, prompting a constitutional crisis implicating all three branches of state government. Having taken the oath of office, New and the other commissioners presented the Supreme Court with their certificates of election, seeking to assume office. The Court declined their request and, in *State ex rel. Hovey v. Noble*, declared the legislation unconstitutional. "Neither the executive nor the legislative [branches] can select persons to assist the courts in the performance of their judicial duties," the Court ruled unanimously.

Of course, *Hovey* did nothing to alleviate the Court's heavy caseload. Rather than creating a new commission, the general assembly in 1891 enacted legislation establishing the state's first intermediate appellate court. Hovey appointed New as one of two Democratic judges from among over fifty candidates for the position.

During his short time on the court, New penned ninety-four opinions—encompassing the first four volumes of the *Appellate Court Reports*—on matters such as taxation, railroad negligence, promissory notes, real estate conveyances, employment contracts, recovery of rewards, double jeopardy, malicious prosecution, and conversion of property.

His popularity as a judge quickly won him the Democratic Party's nomination to the Indiana Supreme Court, but, sadly, tragedy struck months before election day. On the morning of July 11, 1892, the sixty-two-year-old jurist and statesman died at home from a self-inflicted gunshot wound to the heart. One report suggested that New suffered from depression and anxiety, conditions exacerbated by his recent nomination. Most accounts, however, simply attributed the suicide to a fleeting mental delusion following a recent bout of the flu. New's colleagues on the bench likewise struggled to understand this "public misfortune," lamenting the unrealized potential of his election to the "Supreme Bench of the State."

Whatever the reason for his untimely death, New—a pioneer of the appeals court—left behind a legacy of "untiring industry" and a "conscientious regard for right and justice" during an era marked by political corruption and partisan discord.

Selected Bibliography

Indianapolis Journal, February 1, March 11, 29, 1889, February 13, 1891, July 10, 1892.
Indianapolis News, February 23, 1881.
Indiana State Sentinel, March 18, 1891.
Taylor, Charles W. *Biographical Sketches and Review of the Bench and Bar of Indiana.* Indianapolis: Bench and Bar Publishing Company, 1895.
Thornton, W. W. "The Supreme Court of Indiana." *Green Bag* 4 (June 1892): 249–74.

CASE CITED

State ex rel. Hovey v. Noble, 21 N.E. 244 (Ind. 1889).

INDIANA SUPREME COURT

MILTON S. ROBINSON

March 12, 1891–July 28, 1892

DAVID J. REMONDINI

Milton Stapp Robinson, who studied law as a teenager under a father who helped draft the 1851 Indiana Constitution, began a distinguished legal career at age twenty, and became one of the first five judges of the Appellate Court of Indiana. However, after just a brief time on the bench, he died of sunstroke.

Robinson, born in Versailles, Indiana, on April 20, 1832, received his common school education there and in Greensburg, where his family moved in 1842. The future judge began studying law with his father, Joseph R. Robinson, at age seventeen and was formally admitted to the bar three years later. At about that time, he moved to Anderson, where he lived the rest of his life, opened his own legal practice, and became involved in the nascent Republican Party.

Even as a young man, he had gained the attention of the state's leaders. He was appointed by the Indiana General Assembly as one of the directors of the Northern Indiana Prison at Michigan City. But he left that position after a brief time to join the Union army in the Civil War. His friendship with Indiana governor Oliver P. Morton led to his appointment as a lieutenant colonel with the Forty-Seventh Regiment, Indiana Volunteers in December 1861. He declined the governor's offer to be the regiment's colonel, citing his lack of military experience.

Experience came quickly as he was involved in several battles and was later appointed colonel of the Seventy-Fifth Indiana Volunteer Infantry, which saw action at the Union army's defeat at the Battle of Chickamauga. He also fought at the Battle of Vicksburg with a future governor, Alvin P. Hovey, who would later appoint him to the Appellate Court of Indiana.

Following the war, Robinson's interest in politics continued, likely aided by his family name and relationships with Indiana's political elite. Described as a "fine orator of more than ordinary pleasing presence," he was elected to the Indiana Senate, representing Madison and Grant Counties, and served two terms in the U.S. House of Representatives from 1874 to 1878. After leaving Congress, he continued to serve the Republican Party in various positions and was one of the speakers at Hovey's funeral.

In addition to his political activities, Robinson also built a significant legal practice in the Anderson area in a law firm that bore his name from 1873 until he joined the appeals court. In remarks at his memorial service, his longtime law partner, John W. Lovett, revealed that Robinson was in near constant pain from acute neuralgia, "yet he rarely succumbed to its influence or deserted his post of duty on account of it." Lovett also recalled that many Civil War veterans would visit the law office to see "Colonel Robinson" and leave with some "provision" for their needs.

In his brief time on the bench, Robinson was quite productive and authored nearly three dozen opinions. A colleague on the court, Judge James B. Black, noted that Robinson's background made him well-suited to serve on the court. His legal acumen did not come only from dusty law books. "His life had been one of varied experience and great activity," Black said of Robinson. "He had performed with distinguished honor the responsible and important duties of a field officer of volunteers in the civil war, and he had served with great credit and usefulness in the Legislature of the State and Congress of the Nation."

Robinson had been on the appeals court just over a year as Hovey's appointee when he was nominated by the Republican Party to be the nominee for the court in the general election. But during the summer of 1892 he had been in "delicate health" and succumbed to a heatwave that had engulfed the country, dying from sunstroke in his Anderson home just sixteen months after being appointed to the court. According to news accounts, 10,000 people attended his funeral.

Selected Bibliography

Cambridge City Journal, August 13, 1874, citing *Indianapolis Journal.*
Indianapolis Journal, December 1, 1891.
Jackson, Stephen T. "Robinson achieved 'citadel of respect.'" Madison County Historical Society, June 2, 2012.
Jasper Weekly Courier, August 12, 1892.
Noblesville Ledger, September 1, 1882.
Princeton Clarion Leader, March 19, 1991.

INDIANA SUPREME COURT

GEORGE L. REINHARD

March 12, 1891–January 1, 1897

DAVID J. REMONDINI

A German immigrant born in the mid-1800s, George L. Reinhard came to America as a young boy to work in his family's woodshop. Described as both charismatic and modest, he served as a private in the Civil War and opened a law practice in the Ohio River town of Rockport, Indiana. Later, he built a career as a prosecutor, judge, popular law professor, and one of first judges of what is now known as the Court of Appeals of Indiana.

Born on July 5, 1843, in a small village in Bavaria, Germany, he journeyed to America at age fourteen with his mother and stepfather. They settled in Cincinnati, where his uncle ran a woodshop and where Reinhard worked until the family moved to nearby Union County, Indiana. The Civil War was brewing at the time. Reinhard joined the Union side and enlisted in April 1861 before he turned eighteen. He served four years as a private while his unit took part in several major battles. While a soldier, he took time to study American history and constitutional government.

After the war he briefly attended school in Cincinnati and then in 1866 enrolled at Miami University in Ohio, where he supplemented his income by teaching German. He left without graduating and moved to Owensboro, Kentucky, in 1868 to earn money as a schoolteacher and to study law. While in Kentucky, he married Mary Wilson, and in 1869, joined the Kentucky bar. In 1870 the couple moved to Rockport, Indiana, to set up his legal practice.

Quickly, Reinhard entered politics and became, against his wishes, the Democratic candidate for state representative in 1872. Although defeated in a close race, he was elected prosecutor in 1876 and reelected without opposition in 1878 to the Second Judicial District, which included his home county, Spencer, as well as Perry and Warrick. While in office, he wrote his first book, *The Criminal Law of Indiana.* After his term ended in 1880, he returned to his law practice. But in 1882 he was elected judge of the Second Judicial Circuit and served two terms.

Meanwhile, the Indiana Supreme Court struggled to handle its caseload. In 1891, to meet the growing burden, the legislature created a five-judge Appellate Court of Indiana. Reinhard resigned from the circuit court and on March 10, 1891, became one of the first five appellate judges appointed by Governor Alvin P. Hovey. He won election on his own during the general election of in 1892.

While still on the appellate court in 1894, he was nominated for the supreme court but was defeated when Republicans swept statewide races. However, he did not have to give up his judgeship and he remained on the appellate court until the end of his term on January 1, 1897. During the latter part of his time on the court he joined the faculty of Indiana University. As evidence of his popularity, a debate club, the Reinhard Club, was named in his honor because his "life and example inspired the origin of this society." In 1902 he was named dean of the law school and vice president of Indiana University. He was one of the founders of the American Bar School Association and is credited with moving his law school from the long-established "text methods" to the case system.

In 1902 Reinhard published *A Treatise on the Law of Agency in Contract and Tort* while another work, *Cases on the Law of Agency*, was completed by others after his death. It was "presented as a memorial to the late Dean Reinhard, whose high qualifications as a jurist, administrator, author and teacher were so generally recognized during his lifetime." Tellingly, and perhaps as a nod to his own less than aristocratic origins, he also wrote *The Common Sense Lawyer*, which was "prepared for the mechanic, the tradesman, and those in humbler stations in life." In other well-crafted writings, Reinhard was an early adopter of the belief women should be lawyers and an advocate for more stringent requirements to join the legal profession. While still dean, he died in his Bloomington, Indiana, home on July 13, 1906, after several months of poor health. An Indiana University publication marked his passing by noting "his exceptionally meritorious work, . . . his sterling character, loyal nature and lovable personality."

Selected Bibliography

Death of Judge Reinhard Casts Gloom Over University (1906). http://www.repository.law.indiana.edu/reinhard/4?utm_source=www.repository.law.indiana.edu%2Freinhard%2F4&utm_medium=PDF&utm_campaign=PDFCoverPages.

Monks, Leander J., ed. *Courts and Lawyers of Indiana*. Indianapolis: Federal Publishing Company, 1916.

Staton, Robert H., and Gina M. Hicklin. "The History of the Court of Appeals of Indiana." *Indiana Law Review* 30, no. 1 (1997): 208–9.

Taylor, Charles W. *Biographical Sketches and Review of the Bench and Bar of Indiana*. Indianapolis: Bench and Bar Publishing Company, 1895.

INDIANA SUPREME COURT

EDGAR D. CRUMPACKER

March 12, 1891–January 1, 1893

WILLIAM F. GULDE

On May 13, 1902, an overflow crowd composed primarily of African Americans gathered at Faneuil Hall in Boston to rally in support of Section 2 of the Fourteenth Amendment. The event was dubbed the Crumpacker Rally in honor of Edgar Dean Crumpacker, who, as a congressman from the Tenth District of Indiana, sponsored legislation to reduce the number of representatives in Congress from the South because many blacks had been disenfranchised. Lynching, terror, poll taxes, and other tactics had been used in the South to keep African Americans from voting and powerless. In the end, his legislation had little support from either Republicans or Democrats, but he certainly got the nation's attention. For most of his political life, Crumpacker served in the U.S. House of Representatives, but he also served briefly on the Appellate Court of Indiana.

Born near Westville, Indiana, on May 27, 1851, to Theophilus and Harriet Crumpacker, Edgar Dean Crumpacker spent his earliest years on farms. As a young boy, he and his family moved from La Porte County to a farm near Valparaiso. His earliest education was in a nearby schoolhouse, but he later attended the Valparaiso Academy. His early interest in politics might have come from his father, who served in the Indiana House of Representatives from 1872 until 1878.

Unsure of a vocation, young Edgar first rented a thirty-acre farm near Valparaiso. He also married Abbie Parshall on November 10, 1875. She died two years later. Later, he started reading law with William C. Talbott in Valparaiso and then attended Indiana University's law school, where he was allowed to skip grades due to what he had already mastered under Talbott.

By 1878 Crumpacker opened his first law office in Chesterton, but stayed there for only one year before moving back to Valparaiso. Shortly after his return, he married Charlotte Lucas, a schoolteacher, on April 20, 1879. Although he had not lived in the city for very long, the twenty-nine-year-old attorney decided to run for mayor of Valparaiso as a Republican in 1880. He was defeated but undeterred. Two years later he was elected city attorney of Valparaiso. In 1884 and 1886 he was elected Porter County Attorney. He also began to get heavily involved in both state and national Republican politics. Inspired by Benjamin Harrison's presidential campaign, Crumpacker spoke at a huge rally in Valparaiso for the future president in 1888.

When Governor Alvin P. Hovey appointed the first judges of the state's second appeals court in 1891, he chose Crumpacker to represent the court's fifth district. The judges, who were paid $3,500 a year, heard cases involving railroads, property disputes, and insurance claims. By statue, they had to run in the November 1892 election to continue on the bench. Crumpacker lost his by a substantial margin to George E. Ross.

Not content to remain a small-town lawyer in Valparaiso, Crumpacker ran for the Tenth District U.S. Congressional seat in 1896 and received the largest plurality of any Indiana congressional candidate in that election. He was touted as a potential U.S. Senate or gubernatorial candidate, but nothing came of either. As the Calumet Region began to change, more Democrats moved into the area making each of his election campaigns more difficult. He struggled against the tides of change especially when Samuel

Gompers of the American Federation of Labor visited his district in 1906 and denounced Crumpacker as an "enemy of labor." In 1910 he narrowly won his election for Congress, but his fortunes changed in 1912, when he was defeated by Democrat John Peterson.

In March of 1913 Crumpacker packed his bags in Washington to begin the journey back to Valparaiso. Before he left, he issued a press statement noting, "I am quitting public life without any regrets and I intend to go back home and live among the plain people." He died in 1920 at the age of sixty-eight.

Selected Bibliography

Boonville Standard, November 25, 1898.
Greenidge, Kerri K. *Black Radical: The Life and Times of William Monroe Trotter.* New York: Livergiht, 2020.
Indianapolis Journal, March 12, 1891.
Indianapolis News, October 23, 1906.
Indianapolis Star, February 12, 1905.
Inportercounty.org/.
Logansport Pharos-Tribune, February 1, 1890.
Munster Times, March 6, 1913.
Streater (IL) Times, June 27, 1888.

INDIANA SUPREME COURT

WILLARD NEW

August 20, 1892–January 1, 1893

RYAN T. SCHWIER

Willard New ascended to the Appellate Court of Indiana bench under the most tragic of circumstances. Shortly before his appointment, New's father and predecessor on the court, Jeptha Dudley New, committed suicide. Willard served out his father's unexpired term—a term set to end just four months later, making his tenure with the court one of the shortest.

Born December 4, 1862, New grew up with his two siblings—Mary and Burt—in the small, southern Indiana town of Vernon. A student of the common school system, he went on to graduate from Indiana University in 1881 before studying law with his father. Soon after his admission to the bar in 1883, New was elected mayor of his hometown, a post he held for two years before entering private practice.

Considering his limited practical experience, New's elevation to the appeals court may have been a token of political courtesy following his father's death. Some even questioned the need for his appointment, suggesting instead that the vacancy go unfilled until the November elections. The author of only nineteen opinions, New's limited contribution to the court's jurisprudence seems to have justified these concerns. Indeed, his most cited case—holding an urban railway operator negligent for colliding with the plaintiff's horse-drawn carriage—carried no authoritative weight beyond a 1919 Indiana Supreme Court decision on a similar matter.

New's brief and arguably lackluster tenure with the appeals court preceded a flourishing career as a trial court judge and practicing attorney. In 1894, running as a Democrat, he was elected judge of the Sixth Judicial Circuit, encompassing Ripley, Jennings, and Scott Counties. His popularity on the bench quickly attracted the attention of fellow Democrats looking to replace Indiana Supreme Court Judge Leonard Hackney, the party incumbent, in the 1898 general election. Perceived by some within the party ranks as a tool of corporate interests, Hackney posed a threat to the much-needed Populist vote. New, on the other hand, had broad bipartisan support. Alas, party bosses had other plans, forcing New to withdraw from the race just three days after accepting his nomination. Despite this setback, New, after completing his first six-year term with the circuit court, easily won re-election in 1900.

Upon retiring from the bench in 1906, New returned to private practice, partnering with his brother, Burt, for several years before departing for Indianapolis in 1911. There, he established a long-lasting partnership with attorney Bernard Korbly, with whom he argued several high-profile cases, including one involving the appeals court's power of judicial review. In 1911 the general assembly had vested *final* jurisdiction in the court in all but twenty-one types of cases. The measure—known as the Hauck Act—threatened to deprive the Indiana Supreme Court of its authority as a court of last resort. Several interested attorneys filed amicus briefs (at the Court's behest), virtually all of them attacking the constitutional validity of the act.

As the only private attorneys supporting the measure, New and his partner argued that the Indiana Constitution conferred "no vested right in a remedy [of] appeal" from one appellate court to a superior tribunal. Rejecting this argument, the Supreme Court, in *Ex parte France*, struck down the Hauck Act as unconstitutional. In effect, a majority of the justices concluded, the measure withdrew from the Supreme Court "all revising and reviewing power," thus rendering "the Appellate Court supreme."

New's isolated arguments in the case may have been politically motivated. After several years of intraparty strife, the Democrats reemerged as the dominant party in 1909, having found their foothold under popular leaders such as Governor Thomas Marshall. The Hauck Act tracked other Progressive Era reform efforts by the Democratic-controlled general assembly. New was a Democratic loyalist and his law partner Korbly served for several years as the party's state campaign chairman. A decision upholding the act would have vested broad subject-matter jurisdiction in a politically appointed appeals court with no threat of further judicial review, giving Democrats the sheen of authority they needed to validate their legislative agenda.

Though he went on to enjoy several years of successful practice, New seems to have struggled with some of the same demons that haunted his father. In 1918 the *Indianapolis News* reported that, after more than a year of "treatment in several sanitoriums," officials declared him of "unsound mind." Having suffered from "hallucinations" and "destructive mania," New had apparently become so unstable that a justice of the peace ordered him confined. When he died on May 30, 1933, newspapers simply reported that he had passed "after a long illness." He was seventy-two years old. Among those who survived him included his siblings and his wife, Laura Steffens New.

SELECTED BIBLIOGRAPHY

Indianapolis Journal, July 15, 1892.

Indianapolis News, June 15, 18, 1898, July 23, 1900, October 10, 12, 1916, August 28, 1918, May 30, 1933.

Indianapolis Star, March 11, 1911, April 1, 5, 1911, June 22, 1911.

Monks, Leander J., ed. *Courts and Lawyer of Indiana*. Vol. 3. Indianapolis: Federal Publishing Company, 1916.

Stoll, John B. *History of the Indiana Democracy, 1816–1916*. Indianapolis: Indiana Democratic Publishing Company, 1917.

Taylor, Charles W. *Biographical Sketches and Review of the Bench and Bar of Indiana*. Indianapolis: Bench and Bar Publishing Company, 1895.

CASES CITED

Barnett v. Bryce Furnace Co., 62 N.E. 6, 7 (Ind. 1901).

Ex parte France, 95 N.E. 515 (Ind. 1911).

Muncie St. Ry. Co. v. Maynard, 5 Ind. App. 372, 32 N.E. 343 (1892).

WILLIAM HAYDEN ENGLISH FAMILY PAPERS COLLECTION, INDIANA HISTORICAL SOCIETY

HENRY C. FOX

August 20, 1892–January 1, 1893

JAMES E. ST. CLAIR

Henry Clay Fox, according to the late nineteenth-century book, *Bench and Bar of Indiana*, had a "considerable reputation as a lawyer and as a wit . . . and some notoriety as a writer of humorous literature." A sample of his wry humor can be found in his reply to a questionnaire from Charles W. Taylor, the book's author: "I was born in Ohio. The time and place of my death have not yet been fixed. The public can have no possible interest in what I have been doing in the world. I am entirely satisfied with many things that I have done, while there are others I would like to forget."

Fox, who was born on January 20, 1836, was named for the Great Compromiser by his father, an ardent admirer of the distinguished politician best remembered for his efforts to avert civil war. Fox's family moved to Centerville, Indiana, in 1860 and he began studying law with George W. Julian, prominent politician and antislavery activist, and Nimrod H.

Johnson, judge of the Wayne County Criminal Court. Fox was admitted to the bar in 1861 and in the same year was married and went off to fight in the Civil War with the Fifty-Seventh Indiana Volunteer Infantry, seeing action in Kentucky, Tennessee, Alabama, and at the Battle of Shiloh.

Following military service, Fox returned to Wayne County and resumed practicing law. From 1863 to 1867 he was district attorney for Wayne, Union, Franklin and Fayette Counties, and in 1878 he was elected judge of the Wayne Superior Court. In between his stints in public office, he practiced law with several partners, including Judge Johnson. Upon the death of Judge Milton S. Robinson, Governor Ira J. Chase appointed Fox to the appeals court in the summer of 1892. He was a Republican candidate for a full term on the court in the fall of that year but was defeated.

During his brief time as an appeals court judge, Fox participated in about two dozen cases. In *McChesney v. State* he reversed a decision of the Marshall Circuit Court in a paternity case. Fox based his decision on the testimony of two men who said the mother had sex with men other than the defendant. In another case, *Enders v. McDonald,* Fox affirmed a lower court's decision that landowners had the right to keep a hog that had broken through a fence on their property until its owners reimbursed them for the damages to their wheat field. Fox's decision in *Board of Commissioners v. Lomax* upheld a ruling by the Perry Circuit Court that county commissioners had to pay a surgeon retained by the township trustee to amputate the leg of an indigent man. While commissioners had hired a doctor to care for the poor, the person had no experience in surgery and in such circumstances, trustees could act when a physician lacked the skills to perform a needed procedure.

After his defeat Fox resumed practicing law in Wayne County until winning election as judge of the Wayne Circuit Court, a position he held for twenty-four years. During this period, he was also active as an author, publishing three books, two of which illustrate his humor and positive view of life. In *The Adventures of a Philosopher, a Dun Mule, and a Brindle Dog*, Fox writes, "Happy is the man who looks upon the Brightside of the picture of life, and turns from the shadows and walks in the sunshine." He added that "we cannot always laugh, for sorrow has seasons, and comes unbidden to our doors. Then let us laugh while we can, for it is the light of our lives."

His book *Uncle Zeek and Aunt Liza*, published in 1905, is the story of two former slaves who are devoted to good works. They spend their lives assisting in the household of a Quaker brother and sister. Fox also was editor of *Memoirs of Wayne County and the City of Richmond, Indiana*, published in 1912. He wrote a chapter on the homicide trials in the county.

Fox and his wife Helen had two sons and a daughter. She died in 1912 and he died at his home in Richmond on November 22, 1920.

Selected Bibliography

Fox, Henry Clay. *The Adventures of a Philosopher, a Dun Mule, and a Brindle Dog*. Richmond, IN: M. Cullaton and Company, 1888.

____. *Memoirs of Wayne County and the City of Richmond, Indiana*. Madison, WI: Western Historical Association, 1912.

____. *Uncle Zeek and Aunt Liza*. Boston, MA: Mayhew Publishing Company, 1905.

Taylor, Charles W. *Biographical Sketches and Review of the Bench and Bar of Indiana*. Indianapolis: Bench and Bar Publishing Company, 1895.

CASES CITED

Board of Commissioners v. Lomax, 32 N.E. 800 (Ind. App. 1892).

Enders v. McDonald, 31 N.E. 1056 (Ind. App. 1892).

McChesney v. State, 32 N.E. 339 (Ind. App. 1892).

INDIANA SUPREME COURT

FRANK E. GAVIN

January 1, 1893–January 1, 1897

L. MARK BAILEY

In the Tenth Anniversary Report of the Harvard College class of 1873, Frank E. Gavin drolly reported to his classmates that he was "a Democrat and always beaten when running for office." Although over his lifetime Gavin answered his party's call to service as a candidate for prosecuting attorney, the Indiana Supreme Court, and Congress, his election in 1892 to a four-year term on the recently formed Appellate Court of Indiana was his only major political victory.

Born in Greensburg, Indiana, on February 20, 1854, Gavin attended local common schools and Shelbyville preparatory school before qualifying for admission to Harvard at age fifteen. After receiving his bachelor's degree, he studied law in Greensburg and was admitted to the bar in 1875, the day before his twenty-first birthday.

The law was, perhaps, in Gavin's blood. His father, Colonel James Gavin, returned from the Civil War and established a law practice in Greensburg with legal scholar Oscar B. Hord. Their annotated compilation *Gavin and Hord's Indiana Statutes* was "greatly appreciated by the profession in this state." Colonel Gavin later established the Greensburg firm Miller and Gavin with future Indiana Supreme Court Judge John D. Miller, with whom he practiced until his death in July 1873.

Gavin married Ella B. Lathrop in November 1875. She was an 1873 graduate of the Weslyan Female College in Cincinnati, and daughter of distinguished Methodist Episcopal minister Reverend James B. Lathrop. A newspaper account of the ceremony said the marriage was "a matter of the heart as well of the hand." The couple had three children, son James L., born in 1876, and twins William E. and Mary E., who followed thirteen years later.

Prior to his election to the appellate court, Gavin enjoyed a successful eighteen-year career at his father's firm. He was also a founding member of both the Greensburg and Workingmen's building and loan associations, and the area's first coed literary club, the Tourist Club. He was a presidential elector in 1884.

On the appellate bench, Gavin authored approximately 300 opinions, preparing them with "great care and scrupulousness." His opinions reflect that he was "a leader in the progressive thought of the day," such as in recognizing the personal property rights of women, *Parrett v. Palmer*, and the rights of workers to quit employment in concert, *Clemitt v. Watson.*

After losing his re-election bid, Gavin and fellow appeals court judge, Theodore P. Davis, established the Indianapolis firm Gavin and Davis in the Majestic Building. Upon Davis's death in 1907, Gavin was "chok[ed] with grief at the loss of his friend." Sons James and William later joined him in practice, and the firm was then known as Gavin, Gavin and Davis and later Gavin and Gavin. Offices were first in the Lemcke Building and then the Hume Mansur Building.

Gavin held leadership positions in many organizations, leaving a legacy of service instilled in his descendants. He was treasurer of the Indiana State Bar Association for eleven years, then president in 1912; organizer of the Harvard Club of Indiana; president of the Associated Harvard Clubs; president of the Indianapolis Commercial Club (predecessor to the Indianapolis Chamber of Commerce); president of the Indiana Democratic Realty Company; and trustee of the Meridian Street Methodist Episcopal Church.

Aside from his legal and political career, Gavin was "deeply interested" in Masonic matters, becoming "one of the most prominent Masons in the state." He served as Grand Master of the Grand Lodge of Indiana in 1894–95, and as its grand treasurer and general counsel for many years. He joined the Scottish Rite and became an honorary member of the thirty-third degree.

Self-described as "a lawyer in every fiber of his being," Gavin practiced law in Indianapolis until his death on November 1, 1936, at age eighty-two. He was remembered as kind, cheerful, fair, and tolerant. He is buried in Crown Hill Cemetery.

Selected Bibliography

A Biographical History of Eminent and Self-Made Men of the State of Indiana. Vol. 1. Cincinnati: Western Biographical Publishing Company, 1880.

The American Lawyer: A Monthly Journal Serving the Business and Professional Interest of the American Bar. Vol. 4, January–December 1896. Stumpf and Steurer, 1896.

Dunn, Jacob Piatt, Jr. *Greater Indianapolis: The History, the Industries, the Institutions, and the People of a City of Homes. Vol. 2.* Indianapolis: Lewis Publishing Company, 1910.

Harding, Lewis A. *History of Decatur County, Indiana: Its People, Industries and Institutions.* Indianapolis: B. F. Bowen and Company, 1915.

Harvard College Class of 1873, Tenth Anniversary Report. Cambridge, MA: Harvard College, 1883.

Harvard College Class of 1873, Fiftieth Anniversary Report. Cambridge, MA: Harvard College, 1923.

Polk's Indianapolis (Marion County, Ind.) City Directory, 1897, 1910, 1914.

Proceedings of the Annual Meeting of the M. W. Grand Lodge of Free and Accepted Masons of the State of Indiana, 1937.

Taylor, Charles W., comp. *Biographical Sketches and Review of the Bench and Bar of Indiana.* Indianapolis: Bench and Bar Publishing Company, 1895.

CASES CITED

Parrett v. Palmer, 8 Ind. App. 356 (1893).
Clemitt v. Watson, 14 Ind. App. 38 (1895).

Special thanks to Virginia Rabbit-Jenkins, Judge Gavin's great-granddaughter, for sharing with the author her family archives.

INDIANA SUPREME COURT

THEODORE P. DAVIS

January 1, 1893–January 1, 1897

MARY MELLON

In 1892 Theodore P. Davis became one of the first five appellate court judges to be elected to the bench in a statewide contest. Davis learned his profession on the job rather than through law school, earning a reputation as a self-made man, a quick learner, and for possessing an astute legal mind, all of which paved his way to elected office.

Davis, who was born in 1855 in Hamilton County, spent his childhood working on his family's farm in Adams Township and attended the local common school during the winters. At age seventeen, he became a teacher and supported his new choice of profession by completing a term at the National Normal School in Lebanon, Ohio, in 1872; this was his only formal postsecondary education. While he was still teaching, Davis began studying law on his own, and in 1873 he joined the law firm of Moss and Trissal in

Noblesville to formally complete his legal training. In 1874, at age nineteen, Davis was admitted to the Hamilton County bar and became a lawyer at the firm of Moss and Kane. Two years later he left to form the partnership of Kane and Davis.

During his time in private practice, Davis became increasingly involved with the Democratic Party at the local and state level. Beginning in 1873 he attended every state Democratic convention, was elected a school trustee in Noblesville in 1878, and served as an alternate delegate in 1876 to the Democratic National Convention and as a delegate in 1880. According to contemporary accounts, this service, combined with his reputation as a capable lawyer, led Davis's peers to encourage him to seek elected office.

Before his appellate court candidacy in 1892, Davis's campaign experience was limited to a failed bid for judge of the Hamilton Circuit Court in 1890, losing by 181 votes. Newspapers at the time described Davis's candidacy for the Democratic nomination for the Third District appellate court seat as a surprise, and a last-minute coup against a long-established candidate. Upon winning the vote and returning home to Noblesville, Davis was reportedly greeted by a cornet band and crowds of well-wishers. The outcome of the statewide elections in November 1892 was perhaps less surprising: Democratic candidates swept the five appellate seats, as well as all major state offices.

During his four years as an appellate judge, Davis authored about three hundred opinions. At the time, the court was still a temporary institution whose purpose was to ease the case burden of the Indiana Supreme Court Judges. As a result, the jurisdiction of the court was limited to mainly cases involving misdemeanors, recovery of property and of sums less than $3,500, and claims against decedents' estates. Many of Davis's opinions involved railroad companies, whether through property and labor disputes, insurance claims, or issues of liability for property damage or personal injury.

After failing in his bid for re-election to the appellate court in 1896 (this time Republicans swept the seats), Davis formed a new law partnership in Indianapolis with fellow former appellate court judge Frank E. Gavin. Davis continued his service to his party and the legal profession through membership in the American Bar Association and acting as treasurer and later president of the Indiana State Bar Association. Davis died in 1907 at the age of fifty-two; the primary cause of death listed on his death certificate was "exhaustion." He was survived by his wife Anna, whom he married in 1877, and three children. In the official memorial resolution presented to the appellate court after his death, Davis was described as "distinguished for his legal attainments, his probity, and his high conception of judicial duty" and a "marked example of the fact that culture and education are not given by the colleges alone."

Selected Bibliography

Hamilton County Democrat, April 29, July 8, 1892.
"Judge Theodore P. Davis," Court of Appeals of Indiana website. https://www.in.gov/judiciary/appeals/2358.htm.
Madison, James H. *Hoosiers: A New History of Indiana*. Bloomington and Indianapolis: Indiana University Press and Indiana Historical Society Press, 2014.
Monks, Leander J., ed. *Courts and Lawyers of Indiana*. Indianapolis: Federal Publishing Company, 1916.
Staton, Robert H., and Gina M. Hicklin. "The History of the Court of Appeals of Indiana." *Indiana Law Review* 30, no. 1 (1997): 203–31.

INDIANA SUPREME COURT

ORLANDO J. LOTZ

January 1, 1893–January 1, 1897

DONALD B. KITE SR.

An accomplished judge and lawyer, Orlando Jay Lotz lived during an extraordinary time and remained extremely active in Democratic politics and in his community, including the arts, his entire life.

The son of a Lincoln appointee who worked for the Internal Revenue Service for forty-four years, Lotz was born on January 15, 1851, in Jay County, Indiana. In 1873, after working on the family farm, graduating from high school, and teaching for a time, Lotz began studying law. The following year he finished his "private course" at the National Law School in Washington, DC, graduating with honors. In 1874 Lotz was admitted to the Washington, DC, Bar. In 1875 he began practicing law in Muncie. He was appointed judge of the 46th District Circuit Court by Indiana Governor Isaac P. Gray on March 7, 1885, and a year later elected to the same court. Lotz , the first Democrat to hold the office in Delaware County history, served as circuit judge, until his 1892 election to the Appellate Court of Indiana.

Lotz served four years on the court and much of the time served as chief judge. While serving as an appellate judge, he continued to speak at Democratic Party functions. On the morning of October 30, 1896, while he was still on the court, Lotz, introduced Eugene V. Debs, who ran for president on the Social Democratic ticket, when Debs spoke on the steps of the Delaware County Courthouse in Muncie.

The cases that came before the appellate court during Lotz's tenure included numerous appeals involving the railroads. The court also heard appeals involving, among other things, prominent individuals and criminal cases regarding statutory interpretation. On May 14, 1893, Lotz wrote the opinion reversing a trial court's decision against James Whitcomb Riley in a breach of contract action that was brought against the well-known writer and poet by Riley's business manager. In a criminal appeal decided during the same time period, Lotz held that when an individual is over ten years of age and points a firearm at another individual, she/he commits an unlawful act and may be fined whether or not the weapon was loaded, or the act was committed with a mischievous motive.

Trouble seemed to follow the Lotz family. They suffered a series of unfortunate events over their lifetime. In the early 1890s Lotz and his family members narrowly escaped serious injury on at least two occasions. On March 8, 1891, Lotz's wife reportedly nearly lost her life "through the use of chloroform." Two years later, on July 12, 1893, Lotz, his wife, son Walter, and his mother in-law were involved in a serious accident while riding a trolley in Indianapolis. The accident, which led to litigation, involved a sparking trolley and a live wire, resulting in the car being partially surrounded by a "blue electric flame" following the impact. As Lotz's mother-in-law, "a woman well along in years" jumped from the car Lotz jumped after her. In 1889 their family home was destroyed by fire.

In March of 1901 Lotz, who was then a practicing lawyer in Muncie, was punched in the face by the Delaware County Auditor, apparently over a disagreement regarding the auditor's handling of legal documents. Lotz had reportedly stated that he would sue the auditor on his bond. The two punches caused Lotz to fall to his knees but he "made no attempt to fight back," even though the blow caused his glasses to be broken and his hat to be knocked into the gutter. The auditor ultimately pleaded guilty and paid a fine of one dollar and costs.

In addition to his devotion to his legal practice, Lotz was a great supporter of the arts. In 1889, for example, he gave a speech advocating that Muncie embrace the arts if it wished to attract new residents. The following year he displayed his own oil painting, described in a press account as "unpretentious [but] promising," in an art exhibition that included the work of such prominent Indiana artists as T. C. Steele.

On February 5, 1902, following a two-week battle with typhoid fever, Lotz, described as a "lover of art and literature" in one news account, "passed quietly and peacefully" with his family and his law partners at his side, at his home in Riverside, northwest of Muncie. The judge, his wife and their son, attorney Walter J. Lotz, are buried in Muncie's Beech Grove Cemetery.

Selected Bibliography

Indianapolis Journal, March 14, 1902, p. 6 (woman represented by Lotz after he retired from the court of appeals stated she agreed to dismiss law suit because Lotz appeared during a séance and advised her to do so).

Kahn, Edythe T. *Jacob and Sarah Wolf Lotz: Their Ancestry and Descendants, 1760–1994.* LaSalle, MI: E. T. Kahn, 1994.

Muncie Evening Press, November 3, 1937.

Muncie Star Press, August 5, 1900, p. 12 (recounting speech by young attorney Lotz supporting the Republicans'choice of Rutherford B. Hayes but referencing Lotz's then-client Rutherford B. Powell), January 2, 1916, p. 22 (describing Judge Lotz's investment in and ultimately unsuccessful "perpetual motion and power saving machine").

CASES CITED

Riley v. Walker, 6, 622 (Ind. App. 1893).
Graham v. State, 8, 497 (Ind. App 1894).

GEORGE E. ROSS

January 1, 1893–January 1, 1897

TIMOTHY P. SPAHR

Pursuing a career in the law was a natural decision for George Ewing Ross. His grandfather, William Olin Ross, was one of the first attorneys in Wabash County and his father, Nathan Olin Ross, was among the earliest members of the Miami County Bar and enjoyed a sixty-two-year career as an attorney.

George Ross was born in Peru, Indiana, on January 15, 1858, the ninth of ten children. At age fourteen, he entered the Waveland Academy, also known as Waveland Collegiate Institute, in Montgomery County, where he remained for one year. He briefly attended Wabash College in Crawfordsville and then studied law in Logansport under the tutelage of his father. He enrolled as a law student in the fall of 1876 at Indiana University in Bloomington, but soon returned to studying law with his father.

In 1877, at age nineteen, Ross was admitted to the bar in Cass County. In May of that year, he married Martha Boice of Goshen. They had two sons, Nathan O. Ross and George E. Ross Jr., born in 1878 and 1881, respectively.

Just a year after his admission to the bar, Ross gained public attention by representing the plaintiff in a lawsuit against the operators of People's Bank in Logansport. He was up against some of the most experienced attorneys in town, including his father. The case resulted in a hung jury in a trial in in Cass County Superior Court. It was then moved to Miami County, where Ross won for the plaintiff. One of the defendants appealed to the Indiana Supreme Court, which affirmed the trial court's decision in *Uhl v. Harvey*.

For much of his early career, Ross was an assistant solicitor for the Pan Handle Railroad, working with his father, who was the solicitor. In 1888 Ross was the Democratic candidate for the Cass Circuit Court, having beaten then-serving Judge Maurice Winfield for the nomination. However, he lost the election to the Republican candidate, Dyer B. McConnell.

Despite the defeat, Ross again sought elective office. In 1892 he was nominated as the Democratic candidate for judge of the recently established Appellate Court of Indiana for the Fifth District, defeating both John D. McLaren of Marshall County and Robert Effinger, his father's former law partner in Peru. In November 1892 Ross beat the Republican incumbent, Edgar Dean Crumpacker, who had been appointed to the court by Governor Alvin P. Hovey the year before.

Ross served on the appeals court for the next four years, becoming chief judge for the November term in 1894. At the age of thirty-six, he was the youngest judge who had ever served as the presiding judge of either the state's supreme or appellate courts.

During his tenure on the court, Ross was quite active, writing 254 majority opinions, as well as five concurring opinions and twenty-two dissenting opinions. His extensive experience as a railroad attorney obviously served him well in cases involving railroads. He wrote majority opinions in many cases in which a railroad was a named party, and more than half of his concurring and dissenting opinions were in such cases.

Although he was renominated in 1896 by his party for another term, he and the rest of the Democratic members of the court lost in the fall election. Ross returned to practicing law with his father in Logansport in 1897. Unfortunately, he suffered two major blows not long after that. His eldest son,

Nathan, who had been admitted to the Cass County Bar in December 1897 and had attended law school at Columbia in New York City for two years, took ill in February 1898 and eventually died of consumption in Logansport in December 1899. Then, in July 1901, Ross's father died.

Following his father's death, Ross took over as the solicitor of the Pittsburgh, Cincinnati, Chicago & St. Louis Railway Company, later known as the Pennsylvania Railroad Company, a position that he held for the rest of his life.

On June 27, 1928, Ross died in La Jolla, California, just as he was starting his summer vacation. Although his death ended a nearly century-old family tradition of practicing law in north-central Indiana, Ross left a legacy as one of the first judges to serve a full term on what is now the Court of Appeals of Indiana and as the only Miami County native to ever serve on the state appeals court.

Selected Bibliography

Biographical and Genealogical History of Cass, Miami, Howard and Tipton Counties, Indiana. Chicago: Lewis Publishing Company, 1898.

Cass Circuit Court Order Book. Vol. Y. Page 356, Entry Dated May 10, 1877.

Cass Circuit Court Order Book .Vol. 32. Page 378, Entry Dated December 20, 1897.

Indiana Court of Appeals Website. https://www.in.gov/judiciary/appeals/2360.htm and https://www.in.gov/judiciary/appeals/files/bios-hist-ross-george.pdf .

Logansport Pharos, December 18, 1899, July 23, 1901.

Monks, Leander J., ed. *Courts and Lawyers of Indiana.* Indianapolis: Federal Publishing Company, 1916.

Taylor, Charles W. *The Bench and Bar of Indiana.* 3 vols. Indianapolis: Bench and Bar Publishing Company, 1895.

Thomas, John Hardin. "The Academies of Indiana." *Indiana Magazine of History* 10 (December 1914): 331–58.

Weesner, Clarkson W., ed. *History of Wabash County, Indiana.* Chicago and New York: Lewis Publishing Company, 1914.

CASE CITED

Uhl v. Harvey, 78 Ind. 26 (1881).

A BIOGRAPHICAL HISTORY OF EMINENT AND SELF-MADE MEN OF THE STATE OF INDIANA

WOODFIN D. ROBINSON

January 1, 1897–January 1, 1907

JULIE C. S. McDONALD

Woodfin D. Robinson, who returned to his law practice after serving ten years on the Appellate Court of Indiana, was at work in his office the day before he died of a heart attack at home at age seventy-three on May 8, 1930. One of his most newsworthy cases as an attorney was the "Dry Appeal" case in which Robinson reasoned that localities should decide whether to permit the sale of alcohol. He argued on behalf of the F. W. Brewing Company of Evansville about the construction of a law that permitted drinking alcohol but prohibited buying it. Robinson argued that the right to drink the alcohol necessarily presupposed the right to buy and sell it.

Representatives of the Anti-Saloon League and Indiana's attorney general claimed that alcohol was "in a class with smallpox," thereby amply justifying the use of the police power to prohibit its sale. In this climate, Evansville's 200 saloons did a brisk business that nearly depleted their stocks by offering "bargain sales" to friends who would hold or hide liquor in their homes until the Indiana Supreme Court ruled on the constitutionality of the prohibition law.

On June 28, 1918, Robinson lost his argument when the Court held that the act's prohibition on the sale of intoxicating liquors was constitutional. Sixteen months later, Congress passed the National Prohibition Act, enabling legislation to implement the Eighteenth Amendment. Three months after that, Congress ratified the amendment, and nationwide prohibition began the next day.

Robinson, who was born in Illinois on February 27, 1857, moved to Indiana at age eight. He had eight siblings, and his father was a successful farmer in Gibson County. Robinson lived and worked on his father's farm until he was twenty-two. He attended local grade schools and high school at Owensville and then graduated from Indiana University with a bachelor's degree in 1879.

He then taught school in Gibson County, serving as a principal and superintendent of schools in the county, while studying law privately. He then attended the University of Virginia law school and graduated from the University of Michigan law school in 1883. He was admitted to the bar that year and entered practice in Princeton, Indiana.

Robinson practiced with Arthur Twineham from 1883 to 1897 and during this time also founded the *Gibson County Leader* newspaper. He was elected to the Indiana House of Representatives as a Republican in 1894, and then was elected to the appellate court in 1896, serving for ten years and as chief judge for four terms, November 1897 to May 1906.

It was considered a great surprise when Robinson's campaign managers did not secure his renomination for appellate court judge in 1906, as he was considered one of the "safest judges in the state." An acquaintance said, "Probably no other judicial candidate stood higher with the attorneys of the state, but Robinson's friends relied too much on them. They didn't attempt to make a thorough organization that was absolutely necessary to succeed under the circumstances." Spending ten years in Indianapolis might have also hindered his renomination in 1906. One newspaper reported that he even denied living in Indianapolis. "Princeton is my home," he said, adding, "Princeton is my voting place, and it is from Princeton that I am running for renomination." He then lost a race for judge of the Indiana Supreme Court in 1912, and was considered again in 1918, but withdrew his nomination.

Robinson married Jessie Montgomery in 1884, and they had one daughter, Virginia. He was remembered as someone who “manifested a spirit of justice, sweetness of temper, gentle courtesy, and an essential kindliness.”

Selected Bibliography

Dunn, Jacob Piatt, Jr. *Indiana and Indianans: A History of Aboriginal and Territorial Indiana and the Century of Statehood.* Vol. 5. Indianapolis: Federal Publishing Company, 1916.

Hamilton County Times, May 31, 1906.

Indianapolis News, June 9, 1932.

Noblesville Ledger, October 28, 1914, November 5, 1932, May 2, 1955.

Rushville Daily Republican, August 30, 1912.

Tipton Daily Tribune, March 26, 1951.

CASE CITED

Schmitt v. F .W. Brewing Co. 187 Ind. 623, 120 N.E. 19 (Ind. App. 1918).

INDIANA SUPREME COURT

WILLIAM J. HENLEY SR.

January 1, 1897–October 1, 1904

WILLIAM F. GULDE

When famous lawyer Clarence Darrow was in a jam and needed help he turned to William J. Henley, a former judge of the Appellate Court of Indiana. Darrow was struggling for cash in 1912 as he was having his own legal troubles in Los Angeles. To his mistress, Mary Field, back in Chicago, he wrote, "If you haven't enough to get back tell Judge Henley to loan it to you & I will send it to him. He has been in trouble & is all right." Henley had just gone through a sensational trial of his own that made headlines both in Chicago and Indianapolis. In 1910 he had been charged by Illinois officials with embezzlement and creating a slush fund with which to bribe Illinois legislators to curry favor for the Chicago and Western Indiana Railroad, of which he was the acting president. Darrow represented Henley and had managed to get all of the charges dropped. Likely breathing a sigh relief, Henley resumed his legal practice in Indiana.

Born to Thomas W. and Hannah Williams Henley in 1863, Henley grew up in Carthage, Indiana, in northwestern Rush County. Raised in the Quaker faith, young William attended the Friends Academy in Carthage. He later graduated from Carthage High School in 1881 and immediately began studying law in New Castle. By 1885 he had moved to Rushville, where he met and married Sara Monroe. His first law partner in Rushville was Ben L. Smith and later Lot Guffin. Besides running a successful law firm, Henley became interested in Republican Party politics. In 1896, at the of age thirty-three, Henley successfully ran for the Appellate Court of Indiana on the Republican ticket. He was one of the youngest judges to ever serve in that position. His first tenure on the court began in the winter of 1897. He was reelected two other times and served until 1904.

The cases in front of Henley reflected both the societal and economic trends of the day. A substantial amount of the court's docket was lawsuits against railroad companies. Citizens and local governments frequently sued rail companies for damages. For example, in 1899 the court reversed a decision by the Grant County Circuit Court to award damages to the Buboise family. Mrs. Buboise had fallen out of a wagon after her horses became spooked by an electric streetcar in Marion, Indiana. The court ruled that the streetcar company was neither reckless nor malicious. In a similar ruling, Henley wrote an opinion for the court reversing a Sullivan Circuit Court decision awarding a Farmersburg man damages from the Evansville and Terre Haute Railway Company. Charles Welch was standing on a platform at the depot when much to his horror the incoming passenger train struck and killed a nearby man, whose body struck his own. He sued and was awarded $500, but the appellate court ruled that the rail line was not at fault. Henley wrote that "such an injury could not have been foreseen as reasonably anticipated as the probable result of appellant's negligent act." In other words. There were no precautions that the railroad could have taken for the bystander's safety under the circumstances.

In cases involving railroads, Henley was usually inclined to side with the company rather than the plaintiff. His sympathy with the railroads was manifested when he resigned from the court in 1904 to become President and General Counsel of the Chicago and Western Indiana Railroad. He remained with the railroad until 1912, but his indictment in 1910 may have affected his relationship with the company.

Other issues the court wrestled with during his tenure included industrial liability issues and oil and natural gas disputes, alcohol prohibition, workmen's compensation, and easements for telephone companies.

After his brief, albeit tainted, tenure with the Chicago and Western Indiana Railroad, Henley returned to the practice of law in Indianapolis with a variety of partners until his first retirement in 1917 due to ill health. By 1920 he resumed practicing law in Rush County until he retired for good in 1939.

He died in Carthage on April 11, 1944, survived by his wife Myrtle and three daughters. He is buried in Riverside Cemetery in Carthage.

Selected Bibliography

"Charge Against Henley Quashed." *Rushville Republican*, December 21, 1912.
"Embezzlement Charge Against Indiana Man." *Indianapolis News*, May 7, 1910.
"Henley's Bond Arraigned." *Indianapolis News*, May 9, 1910.
"Henley Denies Bribery Charge." *Rushville Republican*, May 7, 1910
Tietjen, Randall, ed. *In the Clutches of the Law: Clarence Darrow's Letters* (Berkley: University of California Press, 2013).

CASE CITED
Evansville and Terre Haute Railroad Company v. Welch, 25 Ind. App. 308, 58 NE 88 (1900).

INDIANA SUPREME COURT

DANIEL W. COMSTOCK

January 1, 1897–January 1, 1911

DONALD B. KITE SR.

On April 14, 1917, shortly after becoming a member of the U.S. House of Representatives, Daniel Webster Comstock, a seventy-six-year-old Civil War veteran, rose to give an impassioned speech on America's entry into World War I. He expressed his support for a substantial war loan to the Allies and his preference for the enlistment of volunteers over conscription.

Comstock, who was born on December 16, 1840, in Germantown, Ohio, was educated in nearby common schools, graduated from Ohio Wesleyan University in Delaware, Ohio, and studied law. Upon the completion of his legal studies, he moved to New Castle, Indiana, where he began practicing law and was elected prosecutor in 1862 with jurisdiction over Henry and Rush Counties. When the Civil War began, Comstock ceased practicing law in order to become a private in the Ninth Indiana Cavalry Regiment, serving until September 18, 1865, and rising to the rank of captain and then assistant adjutant general. Comstock was given military honors for rescuing a superior officer "in the face of a withering fire from the enemy" after the officer was thrown from his horse.

Following Comstock's service in the Civil War, he moved to Richmond, Indiana, where he married, practiced law, was elected Richmond City Attorney in 1867, and was subsequently elected and then reelected Wayne County Prosecutor in 1872 and 1874. In 1878 he was elected to the Indiana Senate, where he served on the judiciary committee. Thereafter, in 1884 and 1890, Comstock was elected judge of the Seventeenth Judicial Circuit, presiding for about twelve years.

During his time as a trial judge, which helped to shape his views as an appellate judge, Comstock presided over a significant number and variety of cases including at least one case where he was compelled to impose the death penalty. As a trial judge Comstock also performed other judicial functions including performing several marriages.

In 1896 Comstock was elected, the first of four times, to the Appellate Court of Indiana. During his lengthy tenure, the court's decisions addressed a variety of issues affecting criminal law, negligence, the railroads, and other areas of public and private concern. Comstock's opinions, including his dissenting opinions, speak both to his intellect and the time in which they were written. In January of 1905 he wrote an opinion holding that when individuals equip their houses as a "blind pig" or "blind tiger," meaning illegally selling intoxicating liquors from their homes, they may be prosecuted for maintaining public nuisance despite the absence of an Indiana statute making such a declaration.

In *Massey v. Massey*, Comstock dissented from the view taken by his colleagues in a divorce case, concluding that the husband's contention that his wife had made a false charge of adultery against him constituted an insufficient ground for a divorce inasmuch as "such a false charge against a man is trivial in its effects compared with the utter ruin it may cause a woman."

In 1911 Comstock retired from the appeals court and began practicing law in Richmond with his son Paul. They practiced law together for several years until Comstock was elected in 1916 to Congress. He also served as department commander of the Grand Army of the Republic, Department of Indiana.

On May 19, 1917, Comstock died of pneumonia at his apartment in the Dewey Hotel in Washington, DC, just three months after he was sworn into Congress and approximately fifteen months after he gave a campaign speech, responding to the charge that he was "old and ha[d] held office long enough, observing that "youth is a blessing but not a merit." Comstock was buried in Richmond's Earlham Cemetery, with both the Senate and the House of Representatives holding memorials in his honor. Comstock was survived by his wife Josephine and his son Paul, who was a Spanish-American War veteran, along with two daughters, Elizabeth and Clara. Neither daughter ever married, according to a family member, both because "their father put to scorn any young men who might have been attracted to them" and that no young man could match their father, whom they considered perfect.

Selected Bibliography

Comstock, D. W. *Ninth Cavalry: One Hundred and Twenty-First Regiment Indiana Volunteers*. Richmond, IN: J. M. Coe, 1890.

Muncie Star Press, January 6, 1906. (Describes Comstock's accident while taking a bath in the statehouse.)

Palladium-Item, August 29, 1922. (Notes Comstock was a charter member of the Taconite Club.)

Richmond Item, July 9, 1896, February 20, 1911. (Describes Comstock being hit by bicyclist in Chicago.)

_______. February 10, 1911. (Report of Comstock's speech about George Washington's traits and imperfections.)

CASES CITED

Massey v. Massey, 80 N.E. 977 (Ind. App. 1907).

INDIANA SUPREME COURT

ULRIC Z. WILEY

January 1, 1897–January 1, 1907

DONALD B. KITE SR.

On May 24, 1901, Judge Ulric Zwingli Wiley spoke to the nine graduates of Irvington High School at its first commencement since the school had received its commission. The judge's topic, "The Perpetuity of Popular Government," focused on the value of education and the dependence of the government on the new generation.

The son of a Quaker preacher and farmer, Wiley was born on a farm near Madison, Indiana, on November 14, 1847, and he attended nearby schools before graduating in 1867 from Hanover College. He attended law school at Northwestern Christian University, which became Butler University, receiving his law degree in May of 1873 while also studying law under Indianapolis attorney William Wallace. Wiley practiced law in Madison beginning in 1869 before moving to Indianapolis in 1871. He also taught school for two years.

In 1874 Wiley married Mary Albert Cole, with whom he eventually had four children, and the couple moved from Indianapolis to Fowler, Indiana, where Wiley opened his law office. One year later Wiley was appointed Benton County's first county attorney and served in this position until 1877. Wiley was elected to the Indiana General Assembly in 1882. He was appointed a Purdue University trustee in 1890. Wiley, who remained a Republican for most of his life, save a short stint in 1912 in the Progressive Party, traveled to Washington, DC, in 1901 to watch the inauguration of William McKinley. In 1892 he was appointed judge of the circuit court consisting of Benton, Newton and Jasper Counties and served until 1896. Wiley was also dean of the Indianapolis College of Law during the early part of the 1900s.

In 1896 Wiley resigned from the trial bench and was elected to the Appellate Court of Indiana on the Republican ticket. He was reelected two additional times, retiring from the court at the end of his term in 1907.

Wiley's opinions were typically anchored to his legal and political philosophy. In addition to opinions that addressed significant societal issues such as the contractual rights of married women, the court addressed issues that were impactful regardless of the underlying subject matter. On May 11, 1899, Wiley, writing for the court in *Schwartz v. Parsons*, reversed a trial court's decision denying the defendant's attorney's request to continue a trial where the defendant was "confined by sickness to his bed" more than 125 miles away from the courthouse. Wiley based the decision on the fact that the defendant was the only defendant in the case and not merely a witness and that according to law "litigants are entitled to be present in court when their rights are being litigated."

In a subsequent but unrelated decision in 1906, *White v. State,* Wiley affirmed the imposition of a fine on a Hancock County druggist who had allegedly exhibited a gaming device when he allowed "dice-shaking for the cigars in his store." He rejected the argument that the pharmacist should not have been fined because dice were not listed as a gaming device under the applicable statute, noting that the language of the statute allowed anything to be considered a gaming device if it was used for the purpose of gambling to win money or other property.

In 1906 newspaper reporters began to speculate as to whether Wiley's prospect of re-election to the appellate court, as well as the prospect of his possible election to Congress as a Bull Moose candidate were negatively impacted by a series of unrelated but unfortunate events. Wiley, a judge on the appellate court at the time, was listed as a director of the Ubero Plantation development company in published advertisements, which sought to entice potential shareholders to invest in the project. Ultimately the project failed. Wiley apparently became caught up in the Ubero Plantation scandal for a time as a result of his being the author of a letter or report that was shown to potential investors referencing the promising returns from neighboring plantations. The suggestion was also made that Wiley had ruled in favor of the railroads "too frequently" and went on to represent a railroad. His electability issue was resolved when he retired from the court just before the election.

Following his retirement from the court, Wiley practiced law in Indianapolis until approximately 1928. During this time he represented the Chicago and Erie Railroad as well as other clients.

On January 5, 1929, when Wiley died of influenza, a memorial service was held in the Indiana Supreme Court courtroom in the Indiana Statehouse. He is buried in Crown Hill Cemetery, in Indianapolis.

Selected Bibliography

Columbus Republic, February 8, 1900.
Hamilton County Democrat, July 4, 1902.
Houston, Florence Wilson, Laura Cowan Blaine, and Ella Dunn Mellete. *Maxwell History and Genealogy: Including the Allied Families of Alexander, Allen, Bachiler . . . Walker, Wiley, Wilson.* Indianapolis: Press of C. E. Pauley, 1916.
Indianapolis Journal, July 17, 1901 (articles addressing the Judge's fishing prowess).
Indianapolis News, April 30, 1904.
Muncie Star Press, June 29, 1902, p. 4.
Wiley, Harvey W. *An Autobiography*. Indianapolis: Bobbs-Merrill Company 1930.

CASES CITED

Schwartz v. Parsons, 340, 53 N.E. 785 (22 Ind. App. 1899)
White v. State, 95, 76 N.E. 554 (37 Ind. App. 1906);

The writer thanks Howard Maxwell of Indianapolis. Maxwell has been helpful on more than one occasion regarding research and suggestions concerning Maxwell descendants, including Judge Wiley and Jerome Wiley Segovia, Washington, D.C., who is a descendant of Judge Wiley's brother Doctor Harvey Washington Wiley.

INDIANA SUPREME COURT

FRANK S. ROBY

March 21, 1901–January 1, 1911

RICHARD E. HUMPHREY

The high regard that legal colleagues held for Frank S. Roby can best be surmised by two references to his judicial acumen in separate addresses to annual meetings of the Indiana State Bar Association. In 1928, at a time when the Indiana Supreme Court was struggling with a "congestion of cases," Justice Clarence Martin, a former law clerk for the judge, said Roby had accurately identified this problem years before "in an able address before this Association in describing the system of administration, and which has not since changed." Again, in 1930, Judge Charles F. Remy of the Appellate Court of Indiana, in an address on "Brief and Oral Argument on Appeal," remarked, "Judge Frank S. Roby, one of the ablest judges who has been a member of either of the Indiana courts of appeal, in one of his opinions, wrote, 'The rules of the Supreme Court . . . are designed to advance justice, and not to defeat it. . . . That they should be observed, goes without saying.'"

Roby was born June 26, 1854, in Leesville, Ohio, to Pliny and Ann E. Roby. Shortly after his birth, his parents moved to Steuben County, Indiana, where he spent most of his boyhood. His primary schooling was overseen by his mother in a one-room schoolhouse. He subsequently attended Angola High School for just a year and was granted a teaching license. Roby taught school during the winter and worked in his father's carpentry business in the summer, reading borrowed law books in his leisure time. He later read law with Robert W. McBride, who was to become a circuit judge and Indiana Supreme Court Judge.

Admitted to the bar in 1876, Roby began active practice in 1882 and was associated with several small firms, finally settling in Auburn, Indiana, in 1894. In addition to his legal occupation, he also served on the board of directors of the Northeastern Indiana Street Railway Company, which was incorporated in Auburn in 1899. Roby was appointed circuit judge in 1897, succeeding Judge William Penfield. He was appointed to the appellate court by Governor Winfield Durbin, on March 21, 1901, and was thereafter elected to the position in 1902 and 1906. Roby was also a charter member of the Indiana State Bar Association.

Of the nearly 400 court of appeals cases upon which Roby rendered an opinion, perhaps the most notable and interesting was *Ramsey et al. v. Hicks*, where he ruled in favor of the appellants, Ramsey and others, who represented a Presbyterian congregation attempting to regain possession of land where their church building and pastor's residence stood. Loss of the property had resulted from the congregation's initial agreement to unite with the Presbyterian Church in the U.S.A. The appellants, in their initial suit, denied that any such union had transpired. The plaintiffs, Joseph P. Hicks and others, asserted that, as the congregation was in fact incorporated into the Presbyterian Church in the U.S.A., ownership of the property had thus reverted to the national organization. The trial court's decision, in favor of Hicks et al., was later affirmed by the Indiana Supreme Court, on March 31, 1910, with Justice Oscar Montgomery's opinion overruling Roby's decision.

In addition to his address at the 1903 Indiana State Bar meeting, Roby's eloquence as an orator is further supported by the preservation of four other speeches that are retained in the Indiana Pamphlet collection of the Indiana State Library. His speech, "Indiana Courts of Appeal," was made before the State Bar Association of Indiana, on July 8, 1903; on January 22,

1906, Roby spoke to the law class of Indiana University (now Indiana University Maurer School of Law) about "Authority of Judicial Decisions"; and his "Toast the Judge," a tribute to Judge Edwin C. Vaughn upon his retirement was made on November 30, 1906, to the Wells County Bar Association in Bluffton, Indiana. At the December 17, 1907, meeting of the McKinley Club in Indianapolis, Roby discussed "Precinct Committeeman," alluding to his experiences in Indiana politics and encouraging integrity and honesty in all endeavors of public service.

Upon leaving the appeals court, Roby returned to private practice in Indianapolis, which he continued for eighteen years until failing health forced him to retire. He died of pneumonia on January 3, 1926, at the home of his adopted children in Zionsville, Indiana, and was buried in the Woodlawn Cemetery in Auburn, Indiana. Perhaps the best summation of his life can be found in the final sentence of his memorial tribute: "That he was a patriotic citizen, a very capable lawyer and an upright judge, those who knew him will freely attest."

Selected Bibliography

https://www.in.gov/judiciary/appeals/2365.htm/.
https://www.in.gov/judiciary/appeals/files/bios-hist-roby-frank.pdf/.
Indiana University Maurer School of Law. "Indiana Bar Proceedings." *Indiana Law Journal*
(1928–1929): 43.
———. "Indiana Bar Proceedings." *Indiana Law Journal* (1929–1930): 26.
———. "Indiana Bar Proceedings." *Indiana Law Journal* (1946–1947): 49.
Skene, W. F. *McGraw Electric Railway Manual*. New York: McGraw Publishing Company, 1913.

CASES CITED

Ramsey et al. v. Hicks et al., 87 N.E. 1091 (1909).
Ramsey et al. v. Hicks et al., 91 N.E. 344 (1910).

INDIANA SUPREME COURT

DAVID A. MYERS*

October 18, 1904–January 1, 1913

JAMES R. WILLIAMS

David Albert Myers, who served on the Indiana Supreme Court as its fifty-eight judge, was a Republican politician and consummate legal fixture in the state of Indiana. His career was marked by remarkable achievement and longevity.

Myers was born on August 5, 1859, in Cass County, Indiana. He was educated at Smithson College, Danville Normal College, and Union University before receiving his law degree from Albany Law School in New York in 1882. Thereafter, he began practicing law in Greensburg, Indiana, being elected city attorney in 1886. In 1890 and 1892 he was elected prosecuting attorney of the Decatur-Rush Judicial District, before his 1899 appointment as judge of the Bartholomew-Decatur Circuit by Governor James A. Mount.

In October 1904 Myers was appointed judge of the Appellate Court of Indiana from the First District by Governor Winfield T. Durbin. In

November of that year and again in 1908 he was elected to the appellate court and served in that capacity until January 1913. Myers was first elected to Indiana's highest court in 1916, a year when Republicans won all the top state offices on the ballot. He was reelected in 1922 and again in 1928, another big year for Republicans. He ran for re-election in 1934 but was unable to weather the Democratic tide that had begun to sweep the state in 1932. He was defeated by another Greensburg attorney, George L. Tremain. In his total of thirty-two years on Indiana's highest two courts, Myers served under eleven governors. Remarkably, the astute Republican politician was reputed to be as amicable with Democrats as he was with members of his own party. During his time on the bench, Myers was on two occasions the only elected Republican in the Indiana Statehouse.

In his first year on the supreme court Myers grappled with the other justices over some key constitutional issues. In 1917 in *Bennett v. Jackson, Secretary of State et al.*, he sided with the court's majority in preventing the general assembly from calling for election of delegates to a constitutional convention. The Court ruled that only the voters had the authority to call a constitutional convention. Myers also joined the Court majority in the case of *Board of Election Commissioners of City of Indianapolis v. Knight* to invalidate the Partial Suffrage Act that would have given women voting rights in some municipal and school board elections.

In his seventeen-year tenure on the Indiana Supreme Court, Myers wrote a total of 292 opinions. Close to 60 percent of Myers's opinions were about criminal appeals. At the time the Court was bogged down with a backlog of cases, due in part to the large number of criminal appeals the Court had to hear.

After retiring from the Court in 1935, Myers returned to Greensburg and practiced law until shortly before his death. He was believed to be the oldest practicing attorney in the Midwest, practicing up until the age of ninety-five. At the age of ninety-two, Myers reflected on a U.S. patent law case that he had recently successfully litigated for which he said he "had to buy an entire new set of law books and 'cram' for more than a month."

Aside from his involvement in political and public affairs, Myers helped to found the Indiana State Bar Association and was a lifelong member and supporter. In 1948 he was presented with a life membership certificate along with the other four surviving founder-members of the association.

Additionally, for more than half a century he was a member of the Knights of Pythias, the Masons, and the Columbia Club in Indianapolis.

The *Greensburg Daily News* wrote in a tribute to Myers's ninety-fifth birthday that he was "[m]aintaining his usual busy schedule . . . at his desk, smoking the inevitable cigar, with things other than his remarkable longevity and state of health uppermost in his mind." Myers died on July 1, 1955, at his Greensburg home.

Selected Bibliography

Greensburg Daily News, May 10, 1951, August 5, 1954.

CASES CITED

Bennett v. Jackson, Secretary of State et al., 186 Ind. 533 (1917).
Board of Education Commissioners of City of Indianapolis v. Knight, 187 Ind. 108 (1917).

*This profile is revised from one that appeared in *Justices of the Indiana Supreme Court* (2010).

CASSIUS C. HADLEY

January 1, 1907–January 1, 1911

GRETA MORRIS SCODRO

Early in his legal career, Cassius Clay Hadley got statewide press coverage as the prosecutor of a notorious Hendricks County murder.

A member of a large, early-pioneer family, he was born August 9, 1862, on a farm in Hendricks County, one of nine children. After finishing local schooling, he studied at Butler University for three years and then earned a law degree from DePauw University in 1886. He had the good fortune to "read law" as a clerk for his uncle, John V. Hadley, who became Hendricks Circuit Court judge and later an Indiana Supreme Court Judge. Shortly after his marriage to Frances S. Reed, the couple moved to Scott County, Kansas, where Hadley opened a law practice. After returning to Hendricks County about 1890 and settling in Danville, Hadley began practicing law with Thomas Cofer.

Statewide attention came in 1895 when he prosecuted a Hendricks County murder case. One snowy night, the Reverend William Hinshaw ran from the Methodist parsonage, having been shot twice in the arm and slashed with a knife, yelling that two intruders had just killed his wife. Investigation produced evidence that a young lady friend visited the parsonage when the wife was away. Hinshaw was charged with murder; the prosecution's theory was that Hinshaw shot his wife in the head at close range while she slept, then wounded himself to conceal his crime.

At trial, with his Uncle John presiding, prosecutor Hadley created a sensation by re-creating the couple's bedroom in the courtroom, furniture and all, to show the jury that Hinshaw's version of events could not be true. Trial proceedings were covered by the press daily and Hadley's closing argument was quoted at length, accompanied by an artist's sketch of him. The courtroom was so full, women fainted, and men were ejected for vocal outbursts. The jury found Hinshaw guilty and the conviction was affirmed by Indiana's Supreme Court in *Hinshaw v. State*, a fact-filled, frequently cited opinion discussing the nature of circumstantial evidence.

Not long after the trial, Hadley and his wife moved to Indianapolis, where he opened a law office and worked as a county deputy prosecutor. In 1899 he was appointed a deputy attorney general, which gave him the opportunity to argue cases before the U.S. Supreme Court, and ultimately, to seek election to the Appellate Court of Indiana.

A Republican, Hadley won election in 1906, a few years after the appeals court had become a permanent court, but while the legislature was actively tinkering with the court's statutory jurisdiction. During his four-year term, he handed down 168 reported decisions, all in civil cases. *Niagara Oil Co. v. Jackson* (addressing the rights of adjacent landowners relative to water discharged by one that flowed onto the land of another) and *Ames v. Ames*, (reversing an award of specific performance in a family real estate transaction on equitable grounds) were the opinions most frequently cited in later cases. His fellow judges described him as a "diligent, painstaking and able" judge who preferred to decide cases on the merits rather than technicalities.

In a 1909 presentation at the annual meeting of the Indiana State Bar Association, Hadley criticized the focus by lawyers and judges on legal technicalities, adding that "we can but wonder, how much speedier and beneficial the results would be if the same research and thought should be expended in the search for the right and justice of the matter."

He pulled no punches in the speech, asserting that too many lawyers and judges were failing to meet the duties they owed each other and the public. Claiming that commercialism and wealth seem to be the ruling passions of the day, Hadley said that "too many of our great lawyers have become mere merchants, offering their wares . . . to the highest bidder without regard to the purposes to which they may be put."

Hadley lost election to a second term, but he had plenty to do after becoming president of the Commercial Club, which was founded by Colonel Eli Lilly in 1890 to promote business growth. In 1912 Hadley oversaw the consolidation of several organizations into the present-day Indianapolis Chamber of Commerce. He was also president of the American Central Law School, one of several Indianapolis schools that formed today's McKinney School of Law.

After suffering a stroke, Hadley died November 24, 1913, at his Indianapolis home. He was fifty-one. Those who had known him described a gracious, well-liked man, good at giving after-dinner speeches, with a keen, but kind, sense of humor.

Selected Bibliography

Indianapolis Star, November 25, 1913.

Indianapolis News, September 28, 1895.

Hadley, Cassius C. "Lawyers & Clients." Paper presented at the Indiana State Bar Association annual meeting, July 1909. Printed in the *Report of the Thirteenth Annual Meeting of the State Bar Association of Indiana* (1909), and available online at https://babel.hathitrust.org/cgi/pt/search?q1=hadley;id=mdp.35112104868908;view=1up;seq=1;start=1;sz=10;page=search;orient=0.

History of Hendricks County, 1914–1976. Danville, IN: Hendricks County Historical Society, 1976 (describing the Hinshaw murder case and what happened to Hinshaw after prison).

Proceedings of the Annual Meeting Indiana State Bar Association. Vol. 18. Hadley's memorial, p. 229; viewable on https://books.google.com/.

"In Memoriam . . . Cassius C. Hadley," 54 Ind. App. ___, ____, ___ N.E. ___ (1913).

In Memoriam, Report of the Eighteenth Annual Meeting of the State Bar Association of Indiana, 1914.

CASES CITED

Ames v. Ames, 91 N.E. 825 9 (Ind. App. 1910).

Hinshaw v. State, 47 N.E. 157 (Ind. 1897) (affirming Hinshaw's murder conviction).

Niagara Oil Co. v. Jackson, 91 N.E. 825 (Ind. App. 1910).

HAZZARD'S HISTORY OF HENRY COUNTY, INDIANA, 1822–1906

JOSEPH M. RAAB

January 1, 1907–January 1, 1911

A. JAMES FULLER

Joseph M. Raab, a longtime jurist and a Civil War veteran who was active in the Grand Army of the Republic, served as judge of the Twenty-First Judicial Circuit, now known as Warren Circuit Court, for twenty-four years before being elected to the Appellate Court of Indiana. Despite being a rather reserved and unassuming man, Raab had a wide influence in Indiana, especially on such fellow Republicans as Governor J. Frank Hanly.

Born on February 14, 1846, in Fountain County, Indiana, Raab enlisted in the Union army and served in the Sixth Indiana Cavalry during the Civil War. He saw action in the Western Theater, including fighting in battles in Tennessee and Georgia. During the campaign to take Atlanta, Raab rode with his unit in Stoneman's Raid as part of a plan to liberate Union prisoners held in Macon, Georgia. The July–August 1864 raid led by General George Stoneman ended in disaster, as the cavalry was cut off by a larger

Confederate force. Although Stoneman was captured, Indiana troops fought valiantly to allow the rest of the men to escape. The Sixth continued its service beyond the final surrenders of the Confederate land forces and was one of the last units to return to Indiana in September 1865.

After the war, Raab studied law and became an attorney in Warren County in 1867. Practicing in Williamsport, Indiana, he won respect for both his sharp legal mind and his sound character, qualities that led to his election as a circuit court judge. In nearly a quarter century on the bench, Raab won praise for his good nature and fair judgments. Known for having a common touch, he related to the Hoosier citizens who came before his court. Among the more sensational cases over which he presided were those involving the rich and powerful.

In February 1903 Raab oversaw a lawsuit brought by Ohio millionaire John W. Brookwalter who sued a poorer man for damages. The defendant had been hired by Brookwalter to oversee an Indiana flour mill he owned while he ran for governor of Ohio. After he lost the election, Brookwalter agreed to cancel debts owed him if the defendant would give up his position in the mill. When the man returned to his job, the wealthy mill owner sued for the canceled debts, but the jury made up of Indiana farmers ruled against him. That same year, Raab presided over a closely watched custody case involving a "demented youth" who was the heir to a fortune. His family members fell out over the estate and sued one another for guardianship of the young man. Raab gave custody and control of the estate to the young man's father.

A lifelong Republican, Raab held fast to the principles of the Party of Lincoln and the nation he had fought to preserve. Taking an active role in both party politics and in the GAR, the judge came to wield considerable influence in state politics, which in part stemmed from his encounter in 1899 on a street in Williamsport with a bright young acquittance in whom he had taken an interest and had encouraged to study law. But the man had been unable to pursue his education because of poverty and was working as a teacher and digging ditches to earn extra money.

Raab told the young Hanly to "quit teaching school and digging ditches" and to come study law with him, using his books, saying, "My office is big enough for both of us." Hanly did so and the judge mentored both his legal and political careers. When he became governor of Indiana in 1905 Hanly praised Raab for taking him under his wing and never forgot what the older man had done for him. The judge also helped his son, Fred, obtain a position on the pension board of appeals, a body that decided cases involving payments to veterans.

Raab's reputation helped him win election to the Appellate Court of Indiana in 1906 and he served one term. Favorable to progressive legislation, Raab continued to play a role in party politics even as he sat on the bench. Defeated for re-election, he returned to practicing law in Logansport, Indiana, where he remained until his death on April 29, 1925.

Selected Bibliography

Evansville Daily Journal, August 12, 1864.
Indianapolis Journal, May 24, 1903.
Indianapolis Star, September 21, 1865.
Indiana Court of Appeals website. https://www.in.gov/judiciary/appeals/files/bios-hist-rabb-joseph.pdf.
Jasper Herald, August 26, 1910.
Muncie Star Press, February 2, 1903, May 25, 1903.
South Bend Tribune, May 21, 1904, August 5, 1905.

INDIANA SUPREME COURT

WARD H. WATSON

January 1, 1907–January 1, 1911

CARL E. KRAMER

Ward Harrison Watson, who served on the Appellate Court of Indiana from 1907 to 1911, boasted a political, legal, and business career that spanned Indiana's rise as an industrial power, the economic crisis of the 1890s, the temperance movement, and the clash between progressives and conservatives for control of the Republican Party.

Watson, born November 7, 1859, to Ward F. and Mary M. Smoot Watson on their Harrison County farm near Corydon, was reared on the farm and educated at local public schools. After completing his education at Central Normal College in Danville, Indiana, he returned to southern Indiana and taught for about five years at public schools in Harrison and Clark Counties. He settled in Charlestown, Indiana, and began studying law with James K. Marsh, a former Democratic state representative, while continuing to teach.

Watson, admitted to the bar in 1883, entered practice with his mentor, a partnership that continued until 1906, when Marsh was elected Clark Circuit Court Judge. Meanwhile, Watson became involved in Republican politics and established a reputation as one of the GOP's "Big Four" leaders in strongly Democratic Clark County. Despite membership in the minority party, Watson won election to the Indiana Senate in 1894 and served from 1895 through 1898, representing Clark and Jefferson Counties. During his tenure he embraced the progressive views of Albert Beveridge and future governor J. Frank Hanley and strove to advance the interests of southern Indiana.

Along with his legal and legislative pursuits, Watson also engaged in banking, joining thirteen other prominent residents in 1891 to form the Bank of Charlestown and was elected to the board of directors. He made his second foray into electoral politics in 1906, when he was elected to the appeals court, representing the First District. As a jurist he was recognized as "a man of deep insight and was always reluctant to decide matters until they had been fully discussed," an observation that suggested that he was influential in judicial conferences.

Watson wrote at least seven majority opinions. Analysis of the cases and his opinions reflect both the court's jurisdictional evolution and Watson's judicial philosophy. At a time when a major function of the appellate court was to reduce the Indiana Supreme Court's caseload, his opinions addressed issues such as child neglect, small estates, divorce and alimony, and collection of local taxes.

Regardless of the subject matter, Watson's opinions reflected strict adherence to statue and case law as written. He usually upheld lower courts' decisions, but he did not hesitate to reverse if an error was apparent. In *Nyce v. Schmoll,* for example, he overturned the Miami County Circuit Court, which had upheld the Peru city treasurer's attempt to collect taxes from a person who had already paid them on property located in another county. Citing statue and case law holding that "the way to discharge a tax is to pay it," Watson ruled for the taxpayer, asserting that he had paid the property tax in good faith in the other county and that requiring him to pay the tax in Peru as well would "work an irreparable damage."

Watson stayed in Indianapolis after leaving the bench in 1911 and continued to practice law in the capital. He also engaged in banking, serving as president and director of Securities Trust Company. Interested as well in higher education, he served for several years as president of the board of trustees at Moores Hill College, located in Dearborn County before it moved to Evansville in 1917 and became Evansville College (now University of Evansville). He also was a member of the Columbia Club and Benevolent Protective Order of Elks.

Watson married Ethel R. Barnett of Charlestown on January 15, 1890. They had no children. She died on January 20, 1910, while he was still on the court. His wife's death had a profound emotional impact, and in her memory, he left the Charlestown home in which she died unoccupied and in the same state it was in at the time of her death. About 1917 he built a beautiful colonial revival house next door to the one in which his wife had died.

Watson maintained his legal practice in Indianapolis until 1931, when he retired to Charlestown. He died at his home on September 19, 1932, shortly after being stricken with paralysis while viewing a horse show at the Kentucky State Fair in Louisville. He is buried in Charlestown Cemetery, where his grave is marked by an imposing art-deco granite monument, whose placement he supervised just two weeks before his death.

Selected Bibliography

Judge Ward H. Watson: In Memoriam Obituary. in.gov/judiciary/appeals/files/bios-hist-watson-ward.pdf).

"Senator Ward H. Watson, 1859–1932." In *Charlestown Community History.* Charlestown, IN: Clark's Grant Historical Society, 1989.

"Watson, Ward H." *A Biographical Directory of the Indiana General Assembly*. Vol. 1, *1816–1899* (Indianapolis: Indiana Historical Bureau, 1980).

CASE CITED

Nyce v. Schmoll, Treasurer, 82 N.E. 539 (Ind. App. 1907).

MOSES B. LAIRY*

January 1, 1911–January 1, 1915

JULIAN L. RIDLEN

Moses Barnett Lairy, born August 13, 1859, on the family farm in Cass County and educated through the eighth grade in a one-room school, thought he was going to be a schoolteacher. It was not uncommon for a student "of promise" to combine winter season teaching with warm-weather farming after little or no training beyond eighth grade. Thus, when his father died in 1877, seventeen-year-old Lairy assumed the farming responsibilities and attended the Northern Indiana Normal School (now Valparaiso University), to prepare himself to teach.

Lairy taught for nine years and was reportedly being groomed for the post of county superintendent of schools. In the meantime, however, he had begun to study law under the tutelage of Judge Dudley H. Chase and began law studies in 1885 at the University of Michigan, graduating with a law degree four years later and returning to Logansport to open a solo practice. After four years, Lairy partnered with veteran attorney Dewitt C. Justice and later with M. L. Mahoney for fourteen years.

In 1894 Lairy ran for the Cass County Circuit Court against Chase, his first law mentor, who had an understanding with sitting Judge Dyer B. McConnell that if Chase won, McConnell would resign, and Chase would be appointed to serve the remainder of McConnell's term. Both events occurred, however, Governor Claude Matthews, a Democrat, found Democrat Lairy more qualified for the interim appointment. Two years later, Chase assumed the judgeship to which he had been elected, only to be defeated for re-election in 1902 by Lairy's younger brother, John.

By 1908 Lairy had gained enough stature in the bar and in political circles to win the Democratic nomination for the Indiana Supreme Court from the Fifth Judicial District. However, he lost the general election to Quincy A. Myers, a fellow member of the local bar, in a cliff-hanger that was not resolved until three days after the election.

Despite the loss, the attention and name recognition gained in the closely contested election served Lairy well. He won election to the Appellate Court of Indiana in 1910, serving one four-year term. Four years later, Lairy reversed the tables of his 1908 supreme court loss, defeating incumbent Myers, who along with other Republicans found himself in the backwash of the 1912 Theodore Roosevelt split that pitted the conservatives against the progressives within the party.

Lairy left the supreme court in January 1921, and shortly thereafter joined the Indianapolis law firm of Myers, Gates and Ralston. He replaced Myers, who had died the previous month, just as he had succeeded his friend and colleague on the court. Thus, the law firm took a distinctly Democratic political flavor, for in addition to Lairy and former governor Samuel M. Ralston, the reorganized firm also added Frederick Van Nuys, who later became a U.S. Senator.

While Lairy earned a reputation as a hardworking judge during his terms on the appeals and supreme courts for his well-reasoned opinions, the cases that brought him more personal attention were those in which he was involved as counsel.

In a case that garnered national press, Lairy was retained to defend Delaware Circuit Court Judge Clarence W. Dearth in the first impeachment proceeding heard in the Indiana Senate since 1835. Dearth was in an ongoing conflict with the editor of a local paper, who had charged him with jury manipulation, making "goats" of a few bootleggers and criminals, and being friendly to the Ku Klux Klan. The editor fled to Ohio to avoid appearing on a charge of criminal contempt. Responding to petitions from Muncie citizens, the House of Representatives approved seven formal articles of impeachment. In the trial before the Senate Lairy and his co-counsel prevailed for their client—two votes short of the two-thirds necessary to convict.

Lairy died at Logansport on April 9, 1927, a little more than one week following the conclusion of the Dearth trial.

Selected Bibliography

"Extemporaneous Remarks of the Honorable Michael L. Fansler to Cass County Bar Association." Transcript of Cass County Bar Association Meeting, April 5, 1961. Recorded by Frank Tolbert.

"In Indiana." *Time*, April 11, 1927. http://www.time.com/time/magazine/article/0,9171,730339,00.html.

"Indiana's Dearth." *Time*, April 4, 1927. http://www.time.com/time/magazine/article/0,9171,723020,00.html.

Logansport Pharos-Tribune, November 7, 1908, April 11, 1927, June 7, 1937.

M.B. Lairy, 67, Ex-Judge Dies. *Indianapolis Star*, April 10, 1927.

Powell, Jehu Z. *History of Cass County, Indiana*. Chicago: Lewis Publishing Company, 1913.

CASE CITED

State of Indiana v. Shumaker et al., 157 N.E. 769 (Ind. App. 1927).

*This profile is revised from one that appeared in *Justices of the Indiana Supreme Court* (2010).

INDIANA SUPREME COURT

MILTON B. HOTTEL

January 1, 1911–January 1, 1919

KRISTA KINSLOW

Some of Milton B. Hottel's most significant opinions during his eight years on the Appellate Court of Indiana supported Progressive Era reforms, particularly workers' compensation laws that had been passed in Indiana in 1915. The appeals court, designated as the court of last resort in matters pertaining to this act, heard numerous cases dealing with this law during Hottel's tenure. For example, his *In re Boyer* opinion was considered at the time to be "one of the leading cases in the United States related to Workmen's Compensation Laws."

Born on May 5, 1860, in rural Harrison County, Hottel attended Indiana University and was originally interested in obtaining a general classical education. However, by the time he graduated in 1882, he had discovered a passion for law. After graduation, he worked briefly at his father's general store before he began to practice law in Salem, Indiana, for the firm Zaring and Hottel. In Salem, he also met and married Cora Harris in 1888; the couple had five children.

Hottel's first attempt for public office was as a Democrat for attorney general, but he withdrew from the race due to family issues. He then ran for the appeals court for the first district in southern Indiana in 1906 but was defeated. Not to be deterred, he tried again four years later for the same position and was successful. It was the only public office he ever held, serving on the bench until 1919. Reportedly "an able speaker," he was also a local celebrity, asked by the Elks Lodge, for example, to give the address at its annual memorial service.

After his tenure as judge ended, he founded the law firm Shea and Hottel with his partner Joseph H. Shea, with whom he had served on the appeals court. Their office was in the Fletcher Savings and Trust Building in Indianapolis. He continued his involvement in community activities, including a Farm Bureau Federation event where he presided as a judge in a mock trial over the constitutionality of the cooperative marketing law that allowed farmers to trade information without breaking antitrust laws. His career as an attorney necessitated travel, and on one occasion, he was involved in a serious automobile accident. In 1931 he and two other lawyers were returning from business in Greenfield when their vehicle collided with another and Hottel broke his collarbone. He subsequently sued the other driver for $15,000.

Hottel later created the firm Hottel, Mote, and Smith, located in the Railway Exchange Building with Donald R. Mote, who later was elected to both the appeals court and Indiana Supreme Court, and Oscar F. Smith. The firm handled a wide range of cases, including civil, probate, and insurance law. Hottel also served as a "special judge" in an embezzlement case involving Indianapolis sheriff Ralph Hitch, who was alleged to have stolen $8,000. Hottel died at the age of seventy-six in Indianapolis on June 12, 1936. He is buried in Salem, Indiana.

Selected Bibliography

Brookville Democrat, June 14, 1906.
Columbus Republic, December 2, 1914.
Greenfield Daily Reporter, March 1, 1931.
Hancock Democrat, February 19, 1931.
Huntington Herald, November 23, 1925.
Indianapolis Star, December 31, 1913, June 2, 1935, June 13, 1936.

In Memoriam. https://www.in.gov/judiciary/appeals/files/bios-hist-hottel-milton.pdf.
Kokomo Tribune, December 6, 1923.

CASE CITED

In re Boyer, 117 N.E. 507 (Ind. App. 1917).

INDIANA SUPREME COURT

EDWARD W. FELT

January 1, 1911–January 1, 1919

WILLIAM F. GULDE

At noon on January 13, 1913, Edward W. Felt administered the oath of office to the newly elected governor, Samuel M. Ralston. The men had been friends since their days at Central Normal College in Danville and with Felt's election to the Appellate Court of Indiana in 1910, both had reached the pinnacles of their careers. In college they had formed a debate team. Now, both men had prominent roles in running the state of Indiana.

Born in Virginia in 1859, Felt moved with his family to Greenfield, Indiana, when he was just a toddler. Greenfield became the center of his life and played an important role in launching his political career. He received his early education there and became active in the Methodist Church. After graduating from Central Normal in 1884, he returned to Hancock County and married Martha Thomas in 1885.

He taught in local schools and he received his first political job when he was appointed a township trustee in 1886. He was admitted to the bar the following year, joined a law firm with James A. New in Greenfield, and was elected prosecuting attorney of Hancock County in 1890 and 1892.

Felt immersed himself in his job, family that eventually included five children, and church. Felt taught an adult Sunday School class, remained active in Democratic politics, and eventually was elected judge of the Eighteenth Judicial Circuit Court, a position he held until 1906.

Following his defeat for the appellate court in 1906, Felt returned to private practice in Greenfield. He ran for the same position in 1910 and was swept into office in a statewide Democratic tidal wave with the party winning eleven of the thirteen congressional offices and a U.S. Senate seat. Democrats also took control of the Indiana legislature.

Some of the issues that Felt faced as a judge reflected the changing times in America. In 1916, for example, he wrote the opinion in the case involving Luella Pence who had been a passenger in a horse-drawn buggy with her husband on a highway in Grant County. Speeding behind the couple was Martin Pence in an automobile. He tried to overtake the couple's carriage but ended up slamming into their buggy, injuring Mrs. Pence. In his appeal, Martin Pence alleged that the Pence couple crossed into the center of the road and that the horse stopped suddenly. Felt cited a lack of evidence for that argument and sided with the couple in *Pence v. Pence.*

In a negligence case involving the town of Monticello, Felt's opinion in *Monticello v. Condo* affirmed a judgment for Catherine Condo, who had fallen from a bridge maintained by the town. The town claimed that Mrs. Condo, who had been crossing the bridge at night to tend to a sick neighbor, should have used a lantern so that she could have seen that the guardrail had fallen off. Felt, however, upheld a jury's verdict awarding Condo damages. Other cases during his tenure involved such issues as rail lines, easement rights, and electric companies.

Felt moved his family from Greenfield in 1910 to the fashionable neighborhood of Irvington in eastern Indianapolis, which was dry and that fit in nicely with his belief in temperance. His children could also attend nearby Butler University. His loyalty to the Democratic Party remained steadfast as he campaigned for Woodrow Wilson's re-election in 1916. He also remained staunchly loyal to the country as it entered World War I. His only surviving son, Truman, left for the Western Front in 1917 and was injured in a gas attack toward the end of the war.

In the summer of 1918, on a visit to Kokomo, the judge had a flat tire. Dust from the highway blew into his throat as he tried to change the tire. Upon his return to Indianapolis, his condition deteriorated, and he was rushed to Methodist Hospital. He was diagnosed with Vincent's Angina and a doctor had to lance his throat, causing him to miss most of the summer campaign season and he subsequently lost the election in November.

Felt did recover and opened a law office in 1919 with William Forney in Indianapolis and began teaching at the Benjamin Harrison Law School. Governor Ed Jackson appointed him an Indianapolis municipal judge in 1925, however, his tenure was cut short when he died after falling from a ladder at his Irvington home in 1926. He was buried in his hometown of Greenfield.

Selected Bibliography

Hancock Democrat, June 10, 1926.

CASES CITED

Monticello v. Condo 94 N.E. 893 (Ind. App 1911).
Pence v. Pence 113 N.E. 751 (Ind. App 1916).

INDIANA SUPREME COURT

ANDREW A. ADAMS

January 1, 1911–September 1, 1913

JEFFERY A. DUVALL

Before serving on the Appellate Court of Indiana, Andrew A. Adams was an active participant in state politics, having been elected as a Democrat three times to the Indiana House of Representatives. During his time in office he served on both the Ways and Means and Judiciary Committees and was best known for his support to change the compensation of public employees from the fee system to fixed salaries. He also served a single term on the Indiana Democratic State Central Committee in 1904.

Adams was born on his family's farm in Whitley County, Indiana, on January 27, 1864, to John Q. Adams, an Irish immigrant who served for four years as county treasurer, and Christina Elliott, a native of Ohio. Andrew began a three-year course of study at Wabash College in Crawfordsville in 1878 before transferring to Washington and Jefferson College in Washington, Pennsylvania, where he graduated in 1884 with a bachelor's degree.

He spent the next two years reading law under the supervision of Colonel R. S. Robertson of the firm of Robertson and Harper in Fort Wayne and was admitted to the bar in 1887. That same year he went into private practice with Judge James S. Collins in Columbia City.

In 1888 Adams made his first successful run for the Indiana House and in 1890 he married Lois Andrews of Louisville, Kentucky. Their son, Robert A. Adams, became a partner in the Indianapolis law firm of Denny, Adams, Baker and Orbison. After dissolving his partnership with Collins in 1896, Adams set up his own practice, which he closed after being elected to the bench in 1910. He resigned from office on September 1, 1913, to become general counsel for Arbuckle Brothers, the famous coffee company based in New York City, where he remained for the rest of his career. During his brief tenure on the court, which took place during the court's first years as a permanent institution, Adams's best-known opinion was rendered in 1911 in the case of *Voss v. Capital Brewing Company*, in which the court affirmed the Superior Court of Marion County's judgment in a case involving tenant's rights.

Adams was generous in his service to various organizations, including as a member of the Uniform State Laws Commission from 1909 to 1913; the board of trustees of Purdue University from 1907 to 1911, including a term as vice president; and as director of both the Columbia City National Bank and Whitley County Telephone Company. While living in Indianapolis he was a member of the Literary Club and during his years in New York City he belonged to the New York City Bar Association, the University Club of New York, and the People's Free Library. Adams was also a member of the Indiana, New York, and American bar associations.

A lifelong Presbyterian, he was a member of the Freemasons and the Phi Gamma Delta fraternity. After a long illness, Adams died in Clearwater, Florida, on May 5, 1936, and is buried in Crown Hill Cemetery in Indianapolis.

Selected Bibliography

Indianapolis Star, May 7, 1936.

Johnston, Thomas R., and Helen Hand. "The Trustees and Officers of Purdue University 1865–1940." *The Archives of Purdue*, 1:243–44.

Memorial Record of Northeastern Indiana. Chicago: Lewis Publishing Company, 1896.

Monks, Leander J., ed. *Courts and Lawyers of Indiana.* Indianapolis: Federal Publishing Company, 1916.

Shepherd, Rebecca A. *A Biographical Directory of the Indiana General Assembly.* Indianapolis: Indiana Select Committee on the Centennial History of the Indiana General Assembly in cooperation with the Indiana Historical Bureau, 1980.
Staton, Robert H., and Gina M. Hicklin. "The History of the Court of Appeals of Indiana." *Indiana Law Review* 30, no. 1 (1997): 210–11, 219.

CASES CITED

Voss v. Capital City Brewing Company, 96 N.E. 11 (Ind. App. 1911).

INDIANA SUPREME COURT

JOSEPH G. IBACH

January 1, 1911–January 1, 1919

KRISTA KINSLOW

The election of Joseph G. Ibach to the Appellate Court of Indiana in 1910 was never in doubt because he was considered to "one of the best known and most highly respected attorneys in Indiana." Once on the court, he presided three times as chief judge but decided not to seek re-election in 1918 after two terms due to "poor health." The *Indianapolis Star*, lamenting his decision, noted how he had "gained the respect and confidence of his associates and the legal profession," adding that his retirement "is a matter of regret in these circles and in his party."

Ibach, who was born on March 15, 1862, in Huntington County, Indiana, attended the county's public high school. He graduated from the Law School of DePauw University in 1883 and married Minnie Friedley two years later. The couple moved to Neff City, Kansas, where Ibach practiced law because "Huntington held no prospects for such an ambitious young man." However, the couple, who had two daughters and a son, moved back to Indiana several years later, settling in Hammond, where Ibach formed a law partnership with his father, Benjamin. Joseph also became active in the community, serving four years on the Hammond school board, two as president.

While on the court Ibach was appointed by Governor James P. Goodrich to the State Council of Defense Committee, which was designed to determine how best the state could support troops during World War I. In that capacity, Ibach headed an investigative team that went to Gary to examine closing-hour regulations, which merchants opposed because it hurt their businesses. Ibach also served as a member of the board of directors of the People's State Bank in Indianapolis, resigning that position when he moved back to Hammond after leaving the bench.

Ibach returned to his law practice and maintained an important role in the legal profession, often addressing bar associations across the state. In 1923 he spoke on the Constitution to the Tippecanoe County Bar Association and in 1927, when speaking to the Huntington County Bar Association, urged lawyers to "speed up litigation" as the length of court cases tended to "discredit lawyers." He sought greater "qualification for the bar" to "lift the profession to a higher plane" as well. Ibach also addressed the topic of Americanization, a key issue in the 1920s, at a meeting of the Hammond Chamber of Commerce. He believed that "a real danger has arisen and the irresponsible foreigner who has not been given an opportunity to acquaint himself with the ideals and institutions of his adopted government . . . must be reached now."

Although Ibach was mentioned as a possible candidate for governor in 1924, he did not pursue that path. He did help to found the People's Cooperative Bank in Hammond and served as its president for a time. It "inaugurated the policy of sharing its earnings with its depositors" and in 1926, "was shattering all records in the state for growth."

Ibach was in two serious automobile accidents, one in 1925 and again in 1936. The first incident occurred because a traffic signal went out during a storm and the second wreck happened after a bumblebee flew into his car. He tried to kill the bee, and in the process, lost control. He broke his leg and a rib and was hospitalized briefly.

After his wife died in 1934 Ibach remarried in 1936 in a midnight ceremony in Crown Point to Lillian Dimmoch, forty years his junior. He died from a streptococcus infection on September 7, 1937, at age seventy-five. The funeral for Ibach, a leader in the Free Masons, was held at the Masonic Temple in Hammond.

Selected Bibliography

Huntington Herald, November 29, 1927.
Huntington Times, December 23, 1936, September 8, 9, 1937.
Indianapolis News, April 19, 1923.
Indianapolis Star, July 17, 1918.
Munster Times, November 10, 1910, November 26, 1912, June 15, August 24, 1918, July 26, 1919, April 28, 1920, December 6, 1923, December 7, 1925, May 19, 1936, August 3, 1938.

INDIANA SUPREME COURT

JOSEPH H. SHEA

January 1, 1913–May 1, 1916

BRADLEY S. BOSWELL

Joseph Hooker Shea enjoyed a long and eventful career, filled with numerous examples of meritorious service. Born to humble beginnings in Scott County, Indiana, Shea used his intellectual and political skills to ascend from small-town lawyer to the position of U.S. ambassador to Chile. He served his state as a longtime trustee of Indiana University, as well as in legislative and judicial branches of government.

Shea was born in Lexington, Indiana, on July 24, 1863, to Irish immigrants Patrick and Bridget Shea. After graduating from the now-closed Lexington High School, he enrolled at IU. In between his coursework, Shea studied law in Scottsburg under a local lawyer. This led to his admission to the Indiana bar in 1885. After graduating from IU in 1889 with a bachelor's degree, he returned to Scottsburg and began practicing law.

In 1892 Shea was elected by fellow alumni to serve on the IU board of trustees, serving from 1892 to 1896, from 1898 to 1916, and from 1918 to

1920. His tenure on the board was marked by several monumental developments: the first African American male and female graduates; the men's basketball team was created; William Lowe Bryan, considered one of the most important figures in the university's history, was hired as president; and the university created the schools of medicine, education, nursing, and business.

Shea, who was also active in Democratic politics, was elected to the Indiana State Senate in 1896, representing Scott, Clark, and Jennings Counties. From 1896 to 1898 he was also the chairman of the Scott County Democratic Committee. After his one term in the state senate ended in November 1900, Shea served as prosecutor for Scott, Jennings, and Ripley Counties from 1900 to 1904. He was the Democratic nominee for Indiana Attorney General in 1904, but lost the election to the Republican incumbent, Charles Miller. In 1906 Shea was elected judge of the Fortieth Judicial Circuit.

In 1912 Shea was elected to the Appellate Court of Indiana, serving from January 1, 1913 to May 1, 1916. Due to his short duration on the court, Shea was not involved in cases of special note or broad interest, however, disputes before the court at that time do reflect the state's economic makeup of that era. In *Watts v. Chicago & E.I.R. Co.*, the case involved railroads; in *Indiana Life Endowment Co. v. Patterson*, the parties were budding insurance companies; oil and mining interests were involved in *Kansas City Oil & Development Co. v. Irick et al.*; the dispute in *Home Telephone Co. v. Weir* concerned new telecommunications; and early automobile parts suppliers were the parties in *McKinzie v. Fisher Gibson Co.*

When President Woodrow Wilson appointed longtime American diplomat Henry Fletcher to be ambassador to Mexico, transferring him from his post as ambassador to Chile, Wilson relied upon the advice of Vice President Thomas R. Marshall, a fellow Hoosier, in appointing Shea as Fletcher's replacement. Shea assumed this new role on May 1, 1916, the same day he left the appeals court, serving as ambassador until May 5, 1921. His tenure was most notably marked by turbulent South American relations, particularly between Chile and Peru.

At the end of the Wilson administration, Shea left his post in Chile, returned to Indiana, and resumed the practice of law in Indianapolis. He ran for election to the Indiana Supreme Court in 1922 but was defeated by Republican David Myers. At the time, the press speculated that Shea's Catholicism cost him the election due to the growing influence of the Ku Klux Klan in the state.

Shea died in Indianapolis on December 22, 1928. After a career spent traversing Indiana and significant parts of the Western Hemisphere, Shea was buried at the Saint Patrick Catholic Cemetery in Madison, less than twenty miles from his native Lexington.

Selected Bibliography

Former Trustees. https://trustees.iu.edu/the-trustees/former-trustees.html/.
Foughty, Trevor. Joseph Hooker Shea. http://www.capitolandwashington.com/politicians/filter/1930/.
History. https://www.indiana.edu/about/history.html.
Lake County Times, November 13, 1922.
New York Times, March 4, 1916, February 11, 1917, December 23, 1928.
Shea, Joseph Hooker. https://www.in.gov/history/markers/445.htm.

CASES CITED

Home Telephone Co. v. Weir, 101 N.E. 1020 (Ind. App. 1913).
Indiana Life Endowment Co. v. Patterson, 103 N.E. 817 (Ind. App. 1914).
Kansas City Oil & Development Co. v. Irick et al., 110 N.E. 566 (Ind. App. 1915).
McKinzie v. Fisher Gibson Co., 108 N.E. 867 (Ind. App. 1915).
Watts v. Chicago & E.I.R. Co., 104 N.E. 42 (Ind. App. 1914).

INDIANA HISTORICAL SOCIETY

FREDERICK S. CALDWELL

September 1, 1913–January 1, 1919

KRISTA KINSLOW

After spending ten years as a teacher, principal, and superintendent, Frederick S. Caldwell left public education in 1892 to become a lawyer in Winchester in Randolph County, having devoted all his available time for several years to the study of law.

Born in Long Bottom, Ohio, on January 17, 1862, Caldwell, at age twenty, moved to Indiana in 1882 to become principal of schools in New Amsterdam in Harrison County. After two years, he went back to Ohio to attend the National Normal University in Lebanon, graduating in 1885 with highest class honors and named class valedictorian. Caldwell then returned to Indiana to teach in Winchester schools, later becoming principal of the high school and then superintendent.

After switching careers in 1892 Caldwell joined a series of partnerships with Winchester attorneys and in 1912 ran for a position on the Indiana

Supreme Court. He lost the nomination at the Democratic state convention to Richard K. Erwin, who went on to defeat the incumbent Leander J. Monks in the general election. In 1913 Governor Samuel M. Ralston chose Caldwell as a legal adviser to review legislation enacted by the general assembly and in the same year appointed him to the Appellate Court of Indiana to fill a vacancy created by a resignation of Andrew A. Adams.

In his first few months as judge, Caldwell was diagnosed with an "illness bordering on nervous prostration" and was confined to his home for two weeks. In 1914 Caldwell was nominated for the court by acclamation at the Democratic state convention and was elected in the fall for a four-year term.

One of his decisions on the court, *Richmond v. Miller,* in part depended on the meaning of a daily newspaper. Helen M. Miller, who owned land adjacent to a public alley, had sought to close a section of the alley that was one-half of a block in length. The city, which lost in circuit court, appealed in part that the notification of the proposed action had to appear twice in a newspaper published either weekly, daily or daily except *Sunday.* Miller's notice appeared in the *Richmond Morning News,* which published every day except Monday. Dismissing that argument, Caldwell wrote that "we have no doubt that said newspaper was popularly classed by the citizens of Richmond as a daily paper."

In *Shaw v. Bankers National Life Insurance Co.,* the issue concerned the management of a mutual life insurance company whose board of directors consisted of a top executive, two associates, and nine board members. After the two associates resigned, the executive claimed he retained sole power to make decisions. Caldwell disagreed, ruling that the resignations of the two associates terminated the original contract.

Leaving the court after one term, Caldwell began a law practice with his grandson, Robert Oliver, in Winchester. He was also active with the Free Masons and was the Master Mason of a lodge in Muncie, and he also made a number of public speeches, including at the Winchester Memorial Day celebration and at a reunion of veterans of the 158th Indiana Volunteer Infantry who fought in the Spanish-American War.

Caldwell was also appointed to a panel investigating whether the Randolph County prosecutor, Eber Brown, had blackmailed a pharmacist, but had to resign, probably due to his declining health. Being a well-known jurist did not make Caldwell immune to crime. While attending a grandson's graduation at Shortridge High School, someone stole his wallet. After a brief illness, Caldwell died on October 13, 1939, at age seventy-seven.

Selected Bibliography

Fort Wayne Weekly Journal-Gazette, March 28, 1912.
Huntington Herald, June 3, 1913.
Indianapolis News, April 22, 1912.
Muncie Evening Press, November 19, 1913, September 24, 1914, October 13, 1939.
Muncie Star-Press, February 21, 1912, September 14, 1913.
Richmond Palladium-Item, October 14, 1939, October 31, 1926, June 8, 1935.

CASES CITED

Richmond v. Miller, 107 N.E. 550 (Ind. App. 1915).
Shaw v. Bankers National Life Insurance Co., 112 N.E. 16 (Ind. App. 1916).

INDIANA SUPREME COURT

FRANK M. POWERS

January 1, 1915–February 3, 1915

JAMES E. ST. CLAIR

Shortly after assuming his position on the Appellate Court of Indiana in January 1915, Judge Frank M. Powers, suffering from pneumonia, returned home to Angola on January 23 and died at the home of his brother-in-law on February 3. "The report of the death of Judge Powers comes as a distinct surprise and is greatly regretted," said Governor Samuel M. Ralston, who had been unaware of the judge's illness.

Powers, a Democrat, had been elected to the court in November, defeating his Republican opponent Ulysses S. Lesh and the Progressive candidate, Homer C. Underwood. Prior to his election, he had been circuit court judge of Steuben and Dekalb Counties for four years. Ralston named James J. Moran, judge of the Jay Circuit Court, to replace him. Moran served on the court until 1919.

Born near Angola on April 3, 1860, Powers studied law in the office of Joseph A. Woodhull and William G. Croxton and was admitted to the bar in

1882. Powers later formed a partnership with Croxton in 1888, which lasted until his death in 1904.

During his brief time in Indianapolis, Powers had prepared two opinions and attempted to work on another after returning home to Angola. In a statement after this death, his colleagues on the court—Joseph G. Ibach, Edward W. Felt, and Frederick S. Caldwell—wrote that "while he was associated with us only a month, we readily observed his sterling worth, and his splendid ability and equipment for the duties and responsibilities which his new office imposed upon him."

In another statement, Representative Cyrus Cline, who served in Congress from 1909 to 1917 and had known Powers for more than thirty years, wrote, "His life ought to be an inspiration to all. The evenness of his temper, the charity of his soul for the unfortunate, the inflexible standard of right and justice that he set up to rule his conduct are monuments along his pathway to success."

Selected Bibliography

Angola Herald, February 12, 1915.
Indianapolis Star, February 4, 1915.

INDIANA SUPREME COURT

JAMES J. MORAN

February 10, 1915–January 1, 1919

A. JAMES FULLER

James J. Moran, who served one term on the Appellate Court of Indiana, was appointed by Governor Samuel M. Ralston to fill the vacancy created by the death of Frank M. Powers, who died within weeks of assuming his position on the court. At the time of his appointment, Moran, a lifelong Democrat, was a widely known judge of the Jay Circuit Court who had presided over many sensational and highly watched cases.

Born in Adams County, Moran attended Ohio Northern University before returning to Indiana, earning a law degree at the Indiana University Law School in Indianapolis in 1896 and practicing law in Portland in rural Jay County in northeastern Indiana. He married Elizabeth Sommers in 1898 and the couple had two daughters. Prominent as an attorney, Moran was elected circuit court judge in 1910 after campaigning widely and earning a reputation as an orator with his stump speeches. During the campaign he was praised for his pleasing personality, handsome good looks, and ability to "make friends easily and quickly."

Moran was dedicated to the law and the Jay County Circuit Court gave him plenty of cases over which to preside. Early in his judgeship, he oversaw the sensational murder trial of Sallie Karney of Corkwell, Indiana, who was charged with murdering her husband, David Karney, a storekeeper. She was initially held without bond and was not allowed to see anyone, including her young children. But Moran, ruling on a writ of habeas corpus, said she could be released pending her trial upon payment of bail of $10,000. A crowd of citizens gathered to help pay her bail, convinced of her innocence.

The resulting case was splashed across the newspapers, as large crowds gathered to watch and hear the trial. Dramatic testimony from the Karney children and other witnesses corroborated Sallie's account of the shooting of her husband, which she said was done by someone else in the store in the front of the building that housed both the business and the family's living quarters. When the prosecuting attorney realized how thin his case was, he dropped the charges and Sallie was released to the overwhelming approval of the people of the area.

Another trial that made Moran a well-known judge involved two men from Massachusetts who were killed in their horse-drawn buggy at a railroad crossing of the Big Four Railroad (Cleveland, Cincinnati, Chicago and Saint Louis Railroad). When the families of the dead men brought a suit for $10,000 in damages, Moran was appointed as a special judge to hear the case. The widows of the deceased traveled to Indiana for the hearing and visited the crossing where their husbands had died. Facing a trial with popular opinion against them and on the side of the grieving women, the Big Four settled the case with a compromise, agreeing to pay the families a smaller amount.

Like other judges of the time, Moran often heard cases involving prohibition under the local option laws that allowed cities and counties to restrict alcohol. He also oversaw lawsuits involving Progressive Era regulations of business. And, of course, the court's docket was filled with the property cases typical in rural and small-town communities. One closely watched case in 1912 involved a suit brought for guardianship over a wealthy eighty-eight-year-old man who was no longer able to manage his affairs. His second wife had taken over the management of his property. His son by a previous marriage wanted to be named guardian and given control of his father's estate, arguing that the woman was making decisions to benefit herself and her children by another marriage. But the old man refused to go along with the guardianship plan, arguing that his wife was conducting his business in accordance with his wishes. Moran eventually ruled that the old man did need a guardian, but appointed the wife as the legal executor, not the son.

After completing his term on the appeals court, Moran returned to practicing law and became an expert in appeals, often arguing cases in higher courts. He died on April 20, 1951, widely regarded as one of the best lawyers in Indiana in the first half of the twentieth century.

Selected Bibliography

Fort Wayne Sentinel, February 13, 1911.
Indiana Court of Appeals Website. https://www.in.gov/judiciary/appeals/files/bios-hist-moran-james.pdf.
Muncie Evening Press, September 22, 1910, June 14, 28, 1911.
Muncie Star Press, August 15, 22, 1910, January 16, 21, 22, 1911, March 3, 1911, May 8, 9, 10, 12, 19, 1912, July 1, 1912.

INDIANA SUPREME COURT

JOHN C. McNUTT

May 1, 1916–January 1, 1917

LINDA C. GUGIN

Perhaps John C. McNutt's main claim to fame was that he was the father of Paul V. NcNutt, one of Indiana's most distinguished governors. While the senior McNutt's record in politics and law was not as illustrious as that of his famous son, nonetheless, he left his mark on the law and local and state politics.

John Crittendden McNutt was born May 25, 1863, in Johnson County, Indiana. His father died when John was four, leaving a pregnant wife and three children. His mother remarried, but within two years her second husband died. Consequently, McNutt's early life was difficult. He hauled logs in the winter and worked on a farm in the summer to put himself through primary school.

McNutt planned to be a teacher after high school and enrolled in a normal school in Morgantown for a year and then completed a six-week course at a teacher's institute. The director of the institute, a man named Vories, allowed McNutt to attend the institute for free. Moved by this gesture, McNutt promised to name his firstborn son after him. True to his word McNutt named his first and only son Paul Vories McNutt.

After teaching for a few years, McNutt decided to be a lawyer. At that time attending law school was not a requirement to become a lawyer. McNutt studied law under the tutelage of his uncle Cyrus McNutt, and at a law office in Franklin. In 1884 he was admitted to the Indiana Bar. Two years later, he started a law partnership in Franklin and married Ruth Neely of Morgantown. McNutt was elected prosecuting attorney for Johnson and Shelby Counties in 1888 and reelected in 1890. Three years later, McNutt became the librarian for the Indiana Supreme Court. In the six years he spent there he catalogued the entire library, and reportedly the catalogue remained in use many years after he left.

Around the turn of the century, McNutt moved to Martinsville and formed a law partnership with John E. Hurt. One of the few Democrats in Martinsville, McNutt was a man of ambition. In 1912 he made an unsuccessful bid as the Democratic nominee for a seat on the Indiana Supreme Court. In May of 1916 Governor Samuel M. Ralston, a Democrat, appointed McNutt to the Appellate Court of Indiana to fill the vacancy created by the resignation of Judge Joseph H. Shea. In November of that year McNutt was the Democratic nominee for the court, but it was a bad year for his party with Republicans winning every office on the ballot. McNutt's term ended on January 1, 1917.

During his brief tenure of the court, McNutt wrote nineteen opinions, none of long-term significance. In eight of those opinions the court affirmed the ruling of the lower court. In *McGee v. Stockton* the court upheld a decision by the lower court rejecting a claim by Landy McGee for damages against the owners of a hotel for injuries he sustained testing a fire escape installed by the hotel. While testing the fire escape, the chain broke and he fell to the cement sidewalk below, incurring serious and permanent damage. McGee claimed he was entitled to compensation for his injuries under a state law requiring employers to take every possible precaution for the safety of their employees. In upholding the lower-court ruling against McGee, McNutt wrote that the statute in question did not apply to McGee's case because he was a contract worker and not an employee and therefore was not entitled to compensation for his injuries.

In six of the cases for which McNutt wrote the majority opinion, the court reversed the lower court. In *Hollander v. Fletcher*, a sad tale of love gone awry, a boyfriend had given some jewelry to his girlfriend, whom he intended to marry. However, the father refused to let the girl marry the boy claiming he was unfit fit to marry his daughter. The boyfriend then sued the father for the value of the jewelry he had given to the girl, and the lower court had ruled in the boyfriend's favor, after affirming his motion to strike a part of the father's responses to interrogatories. McNutt, writing for the majority, said that the trial court had erred in granting the boyfriend's motion to strike part of the father's answer without enough review of all the evidence.

Following his tenure on the court, McNutt returned to Martinsville and continued his law practice. He remained in Martinsville until the death of his wife, then moved to New York to live with his son Paul. He died there December 10, 1949.

Selected Bibliography

Blake, I. George. *Paul V. McNutt Portrait of a Hoosier Statesman.* Indianapolis: Central Publishing Company, 1966.

Kotlowski, Dean J. *Paul V. McNutt and the Age of FDR*. Bloomington: Indiana University Press, 2015.

In Memoriam: Memorials of the Johnson County Bar Association and the Morgan *County Bar Association.* December 15, 1949 (available at the website for the Indiana Court of Appeals, www.in.gov).

CASES CITED

Hollander v, Fletcher, 60 Ind. App. 149 (1916).

McGee v. Stockton, 62 Ind. App. 555 (1916).

INDIANA HISTORICAL SOCIETY

IRA C. BATMAN

January 1, 1917–January 1, 1925

DONALD B. KITE SR.

Ira Coleman Batman, an accomplished attorney, judge, and community leader, displayed ambition and passion at every turn. On June 11, 1915, Batman and his fellow Republican candidates met under Indiana's historic Corydon Elm, which members of the Indiana Constitutional Convention had met ninety-nine years earlier, to participate in a humorous mock trial. When "cross-examined" during the trial, Batman admitted he aspired to be on the Appellate Court of Indiana followed by the Indiana Supreme Court. He "was fined $2 on each aspiration."

Batman was born in 1862 on a Lawrence County farm. After graduating from Indiana University, he taught school in Columbia City for one year before he began his legal studies. He read law with the Bloomington law firm of Buskirk and Duncan and obtained his law degree from Indiana University in 1885. He also served as principal of Columbia City High School from 1885 through 1886.

Batman practiced law briefly in 1886 in Grant County, Nebraska, having been appointed county prosecutor. By 1888 he had married Mary T. Waldron and had begun practicing law with Judge Henry C. Duncan of Bloomington, Indiana, with his office located over the shoe store on the west side of the public square.

In 1904 Batman was elected to the Indiana General Assembly as the Brown and Monroe County representative. While a member of the judiciary committee, he championed a proposal requiring that schoolbooks be revised no earlier than once every ten years, Batman's argument being that this would result in a savings.

While Batman would eventually be considered "one of the towers on the Republican side" in the Indiana House of Representatives, he declined to run for the legislature in the following election. Instead, Batman was elected Monroe County attorney on May 12, 1906. He served for two years in this position and thirteen as Bloomington city attorney. Appointed to the Indiana University Board of Trustees in 1908, Batman served as a trustee for twenty-five years. His work on behalf of IU lasted for decades and was quite important to Batman.

After Batman's law partner Duncan passed away in 1911, Batman practiced with the law firm of Batman, Miller and Blair. He also served as a deputy prosecutor for Monroe and Owen Counties. A frequent speaker and strong campaigner, Batman participated in the Republican candidates' auto tour of Indiana counties in 1914. The Miami County tour alone consisted of a caravan of at least a hundred automobiles that stopped at seventeen towns. In 1916 Batman ran on the Republican ticket and was elected to the Appellate Court of Indiana. He served on the appellate court bench until 1924.

The court heard a variety of cases from contract disputes and the interpretation of criminal statutes to negligence matters. In 1919 Presiding Judge Batman, writing for the court, affirmed a Rush County trial court's decision that a hotel owner did not have a right to keep a piano and stool that had been left by a guest who had not paid his bill. Batman reasoned that the hotel owner did not have this right because the piano was not the property of the guest for whose bill it had been held, and the hotel owner knew it. Three years later, in a 1922 decision, Batman affirmed the Industrial Board's award to a cabinet factory employee who had contracted typhoid fever from water provided by his employer, the contamination resulting from seepage from a toilet. He reasoned that the act of drinking water was necessary "to the life, comfort, and convenience of the workman while at work."

The early 1920s brought a mixture of life's best and worst for Batman and his family. Prior to his re-election to the court of appeals in 1920, Batman walked his only child Emma down the aisle when she married Maurice Riley. However, two days before Christmas in 1922 Batman's eighty-nine-year-old aunt, Catheryne Batman, burned to death, apparently as the result of a lamp-lighting accident.

Influential in the establishment of Indianapolis's James Whitcomb Riley Hospital, Batman, who was then a member of the IU Board of Trustees subcommittee working on the project, drafted the initial proposed bill for the hospital and was a strong advocate for its creation.

During the evening of April 10, 1934, Judge Batman suffered a heart attack and passed away at his Bloomington home. IU canceled classes and his funeral, which was well-attended, was held at the First Christian Church in Bloomington. He was buried at Bloomington's Rosehill cemetery.

Selected Bibliography

Indianapolis Star, May 15, 1913.
Logansport Pharos-Tribune, December 4, 1916.
Muncie Evening Press, October 31, 1926.

CASES CITED

Nicholas v. The Baldwin Piano Company, 123 NE 226-227; 71 (Ind. App 1919).
Wasmurth–Endicott Co. v. Karst, 133 NE 606, 611 (Ind. App 1922).

INDIANA SUPREME COURT

ETHAN A. DAUSMAN

January 1, 1917–September 21, 1928

DONALD B. KITE SR.

Ethan Allen Dausman was an idea man. He scrutinized "the system" and made concrete, albeit occasionally partisan, proposals for change. While serving in the Indiana General Assembly he proposed establishing an expert commission that would examine each male inmate's case to provide treatment needed for physical or mental illness. He later argued that judges, sheriffs, and other court officials should be appointed and hold their positions during good behavior and proposed a measure establishing qualifications for admission to the bar. Dausman's passion remained constant throughout his life.

Dausman, who was born January 3, 1861, on the family farm east of Elkhart, attended nearby public schools. In February 1878 a close friend suggested they take a teacher's examination, given monthly at the Elkhart County Courthouse. While the sixteen-year-old Dausman passed the test and received his teacher's license, his friend failed. Dausman was interviewed by the Union Township Trustee who told him that although he was young and "rather small," he would offer him "a trial" given the scarcity of teachers.

The next several years were a blur of activity. Beside teaching in Nappanee, he began studying law with Nappanee lawyer Daniel Zook, married Mary A. Stauffer in 1883, attended Valparaiso University, and was admitted to the Elkhart County bar. When Zook was elected county clerk in 1886, Dausman took over his practice, which he maintained for eight years before moving to Goshen and opening a law office there on May 1, 1892.

Dausman served for a time as chairman of the Elkhart County Democratic Central Committee and remained a Democrat until the Free Silver campaign of 1896. He became a Republican and eventually was chairman of the Elkhart County Republican Committee. Four years later Dausman was elected to the Indiana Senate as a Republican. He represented Elkhart County from 1900 to 1904 and served as a state representative for the next two years. From 1910 to 1916, Dausman was Goshen City Attorney and practiced law in Goshen with his son.

Elected to the Appellate Court of Indiana in 1916, Dausman was reelected in 1920 and 1924, serving as chief judge during a portion of his tenure. He recognized, of course, that cases before judges "appear to be a jungle of contradictions [and that the court] can no more follow them than one can follow all the roads." His opinions reflect an effort to identify and apply guiding principles that logic suggests or that a majority of a panel of judges agrees should be applied.

In *Drury v. Krogman,* the guiding principle was statutory interpretation. In this case the plaintiffs' neighbor, Joseph Weigand, described by Dausman as "an old reprobate and habitual drunkard," allegedly purchased a quart of whisky from the defendant, William Krogman, who was not licensed to sell liquor. Hours later Weigand left his house only to shoot his next-door neighbor, a mother of five who was simply working in her yard, without provocation. She died eight days later, and her five children were eventually substituted for their father as plaintiffs. Discussing applicable common law principles and legislative intent underlying the applicable statute, Dausman determined that the plaintiff children could not recover damages because they "were wholly dependent on their father, and in no lawful sense can they be regarded as dependents of their deceased mother."

Dausman's dissent in a 1918 workers' compensation case later would be cited in a 1975 Court of Appeals of Indiana opinion as "accurately forecasting the results of judicial legislation that equated normal exertion with an accident." Dausman had reasoned that there was no "accident," as required by the applicable statute, because the decedent "was shoveling coal in the usual way, and while his muscular activity was accompanied by the natural and normal blood pressure, the aorta burst, because it had been thinned and weakened by disease."

In 1928 Dausman announced that due to ill health he would not be a candidate for the court. Unable to complete his third term on the court, he died at his home on September 21, 1928, following "a long illness of heart trouble." His funeral, attended by the other five sitting appellate court judges, was held at the Goshen home of his son and former law partner Guy W. Dausman, who, along with the judge's wife and daughters Gertrude and Inez, survived him.

Selected Bibliography

Dausman, Ethan Allen. "Address of Welcome to the Third Semi-Annual Meeting at Nappanee of the Elkhart County Teachers Association." Unsourced Clipping.

______. Letter to grandson and namesake, December 28, 1926.

______. Letter to C. D. Elliot, September 22, 1925.

______. Letter to Daniel M. Donahue, September 20, 1924.

______. Letter to Mary Dausman, August 31, 1910.

Monks, Leander J., ed. *Courts and Lawyers of Indiana.* Indianapolis: Federal Publishing Company, 1916.

CASE CITED

Indian Creek Coal & Mining Co. v. Calvert, 119 N.E. 519, 528 (Ind. App. 1918).

INDIANA SUPREME COURT

ALONZO L. NICHOLS

January 1, 1919–January 1, 1931

SUZANNE S. BELLAMY

Coming from a humble background and with minimal education and training, Alonzo Lee Nichols was a self-made man, creating his own destiny. He worked first as a teacher in Randolph County schools, then as county deputy clerk and clerk, followed by working as a student in a law office, becoming a member of the bar, and finally being elected a judge of the Appellate Court of Indiana. Nothing was given to him except that which he worked diligently throughout his life to attain.

Born on a farm in Lynn, Indiana, on August 3, 1856, Nichols was the second in a family of eleven children. While both his parents were native Hoosiers, all his grandparents came from North Carolina. The story goes that his maternal grandparents walked most of the way to reach Indiana. Nichols was educated in the common schools of Indiana, including Winchester High School, and spent one year at the Indiana State Normal School at Terre Haute, where he met his future wife. While still a teenager, he became a teacher in his hometown, a profession he continued for twelve years. While working as a deputy county clerk from 1885 to 1889, Nichols studied law and opened a law practice in Winchester after being admitted to the bar. He was elected clerk of Randolph County on the Republican ticket in 1892; after his four-year term, he resumed his law practice in Winchester.

Nichols was first elected to the appellate court in 1918 on the Republican ticket and was reelected in 1922 and 1926 with his final term of office ending on December 31, 1930. He served as chief judge five times: for the May 1919, May 1922, November 1922, November 1925, and May 1928 terms. During his twelve-year tenure, Nichols won the reputation of handing down more decisions than any other judge in the same period. In 1926 he reported that the court had largely caught up with the 550 cases in which it was behind when he was elected. Overcrowding of the appellate court and Indiana Supreme Court dockets was a chronic problem throughout the 1920s. In 1929 the Indiana General Assembly passed a measure, the Street-McGriff law, transferring jurisdiction until January 1, 1931, of almost all appealed cases in which the offenses were misdemeanors from the Supreme Court to the appellate court. The court proved up to the challenge of disposing of the additional workload. One tactic on which all the appellate court judges agreed was that they would be less generous in granting extensions to attorneys representing appellants, requiring that cases be briefed within the legally allotted time.

Nichols was ahead of his time in recognizing the contributions of women attorneys. The *Indianapolis Star* reported in 1921 that he had a female law clerk, one of only two female graduates of the Indiana Law School in Indianapolis that year.

In the 1930 election Nichols lost his bid for re-election as part of a sweep by Democrats of eleven state offices. The Democratic platform demanded tax reform through a graduated state income tax. After his term ended, Nichols returned to the practice of law with his son Merrill in Winchester. Nichols remained active in his church and other civic activities in his community until his death on June 9, 1937.

Selected Bibliography

Indianapolis News, March 15, 1929, November 10, 1929.
Indianapolis Star, May 27, 1921, June 10, 1937.
Muncie Evening Press, August 28, 1926.
Richmond Palladium-Item, June 9, 1937.
Roll, Charles. *Indiana: One Hundred and Fifty Years of American Development*. Chicago and New York: Lewis Publishing Company, 1931.

INDIANA SUPREME COURT

WILLIS C. McMAHAN

January 1, 1919–January 1, 1931

DONALD B. KITE SR.

On Sunday, October 31, 1915, conferees gathered at Richmond, Indiana's East Main Street Friends Church to discuss child welfare during the Indiana Conference of Charities and Corrections. Lake Circuit Court Judge Willis Creighton McMahan, giving an address under the innocuous title "Some Problems of the Courts," offered an increasingly popular but controversial solution: "Let us solve the problem of the mentally defective criminal and pauper, the great social problem of prostitution and dispose of 'our damaged goods' all at the same time and with the same weapon—sterilization."

Reponses from other speakers to McMahan's comments ranged from pointing out that sterilization had been abused in the past to cautioning that it was not an effective solution or that it should be a last resort. McMahan's actions throughout his career, however, show a more progressive side.

He established and presided over proceedings in the first juvenile court in Lake County, helped to develop and monitor a residence for homeless children in Crown Point, appointed an additional probation officer, and created a master commissioner position to relieve the congested court calendar.

Born on August 2, 1858, near Delphi, Indiana, McMahan attended local schools, Central Normal College, and the University of Michigan Law School. After teaching school for a time, he was admitted to the bar in 1883 after which he began his law practice in Crown Point. He married Irene Allman on January 23, 1888, became editor and publisher of the *Crown Point Register*, and president of the Camden Bank.

A lifelong Republican, McMahan was elected and then reelected prosecuting attorney for Lake and Porter Counties in 1890 and 1892. From 1902 to 1913, he served as Superior Court Judge for Lake and Porter Counties and then as judge of Lake Circuit Court from 1914 to 1918, resigning in December of 1918 to seek higher office. During this period, he also served for a time as county attorney. McMahan's time on the trial bench was eventful. In addition to large numbers of more routine matters, he tried political corruption cases and sensational murder cases in which he sentenced men to death. McMahan also handed down new rules to prevent naturalization fraud.

In 1918 he was elected to the Appellate Court of Indiana and then reelected for two additional four-year terms. Cases heard during his tenure varied and included those involving monetary judgments, quiet title actions, contested wills, juvenile cases, and workmen's compensation. In *City of Frankfort v. Slipher,* McMahan, writing for the court, affirmed a stream pollution verdict against the city of Frankfort, noting that the city could have constructed a sewage treatment plant to prevent the contamination.

McMahan's opinion in *Stadia v. State* affirmed Belle Stadia's conviction for bootlegging, notwithstanding the common-law principle that, with the exception of murder and treason, a woman who commits a crime in the presence of her husband is presumed to have been coerced by her husband. McMahan found no evidence that the defendant was acting at her husband's behest. He also wrote the opinion reversing the trial court in a case that ultimately prohibited the manufacture of floral baskets at the state penal farm. McMahan reasoned that the pertinent statute did not contemplate the manufacture of floral baskets, which were not articles used by state or county institutions.

Defeated by Harvey J. Curtis in a Democratic landside in 1930, McMahan ended up for a time working in his opponent's former law firm. He practiced law with J. Edwin Smith for two years and then with Oscar C. Strom and George Hulbert before retiring in 1940. The law firm the three men started was then dissolved.

On May 5, 1948, eight years after he retired from the active practice of law and three months shy of his ninetieth birthday, McMahan died at his home in Gary, Indiana.

Selected Bibliography

Indianapolis News, January 28, 1902.
Munster Times, July 2, 1907.
Porter County Vidette-Messenger, December 27, 1983, April 29, 1988, April 26, 1989.
Vidette Messenger of Porter County, December 27, 1983.
"W. C. McMahan Tells of Court Life." Unsourced newspaper clipping.

CASES CITED

City of Frankfort v. Slipher, 162 N.E. 241 (Ind. App. 1928).
Stadia v. State, 166 N.E. 25, 26 (Ind. App. 1929).

INDIANA SUPREME COURT

SOLON A. ENLOE

January 1, 1919–January 1, 1931

LIBBE K. HUGHES

Elected three times to the Appellate Court of Indiana, Solon A. Enloe was, in the words of his peers, "able, conscientious and thorough." He brought a comprehensive knowledge of law to the bench based on years practicing and teaching law. Enloe, born August 28, 1860, in Mulberry Grove, Illinois, to Isaac and Sophronia Hensley Enloe, was the second of five children. After completing his early education in the Greenville, Illinois, schools, Enloe taught there for three years before heading west in an attempt to improve his health. After two years in Wyoming and Colorado cattle ranching and railroading, he returned to the Midwest and further educational pursuits.

Enloe graduated in the July 1884 scientific class of Central Normal College, a teaching college located in Danville, Indiana. After briefly teaching school in Illinois, he returned to Central Normal to complete the classics course studies in 1886. He married Danville native Cora Dooley on December 25, 1886, in a ceremony officiated by future Indiana governor Ira J. Chase. The couple settled in Greenville, Illinois, where Enloe was employed as principal of Greenville schools. He also studied law and was admitted to the Illinois bar.

The family, which now included daughter Dana, returned to Danville in 1897 and Enloe was admitted to the Indiana bar. He quickly established a law practice with prominent Danville attorney Thad S. Adams and began teaching law at Central Normal's law department.

When the Spanish-American War erupted in April 1898, Enloe, leaving behind his family and career, enlisted in the Indiana Volunteer Infantry. His unit was sent to Camp Thomas in Georgia for training, where it remained until the war ended in July 1898. He was promoted to corporal and although he demonstrated skills as a solider, his health suffered immensely. His unit was sent back to Indianapolis by train in September. Enloe, seriously ill and desperately attempting to avoid being sent to a camp hospital, was discovered, purely by chance, by his former law partner Adams. Adams arranged to have the sick soldier returned to Danville for medical care while awaiting his discharge. His experiences as a soldier ignited an interest in the military that would influence him for the remainder of his life.

Enloe returned to his law practice and teaching duties but was swept up in the fervor surrounding the Philippine Insurrection. In November 1900 he disappeared, writing a letter home informing his family that he was on his way to Manila to join the regular army, adding that he was "cut out for a soldier" and nothing else will suit him. He served in an infantry unit until June 1903 when he returned once again to his family and resumed his law practice. Enloe was also named to head the Central Normal College law department, a position he held until 1929, and elected director of the home guards, a local militia unit formed to replace the Indiana National Guard troops who would soon be deployed into regular service in World War I. He continued to be active in organizations such as the Veterans of Foreign Wars and the United Spanish War Veterans.

Shortly after his wife, Cora, died in early 1918 at age fifty-six, a victim of the country's influenza epidemic, Enloe, a lifelong Republican, announced his candidacy for the appeals court. He won the nomination in the spring and was elected in November. He easily won re-election in 1922 and 1926 but lost in November 1930 to Democratic nominee William H. Bridwell when the Democrats swept the state elections. Enloe and his fellow Republican judges were credited with improving the efficiency of the court and reducing the backlog of cases. It was noted that "his defeat in the landslide of 1930 is generally listed as one among the very potent arguments in favor of nonpartisan voting on candidates for the judiciary."

Enloe, having moved to Indianapolis during his time on the appeals court, returned to private law practice and enjoyed long summer holidays fishing at his vacation home at Long Lake in LaGrange County. He suffered a stroke there in August 1932 and was brought back to his Indianapolis home where he died on October 15, 1932. He was buried in Danville South Cemetery following a memorial service attended by the leading figures of the state's judicial system and veterans' organizations.

Selected Bibliography

Hubbard, Kin, L. G. Ellingham, W. E. Sutton, E. M. Souder, et al., eds. *A Book of Indiana: The Story of What Has Been Described as the Most Typically American State in the American Democracy Told in Terms of Biography.* Indiana Biographical Association, 1929.

Danville Republican, January 31, 1918, October 20, 1932.

INDIANA HISTORICAL SOCIETY

CHARLES F. REMY

January 1, 1919–January 1, 1931

JANE A. SEIGEL

Consistently active. Committed involvement. Conviction of his beliefs. Community oriented. These phrases represent the themes of Charles Frederick Remy's life. The number of organizations and causes to which Remy devoted his life is impressive. He made significant contributions to the public discourse on politics, religion, education, law, and family.

Remy was born on February 25, 1860, in Bartholomew County, near Hope, Indiana, to Calvin Jones and Miranda Essex Remy. He was one of five children growing up on the family farm, and his early life provided much of the foundation for his devotion to education and to his church. His family regularly attended Hawcreek Baptist Church, where Remy learned the value of Bible study and faithfulness.

As an adult, he and his family were members of First Baptist Church in Indianapolis, where for over forty years he taught a Bible class in Sunday school. Church service and attendance were cornerstones of his life. Commenting on Remy's thirty-year tenure on the board of trustees, his pastor said that he "served with unusual discernment, good judgment, and unswerving cooperation based on his ability to understand another person's point of view."

Remy earned a bachelor's degree from Franklin College in 1884. His parents provided the first year's expenses, but after that, it was up to each of the five children to figure out how to complete their education. Remy later said that his parents possessed great wisdom in making him work for his education, believing that the planning, work, and saving required were likely the most important parts of his education. Not that he did not value what he received from Franklin College—on the contrary. He maintained a great loyalty to Franklin, exhibited by serving on its board of directors for more than thirty years. He also served for a time as president of the alumni association, and received an honorary doctor of law degree from the college. Ultimately, he received his law degree from the University of Michigan Law School in 1888. He was also devoted to the law school, attending the sixtieth reunion of his class shortly before his untimely death.

Following graduation from law school, Remy returned to Columbus, Indiana, and began to practice law. He was elected to the Indiana House of Representatives for a term, and then was elected as reporter for the supreme and appeals courts, a position he held for two terms. He then practiced law in Indianapolis from 1905 to 1919. During this period, he also served as special counsel to Governor James P. Goodrich. He was elected to the Appellate Court of Indiana in 1918 and served three terms. His distinguished career on the court included serving as chief judge five times. Upon completion of his service on the court, he resumed practicing law in Indianapolis.

Remy was a founding member of the Indiana State Bar Association, and a member of the American Bar Association as well as the Indianapolis Bar Association. He was an active member of the Columbia Club, Century Club, Society of Indiana Pioneers, the Indiana Historical Society, served as grand chancellor of the Knights of Pythias, a philanthropic organization, and as president of the Indiana Society of the Sons of the American Revolution. He was always active in Republican politics.

A popular and frequent guest speaker at a variety of venues, Remy's topics ranged from "A Father's Relation to His Son," "Christian Citizenship," and state finances to advocating for property tax reform and a constitutional convention.

In a bizarre twist of fate, he experienced the sudden death of a friend from Pittsburgh in his chambers at the statehouse. And later in life he was critically injured in front of the statehouse when he was pinned under a speeding car.

Remy married Deborah Henderson on November 25, 1891. She preceded him in death. Their son, William Henderson Remy, who served as Marion County prosecutor from 1923 to 1928, won a conviction of D. C. Stephenson, the Grand Dragon of the Ku Klux Klan, for the murder of a young statehouse worker. Father and son later practiced law together in Indianapolis. Remy remained active in work and civic engagement until he died suddenly on September 28, 1948.

Selected Bibliography

Indianapolis Journal, June 12, 1902.
Indianapolis News, November 18, 1916, March 19, 1920, November 26, 1923, May 1, 1926, September 28, 1948.
Indianapolis Star, April 30, 1914, October 31, 1916, March 5, 1917, May 25, 1932.
Notes from Doctor Carleton W. Atwater, pastor of First Baptist Church, Indianapolis, who conducted the funeral service of Charles F. Remy on October 1, 1948.

INDIANA SUPREME COURT

FRANCIS M. THOMPSON

January 1, 1925–January 1, 1929

MICHAEL J. DeBOER

Francis Marion Thompson came to the Appellate Court of Indiana toward the end of his varied career as a schoolteacher, an attorney with a private practice in Indiana, Kansas, and Colorado, a prosecuting attorney, and a circuit judge. He was a Republican, a member of the Methodist Episcopal Church, the Masonic Lodge, and the Knights of Pythias Lodge, and an active member of several bar associations. His one four-year term on the appeals court began several years after the conclusion of World War I and ended nearly eleven months before the beginning of the Great Depression.

Thompson, who was born on a farm in Ripley County, Indiana, on July 12, 1857, received a common school education in that county, and then, from the age of seventeen to twenty-two, taught school there. During the summers, he studied in neighboring Dearborn County at Moores Hill College, which in 1917 moved to Evansville and later became the University of Evansville.

After additional study at Indiana University in Bloomington, he began studying law in 1881 in the offices of two prominent lawyers in Versailles, which was the seat of government for Ripley County. He was soon admitted to the practice of law and in 1883 married Malinda M. Harper, a granddaughter of Armit and Malinda Jarvis Robinson and a daughter of Sarah Martha Robinson Harper, one of the pioneer families of Ripley County. Thompson moved west in 1887, practicing law in Kansas and Colorado before returning to Indiana in 1891 to practice law in Versailles.

His professional career at that point included a combination of both private practice and public service. In 1894 he was elected and served one two-year term as prosecuting attorney of the judicial circuit for Jennings, Ripley, and Scott Counties. After his term ended as prosecuting attorney, in the late night and early morning hours of September 14–15, 1897, vigilantes stormed the Ripley County jail and shot and hanged from the branches of an elm tree—the infamous "hanging tree"—five white men who were suspected of being members of a gang that had repeatedly robbed local farmers and others.

In 1906 Thompson was elected and served one six-year term as judge of the judicial circuit for Jennings, Ripley, and Scott Counties. Several of his decisions were reviewed by the appeals court and the Indiana Supreme Court, and the opinions of the reviewing courts show that Thompson adjudicated civil cases that presented an array of issues and claims, including the care and custody of a child, the injuries suffered by a railroad employee and by railroad passengers, the wrongful death of a vehicle operator at a railroad crossing, a contested will, and challenges to actions by local government officials. After serving as a circuit judge, he returned to private practice, appearing as counsel in several cases heard in the appellate court.

Thompson was elected to the appeals court in 1924, which was then a statutory court. He was on the court for four years, serving as chief judge during the May 1927 session. He authored ninety-seven opinions, addressing substantive issues in various areas including agency law, business associations law, contract law, decedents' estates law, insurance law, municipal law, negotiable instruments law, property law, remedies law, tort law, and workers' compensation law. His opinions also addressed procedural issues such as appellate court and trial court procedure, admissibility of evidence, jury instructions, scientific or expert testimony, and statutes of limitations.

After his service on the appeals court ended in 1929, he returned to private practice in Versailles, forming a partnership with his youngest son, Curtis W. Thompson, who later served as a judge in Ripley County. His oldest son, Robert Earl Thompson, also served as a judge in Winamac, Pulaski County, Indiana, for nearly three decades. Thompson died in Versailles on February 18, 1936; his wife and five children survived him.

SELECTED BIBLIOGRAPHY

Staton, Robert H., and Gina M. Hicklin. "The History of the Court of Appeals of Indiana." *Indiana Law Review* 30, no. 1(1997): 203–31.

Stoner, Andrew E. *Notorious 92: The Most Infamous Murder from Each of Indiana's 92 Counties*. Bloomington, IN: Rooftop Publishing, 2007.

Thompson, Francis Marion obituary. https://www.in.gov/judiciary/appeals/files/bios-hist-thompson-francis.pdf.

_______. https://www.in.gov/judiciary/appeals/2388.htm.

INDIANA SUPREME COURT

NOEL C. NEAL

January 1, 1929–January 1, 1933

JULIE C. S. McDONALD

Noel C. Neal came from a family of lawyers—his grandfather, William Neal, was a pioneer lawyer in Cicero, Indiana, and his father, John Neal, was judge of Hamilton Circuit Court in Noblesville. His youngest daughter, Frances N. Ellis, continued the family tradition, becoming Indiana's only female county prosecutor at the time. After his service on the appeals court ended, Neal and his daughter became law partners, and he assisted her in a first-degree murder case that received extensive news coverage.

Neal's road to the bench and bar started when he worked his way through Wabash College by operating a farm, delivering newspapers, and working on construction of the interurban railroad. A newspaper account described him as a "hustler . . . blessed with the value of the coin of the realm. He always was a hard-working boy and when other boys were playing ball, Neal could be seen behind a lawn mower, pushing it over the grass, or engaged in some other labor." He received his law degree from Indiana University and joined his father's practice in 1910.

He was elected to the Appellate Court of Indiana in 1928 but began work early to complete the term of Ethan A. Dausman, who died in office. Neal quickly earned respect on the bench and served twice as chief judge. One newspaper noted that in his first term "none of his opinions [was] taken over by the [Indiana] Supreme Court." His chambers were, however, "taken over" by a thief, who stole Neal's clothes from his office on the fourth floor of the statehouse during a crime spree in the building.

Neal, a Republican, was defeated for a second term on the court in 1932, losing to Ralph N. Smith as the Franklin D. Roosevelt Democratic juggernaut swept across the state. After his term on the court ended, Neal formed a partnership with Elmon Williams in Indianapolis. His daughter Frances joined him in 1948 in a practice in Noblesville. During his career, he also served as the city attorney for Noblesville. He remained active in Republican politics, serving as campaign manager for Raymond E. Willis, who lost in his U.S. Senate race in 1938 to incumbent Frederick Van Nuys.

Because of his experience and expertise, Neal was called upon many times by other lawyers to assist with writing briefs in cases appealed to the appellate and supreme courts of Indiana. Neal, who was born February 4, 1885, died in a car crash in May 1955 after falling asleep at the wheel driving alone from Attica to Noblesville.

In addition to Frances Ellis, Neal and his wife, Mabel, had two other daughters, Elizabeth Owens and Virginia Spannuth, along with his six grandchildren. His home on Conner Street in Noblesville was built in 1924 for his family, and his wife taught ballet lessons in the basement. The ballet bars were still on the walls as late as 2012.

Selected Bibliography

Indianapolis News, June 9, 1932.
Noblesville Hamilton County Times, May 31, 1906.
Noblesville Ledger, October 28, 1914, November 5, 1932, May 2, 1955.
Tipton Daily Tribune, March 26, 1951.

INDIANA SUPREME COURT

ELMER Q. LOCKYEAR

January 1, 1929–January 1, 1933

RANDALL T. SHEPARD

In the early decades of the twentieth century, when energetic reformers such as Theodore Roosevelt and the LaFollette brothers held center stage, Indiana and other midwestern states served as special centers of a coalition for social change that became known as the Progressive Movement. Progressives campaigned for improvements from workers compensation to child labor to women's rights to busting trusts. One of the Indiana's lawyers most prominent in developing such reforms was Elmer Quincy Lockyear of Evansville, later a member of the Appellate Court of Indiana.

Lockyear was particularly inventive and forceful about protection of children, services for the mentally ill, and creating caring residential facilities. Indiana was the second state to establish separate courts for children, keeping delinquents and the abandoned out of adult criminal court and jails, and the first judge of the new probate court at Evansville, appointed in

1919, was Lockyear. In his decade of service there, he launched such initiatives as putting children in the care of a temporary guardian, under court supervision and assisted by payments to meet their needs. It was the beginning of what we would call today placement of a neglected young person as a "child in need of services."

Lockyear's ideas about treatment of children gained such widespread interest that speakers at a statewide child welfare conference could be heard quoting him within his first year in office. His own speech to that same conference urged that Indiana upgrade its care for the mentally disabled, mentally ill, and the impoverished. "Any state that is so stingy that it fails to make adequate provision for all its dependent should be held up to the scorn of modern civilization," he declared.

Lockyear earned considerable standing inside the legal profession as well. When the state bar annual meeting occurred at French Lick in 1923, Lockyear took the stage alongside a member of the Indiana Supreme Court, a former solicitor general of the United States, and a leading judge from Oregon.

Born in Warrick County in 1869 to Levi and Venturia Lockyear, Elmer began his professional career as a teacher in Warrick County. His four years at teaching were so remarkable that he was soon part of the training program for new teachers.

Lockyear then decided on a career in law and entered the DePauw University School of Law. The record of that experience reflects well on his legal talent and his personality. He became an officer of the moot court board, and the seniors chose to add him to their governing committee by naming him class poet.

Lockyear practiced law in Evansville, where he also became part of the reformist political movement, serving as chair of the Progressive Party and running for judge on the progressive ticket in 1914. This was characteristic of his willingness to pursue causes even when they were not altogether popular, such as supporting the effort by local churches to shut down baseball on Sundays or joining with the National Association for the Advancement of Colored People to prevent the execution of a convict whom he believed had not received a fair trial. On the other hand, he engaged in traditional economic development in fields such as manufacturing and retail business. He also periodically contributed to serious history projects, including the

"Lincoln Inquiry" conducted by the Southwestern Indiana Historical Society during the 1920s and 1930s.

Running as a Republican, Lockyear was elected to the Appellate Court of Indiana in November 1928 and his record there, as reflected in his written work, echoed both his earlier focus and the demands of the times. He led the court on issues such as family law reform, workers compensation, and litigation prompted by Prohibition. His colleagues demonstrated their own admiration by choosing him to be chief judge, even at a point when most of the court was Democratic.

Running for re-election as a Republican in 1932 was understandably unavailing, and Lockyear returned to his law practice, first in Indianapolis then in Evansville. He continued speaking out for reformist causes at statewide meetings and local assemblies throughout the decade. Lockyear pursued his law practice until the very week of his death in 1949, having been preceded in death by his wife, the former Letitia Miller.

Lockyear was an inspiration to the bar and to his family, launching four generations of respected Evansville lawyers.

Selected Bibliography

"County's First Probate Judge, Elmer Lockyear, Dies at 80." *Evansville Press*, March 12, 1949.

Elmer Q. Lockyear Remarks, Twenty-Eighth Conference, Charities and corrections. *Indiana Bulletin* 180 (1920): 120.

_______. "The Relation of Courts to Institutions." *Indiana Bulletin* 346 (1922): 131.

INDIANA SUPREME COURT

POSEY T. KIME

January 1, 1931–September 18, 1938

LINDA C. GUGIN

Most of Posey Thornton Kime's adult life was dedicated to public service, including his military service during World War I, teaching in public schools, serving eight years on the Appellate Court of Indiana, and working for various federal agencies.

Born in Petersburg, Indiana, on August 6, 1895, to Doctor John T. and Effa Posey Kime, Posey, his mother's maiden name, was educated in Petersburg schools and attended Purdue University before service with the U.S. Army in France during World War I. After the war he briefly taught school in South Dakota and then enrolled at Indiana University Law School in Bloomington. After graduating in 1922 he practiced law in Evansville until his election to the appellate court in 1930, a year Democrats swept all the offices.

In his first term on the court Kime became a prominent member of the political machine created by Governor Paul V. McNutt. Also prominent in the McNutt machine was Sherman Minton, who was elected U.S. Senator in 1934, the year that Kime was up for re-election. He easily won re-election to the court in 1934, aided in part by President Franklin D. Roosevelt's and Minton's names at the top of the ticket.

In Kime's second term there were rumblings that judges and other public officials would be limited to two terms by the Democratic Party, which meant that he would not be eligible for renomination. Kime began to look for future opportunities. He was in the running for a position on the U.S. District Court in Washington, DC, but was not chosen. In 1938 he was listed as an eligible candidate for a vacancy created on the Indiana Supreme Court, but nothing materialized there.

In September 1938, with three months left in his term, Kime resigned to accept the position as chief counsel for the Federal Power Commission in Washington. Minton was instrumental in obtaining this appointment, but there was much more to the story. It appears that Kime was encouraged to resign from the court because then Governor M. Clifford Townsend would not allow Kime or Alphonso C. Wood, elected at the same time, to be renominated. But two other judges William H. Bridwell and Harvey J. Curtis, both elected as the same time as Kime and Wood, were renominated and reelected. The discrepancy in the treatment of the judges is unclear.

Kime was a productive member during his eight years on the court. He wrote more than 300 opinions. Wood, who served the same amount of time, wrote only 249. Bridwell, who was on the court for ten years, wrote 223. Curtis in his twelve years of service wrote 361. A sampling of Kime's opinions reveals a strong tendency to resolve a case based on the relevant controlling statue. In a 1934 opinion, *Williams v. Michigan City,* Kime was adamant in his commitment to follow statutory intent. He said that an attorney who provided services to city officials but was not the city attorney was not entitled to make a claim for fees. He wrote, "the intent of the legislature, which is written in plain and unequivocal language, is clear. That statute means just what it says and therefore needs no construction."

Similarly, in a 1932 case, *Lee v. Browning,* Kime sided with the advisory board of a school corporation that had granted a school bus contract to a company whose bid was higher than another company's. He argued that a state statute gave the advisory board the discretion to award the contract to "lowest and best responsible bidder." He said that the "Court's judgment could not be substituted for the judgement of the body entrusted with that responsibility."

After leaving the court, Kime served four years as chief counsel for the Federal Power Commission. His next position was as special assistant to the U.S. Attorney General, assigned to the Anti-trust Division of the Department of Justice. On loan from the Justice Department to the War Department in 1946 he undertook a yearlong legal mission to Tokyo to help draft an antitrust code for Japan. In 1952 he was assigned to the antisubversive division of the Department of Justice, acting as a prosecutor for the congressional Subversive Activities Control Board.

Kime died on June 9, 1958, at the age of fifty-eight, at the National Institutes of Health, where he had been hospitalized for several months.

Selected Bibliography

Cincinnati Enquirer, October 16, 1938.
Daily Worker, May 24, 25, 1952.
Indianapolis Star, April 26, 1921, June 11, November 5, 1930, July 17, 1932, June 13, 14, September 3, 26, 1934, December 12, 1937, January 21, October 18, 1938.
New York Herald Tribune, June 9, 1958.
New York Times, January 5, 1946.

CASES CITED

Lee v. Browning, 96 Ind. App. 282 (1932).
Williams v. Michigan City, 100 Ind. App. (1934).

INDIANA SUPREME COURT

ALPHONSO C. WOOD

January 1, 1931–January 1, 1939

JASON S. LANTZER

Alphonso C. Wood, who was well known throughout northeastern Indiana's legal circles, ran on the Democratic ticket in 1926 for a seat on the Indiana Supreme Court. He was defeated, but four years later, Wood, who had proven himself able to attract Republican votes, was elected to the Appellate Court of Indiana, both on his own strength and because of the Great Depression, which turned even solidly Republican areas like Steuben County Democratic. Wood was easily reelected to the court in 1934.

Wood, who was born in Metz, Indiana, on January 23, 1874, attended local schools and graduated from what was then known as Tri-State College in 1895. He graduated from the University of Michigan Law School in 1899, though this was largely a professional formality, having already been admitted to the bar in 1897. Wood and his wife, Mayme Moffett, had one son,

Theodore, who followed closely in his father's footsteps, becoming a lawyer and prosecutor in Angola and judge of the Steuben Circuit Court. He also served as president of Tri-State College.

Although Steuben County was heavily Republican, Wood became Angola's town clerk in 1901 and city attorney in 1905, a post he held until 1909. During this time, he wrote and supervised the publication of city ordinances, which were then adopted by the city council. He spent two years working as secretary to Democratic U.S. Congressman Cyrus Cline. In 1919 Wood helped found Angola's Rotary Club and was a longtime member of the board of directors of the Steuben Printing Company. From 1921 until 1930, Wood was on Angola's school board of trustees. He also started a law practice with his son, which lasted from 1929 to 1930. Additionally, Wood was active in the Masonic Lodge, eventually rising to the rank of 33 degree, and in the Congregational Church.

On the appeals court, Wood presided as chief judge for the May 1932, November 1933, and November 1936 terms. Many of the cases he heard and opinions he helped author were directly tied to the Great Depression that had aided his election. With a host of new laws and regulations at both the state and federal level being enacted, Hoosiers sought legal guidance through the courts. Wood's docket included cases that dealt with the failure or reorganization of businesses, as well as workers compensation, creating precedents that shaped the Hoosier landscape for decades to come.

While on the court, Wood saw the two parts of his professional life come together. From March 1927 to December 1930, he had served as the attorney in the administration of a receivership of the Angola Bank Trust. Believing he was entitled to more compensation for his work than he received, Wood sued in Steuben Circuit Court, which ruled against him. In 1937 he appealed, and the appellate court reversed the decision and ordered a new trial. Wood took no part in the deliberations or decision in the case.

After failing to win renomination in 1938 for a third term on the court, Wood returned to Angola and the practice of law. He died nearly thirty years later, in 1968, at the age of ninety-four in Angola's Cameron Hospital after a yearlong illness. He had practiced law for sixty-four years, only retiring in 1961, and had celebrated his final birthday with members of the Steuben County Bar Association.

Selected Bibliography

Angola Herald, October 24, 1930, November 7, 1930, November 2, 1934, November 9, 1934, February 21, 1968.
Angola Steuben Republican, November 9, 1938, February 21, 1968.
Indianapolis Star, March 1, 1938, February 22, 1968.

CASE CITED

Wood v. Pogue, 5 N.E. 2d 1011 (Ind. App. 1937).

INDIANA HISTORICAL SOCIETY

WILLIAM H. BRIDWELL

January 1, 1931–March 30, 1941

A. JAMES FULLER

William H. Bridwell, a highly regarded jurist and loyal member of the Democratic Party, served as a deputy prosecutor and circuit court judge in Sullivan County, Indiana, before being elected to the Appellate Court of Indiana. His career before ascending to the appeals court was filled with colorful incidents as he worked in a county infamous for its deep class and political divisions.

Born in Owensburg in Greene County on October 14, 1871, Bridwell graduated from Indiana University and worked as a schoolteacher before returning to Bloomington to earn a law degree. He was elected as a deputy prosecuting attorney in Sullivan County and served two terms in that position before Governor Thomas R. Marshall appointed him judge of a newly created circuit court. The court's docket was filled with cases that reflected rural Sullivan County's violent reputation. The area was also known for its vigilante justice usually administered in the form of lynching.

Not surprisingly, many of Bridwell's cases sprung from the context of the county. In 1914 Bridwell oversaw the case of Ira Meldey, a coal miner who murdered a fellow worker by beating him with a piece of pipe during a fight in the coal mine. A few months later, Bridwell sentenced a man to life in prison for killing his neighbor because he said the other man "was making so much noise at night that he could not sleep." A year later, the judge sentenced a woman to two to twenty-one years in the state women's prison for killing her husband when he came home drunk and tried to kick down the door when she refused to let him in. Newspapers noted that she had "been married and divorced seven times." In 1919 Bridwell sentenced another man to prison for the murder of his wife, a teenager whom he had bought from her father for $500. The girl fled from her new husband, but he and her father tracked her down in Saint Louis and brought her back to Terre Haute. There, in her father's home, she quarreled with her husband and, in what the police described as "a most fiendish act," he slashed her throat with a razor.

The judge ordered four black men accused of assaulting three white women out of the county for safekeeping in the summer of 1921. Fear of a mob lynching spurred Bridwell to order the sheriff to take the men to the Knox County jail, but the sheriff there was afraid that the racist mob would follow and carry out its threat and refused to receive them. The Sullivan sheriff and his deputy then took the four accused men to Jeffersonville to the state reformatory, a 200-mile "wild ride" through the southern Indiana hills.

But southern Indiana culture did have its lighter moments, as in November 1919, when "business was practically suspended" in town by a charivari, a noisy public ritual that on this occasion included an automobile procession staged in celebration of Bridwell's marriage to Elsie Denney. The couple had no children, but they were both active in their community. Bridwell was a devout Methodist, but was also a member of the Shriners, the Odd Fellows, the Elks, and the Scottish Rite Masonic Order.

Bridwell's cases often involved coal mining companies, with some suits involving implementation of Progressive Era regulatory laws. He stopped expanded oil drilling in the county when a British company started exploratory drilling on the Methodist church lot in one township. Others involved prohibition laws and Bridwell navigated the legal minefield between the wets and the drys on the issue. He won praise from antiprohibitionists when he quashed indictments of brewery owners in 1915, but drys hailed Bridwell for his tough stand against "blind tiger" operations in which saloons posed as legitimate businesses. He also dealt with cases involving corruption, including election fraud and local political fights over infrastructure.

He left the circuit court in 1922 to practice law but returned to the bench after his election to the appellate court in 1930, most likely aided by his reputation as a fair judge. He served there for a decade, including four terms as chief judge, before his death on March 30, 1941.

Selected Bibliography

Brazil Daily Times, October 30, 1915.
Huntington Press, June 10, 1914.
Indianapolis News, February 17, 1911, May 25, September 22, 1914, November 30, 1915, March 31, 1941.
Indianapolis Star, January 9, 1912, April 16, 1916, November 26, 1919, August 23, 1921.
Princeton Daily Clarion, June 21, 1919.
Richmond Palladium-Item, August 23, 1921.

INDIANA SUPREME COURT

HARVEY J. CURTIS

January 1, 1931–January 1, 1943

RICHARD E. HUMPHREY

Harvey J. Curtis was a visionary leader, perceiving early on that Gary, Indiana, was destined to become a burgeoning steel town and positioning himself to become one of the city's leading citizens. He had practiced law briefly in Walkerton, Indiana, but as Gary was growing he moved there in 1908, and by 1910 had so established his professional reputation that he was appointed the first city attorney, a position he held for the next four years. Curtis's legal acumen, honesty, and fairness served him well as Gary developed, and, never one to shrink from worrisome circumstances, he was called upon to guide the city's leadership through numerous governmental tribulations.

As noted in his Memorial tribute, "those were turbulent years, filled with a multiplicity of problems that could arise only in a city growing and expanding as Gary was . . . but, through it all Judge Curtis guided the city and all its officials and departments legally with the dignity, patience, industry, and profound legal ability that has ever characterized his practice."

Curtis, born on January 20, 1876, to Richard and Jane Curtis of Argos, Indiana, was educated in the Argos school system and, following graduation, served as superintendent of schools in Tyner, Indiana, for four years. He was admitted to the bar at Plymouth, Indiana, on December 29, 1901, and graduated from the University of Michigan School of Law in 1903. In 1904 Curtis married Bessie Edna Johnson of Walkerton, Indiana. The couple had a daughter, Ruth Isabelle, and a son, John Richard.

Curtis, elected to the Appellate Court of Indiana in 1930, served on the bench from January 1, 1931 until January 1, 1943. He became chief judge for four different terms, in 1932, 1935, 1938, and 1940. His opinions number more than 475 and run the gamut of legal issues, but a significant percentage involved labor, workers' compensation, and personal injury. One of the most interesting of these opinions was *Inland Steel Co. v. Barcena*, in which the deceased worker was a Mexican and his common-law wife was African American. State law at the time declared that a marriage was void when one of the parties was a white person, while the other possessed one-eighth or more African American blood.

The employer argued that the Indiana Industrial Board erred in granting the common-law wife legitimacy, claiming the marriage was void and therefore she was not entitled to the workers' compensation benefits the board had granted. The court affirmed the Industrial Board's decision, holding that the statute did not apply because the worker was a Mexican, not a white person. The court reasoned that it was no more logical or consistent to say that all Mexicans were white persons than to say that all inhabitants and residents within the United States were white persons. The court noted that 20 percent of Mexicans were white, 40 percent were Indians, and the remaining 40 percent were mixed. Further, the court held that there was a strong presumption in favor of the marital status.

After Curtis retired from the bench, he became chairman of the board of Mid-City Investment Company in Gary and was sometimes called upon to hear labor dispute cases as a hearing judge. He was an early member of the Gary Bar Association and was also active in the Indiana State Bar Association, the American Bar Association, the Elks Club, the Masons, and was a member of the Episcopal Church of Gary. Curtis made an unsuccessful bid in 1917 as the Democratic candidate for mayor of Gary. In later retirement, Curtis and his wife relocated to Orlando, Florida, where he died on December 27, 1954. He was interred at the Glen Haven Memorial Park and Mausoleum in Winter Park, Florida.

Selected Bibliography

https://www.in.gov/judiciary/appeals/2394.htm/.
https://www.in.gov/judiciary/appeals/files/bios-hist-curtis-harvey.pdf/.
Indiana University Maurer School of Law. "Indiana Bar Proceedings." *Indiana Law Journal* (1931–1932): 1–6.

CASE CITED

Inland Steel Co. v. Barcena, 39 N.E. 2d 800 (Ind. App.1942)

INDIANA HISTORICAL SOCIETY

RALPH N. SMITH

January 1, 1933–October 31, 1935

MICHELLE C. GOODMAN

Ralph N. Smith served the citizens of Indiana through his work as a lawyer, prosecutor, county attorney, and judge of the Appellate Court of Indiana, becoming known for his "dynamic oratory" and his "work in the interest of Democracy."

Born to Otis and Mary Welch Smith on June 9, 1877, in Huron County, Ohio, Smith was raised on the family farm along with five siblings. Upon completing school, he attended Ohio Northern University, graduating from the classical course and then set his sights on law school. He attended law school at Valparaiso University, graduating in 1896 with high honors. That same year, he married Olive McBride and moved to Illinois, where he practiced law for five years. While in Illinois, their only child, Russell, was born. Smith moved his family to La Porte, Indiana, in 1901 and became a prominent, skilled attorney and a respected community leader. In addition to participating in the Masons, Elks Lodge, and Kiwanis Club, he was a leader in the Methodist Church, serving as a delegate to conferences, a speaker at Sunday school conventions, and other church meetings.

Smith's legal practice included a variety of cases, from contracts, personal injury, and estates to questions involving liability for damaged goods transported via railroad as well as cases before appellate courts. Smith also was elected La Porte County prosecutor for three terms. His most well-known case involved the prosecution of Ray Lamphere for the murder of infamous alleged serial killer Belle Gunness, a case shrouded in mystery that received widespread media attention.

In 1920 Smith entered the Democratic primary for U.S. House of Representatives for the Thirteenth District. News articles described him as a defender of the Woodrow Wilson administration and a "man of the people, man of sense, learned, keen with ideals . . . a student of public affairs, and not afraid to champion a cause in which he believes." Reports leading up to the primary named Smith as the front-runner, but he was defeated in a close race. Smith conceded via telegram offering to aid the victor in his campaign. Later, Smith declined an invitation to seek the nomination for U.S. Senate.

Smith went on to serve as La Porte County attorney and continued to practice law. In 1928 Smith represented the La Porte Circuit Court Judge before the Indiana Supreme Court on the issue of whether the circuit court or Supreme Court had the ability to release a prisoner on bail pending appeal. The case was prompted by a request from D. C. Stephenson, former grand dragon of the Ku Klux Klan, following his murder conviction. After the arguments, the petition for release was dismissed, so the supreme court did not render an opinion.

The next move in Smith's career was to run for election to the appeals court. He campaigned and spoke at numerous events across the northern part of the state, including at a rally for gubernatorial candidate, Paul V. McNutt. Smith won and assumed the bench in 1933. The court was just three years into writing opinions for all appeals, not just reversals, building Indiana's case law and revealing the court's reasoning for each case. Smith was chief judge toward the end of his time on the bench.

The court's docket covered diverse subjects, including estate cases, contracts for sale of vehicles, injuries resulting from railroad accidents, and bank liquidations. One appeal presented an issue of first impression:

whether the operation of a mortuary in a purely residential area was a private nuisance under the circumstances before the court. In *Albright v. Crim*, Smith analyzed several cases from other states holding that evidence supported the finding of a private nuisance since the mortuary would depreciate the values of surrounding properties and impair the owners' enjoyment of their property.

Smith also wrote for the court in *Chesapeake & O.R. Co. v. Patchett* on the exercise of reasonable care to avoid injury when travelers pass over railroad crossings and the application of contributory negligence, concepts which are still analyzed today.

As an appellate judge, Smith participated in speaking engagements at clubs, Democratic party meetings, and civic organizations. In March 1935, after one engagement in Vincennes, Smith suffered a heart attack and was later moved to Indianapolis for further care. Reportedly improved after leaving the hospital, Smith suffered another heart attack and died on October 31, 1935, at his home in La Porte.

Selected Bibliography

Cairo (IL) *Bulletin*, May 7, 1980.
Citizens Historical Association, No. 2 B817 D12 E46 F32, July 17, 1937.
Delphi Citizen, October 6, 1932.
Hammond Lake County News, November 13, 1908.
Hammond Lake County Times, August 12, September 22, 26, 1913, August 23, 1928, December 17, 1931, February 12, 15, August 13, October 29, November 1, 1932, January 13, February 2, 1933.
Indianapolis Star, March 31, April 6, November 1, 1935.
Monks, Leander, J. ed. *Courts and Lawyers of Indiana*. Indianapolis: Federal Publishing Company, 1916.
Marion Daily Mirror, May 16, 1908.
Richmond Palladium and Sun Telegraph, May 7, 1908.
South Bend News-Times, March 6, 1920.
Staton, Robert H., and Gina M. Hicklin, "The History of the Court of Appeals of Indiana," *Indiana Law Review* 30, no. 1 (1997).

CASES CITED

Albright v. Crim, 185 N.E. 304 (Ind. App. 1933).
Chesapeake & O.R. Co. v. Patchett, 184 N.E. 789 (Ind. App. 1933).
Jones v. Lathrop-Moyer, 190 N.E. 833 (Ind. App. 1934).
Lantz's Estate v. McDaniel, 190 N.E. 130 (Ind. App. 1934).
Warnock v. Fogle, 186 N.E. 889 (Ind. App. 1933).

INDIANA SUPREME COURT

WILLIAM F. DUDINE

January 1, 1933–January 1, 1941

THOMAS E. WHEELER II

William F. Dudine spent his life in service to others. He was a soldier, teacher, lawyer, and prosecutor, and served as a judge for more than twenty years. Born on September 6, 1896, in Dubois County, Indiana, to Henry P. and Agnes S. Dudine, he graduated from Jasper High School in 1913 and spent a year at the Indiana State Normal College in Terre Haute earning his teaching degree. He taught school for four years in Dubois County, where he acted as a drill leader for students interested in military service and organized them to march in various parades.

He enlisted in the U.S. Army in 1918 during the waning days of World War I and served briefly with the American Expeditionary Force in Europe. He was discharged following the armistice on November 11, 1918. Upon returning from Europe he enrolled at Catholic University of America in Washington, DC. While attending law school there Dudine excelled at debate and won a gold medal as the top debater in his class. The debate focused on the expulsion of five members of the New York State Assembly for being socialists. He opposed the expulsion and won a unanimous decision by the judges.

After graduating from law school in 1922, he returned to Jasper to begin his law practice and in June of that year, he married Margaret L. Grenough; the couple had four daughters and a son. During his time in private practice he also worked as Jasper city attorney and Dubois County Attorney.

Active in religious, civic, and political affairs, Dudine was commander of the Jasper post of the American Legion and belonged to the Knights of Columbus. A lifelong Democrat, he was elected at age twenty-eight as prosecuting attorney for the 57th Judicial District (Dubois and Pike Counties). Some of his more colorful cases involved prosecuting individuals for illegally manufacturing liquor in violation of Prohibition. For example, he won a conviction of Albert Doench for operating a still that produced about five gallons a week. Doench appealed his conviction to the Appellate Court of Indiana, claiming he was unfamiliar with courts and legal proceedings, did not have access to an attorney, and was unaware of his rights. In *Doench v. State of Indiana*, the court denied his appeal.

In 1932, at age thirty-six, Dudine sought the Democratic nomination for a seat on the appellate court. He was opposed by George L. Tremain, a more experienced lawyer who nevertheless lost in a controversial race at the Democratic convention. During the voting, a fistfight broke out on the convention floor as delegates changed their votes from Tremain to Dudine, giving him a 100-vote margin. Tremain later was elected to the Indiana Supreme Court, serving from 1935 until 1940.

Dudine won in the general election and served two terms on the appeals court, from January 1, 1933 to January 1, 1941, and was chief judge for two of the court's terms. Among his many decisions were several reflecting the labor strife of the time. One case, *Bedwell v. Dixie Bee Coal Corp.*, involved an armed confrontation between striking union miners at a coal mine and workers hired to replace them. One replacement worker, Elmer Bedwell, was shot in the arm by one of the striking miners and sought workers' compensation from the Industrial Board of Indiana, which was denied. The case was appealed and Dudine's opinion reversed the board's finding, ruling that the "evidence conclusively shows that appellant's injury arose out of and in the course of his employment by (the coal mine operator)."

After losing his race for re-election in 1940, Dudine returned to Jasper in 1941, reentering private practice. In 1954 he was elected as judge of the 57th Judicial Circuit and served two six-year terms. In 1966 when he stepped down from the bench, he practiced for a year with the Jasper law firm of Schneider and Lyons, before retiring completely in 1967. Dudine died on September 27, 1971, at age seventy-five while visiting two of his daughters in South Bend. He is buried beside his wife Margaret, who died in 1948, in the Fairview Cemetery in Jasper.

Selected Bibliography

Jasper Weekly Courier, June 21, 1918, April 30, 1920.

CASES CITED

Doench v. State, 165 N.E. 777 (Ind. App. 1929).
Bedwell v. Dixie Bee Coal Corp., 192 N.E. 723 (Ind. App. 1934).

INDIANA HISTORICAL SOCIETY

FRED A. WIECKING

November 4, 1935–July 28, 1936

TREVOR FOUGHTY

In describing Judge Fred A. Wiecking, Governor Paul V. McNutt remarked that his close friend was "possessed of those fine qualities we seek for faithful public service." Wiecking's sudden death at a young age—and less than a year into judicial service—kept him from fully realizing the potential McNutt recognized in him. But his path to the bench makes clear that his life was devoted to public service—often at the behest of his law school classmate McNutt.

Born in Bluffton on August 15, 1892, Wiecking enrolled at Indiana University in the fall of 1909. His studies were interrupted during World War I when he enlisted in the army, and he was assigned to a reserve unit at Camp Hancock in Georgia. The experience instilled in him a lifelong devotion to the military: When he returned to Bloomington, he helped establish the university's Reserve Officers' Training Corps program, and even after earning his law degree in 1919 Wiecking stayed active in the Indiana National Guard. At the time of his death he was serving as a major in the ordnance corps.

After establishing a law practice in Bluffton in 1920, Wiecking became active in the American Legion, helping to establish a post there. His involvement with the legion ultimately provided him an unexpected path into politics and government. In August 1928 he was chosen to serve as state commander. Shortly thereafter, his fellow legionnaire (and former state commander) McNutt made a bid for national commander at the national convention in San Antonio, Texas. With Wiecking serving as his campaign manager, McNutt won a come-from-behind victory on the third ballot.

His wagon now firmly hitched to McNutt's rising star, Wiecking became increasingly involved in partisan politics. When McNutt began running for governor in 1931, Wiecking briefly flirted publicly with running for Congress in the newly redistricted Fourth District. Instead, he spent 1932 managing the campaign for attorney general candidate Philip Lutz Jr., a close McNutt ally.

McNutt and Lutz both won handily in the Democratic wave of 1932, and Wiecking was rewarded by being named chief assistant attorney general for Lutz, the top appointed position in the office. From that perch, he worked closely with the general assembly in the 1933 session to write and pass the Indiana Financial Institutions Act, a major priority of McNutt's that allowed for reorganization of all the banking institutions in the state. Ahead of the 1935 session, Wiecking also helped draft liquor control legislation as the country came out of Prohibition.

But before the session began, Wiecking was again rewarded for his efforts to assist McNutt. In the summer of 1934, future U.S. Supreme Court Justice Sherman Minton became the Democratic nominee for U.S. Senate, resigning his position as public counselor to the Public Service Commission; McNutt replaced him with Wiecking, who also retained his role in the attorney general's office, though without pay.

Just over a year later, McNutt promoted Wiecking again when the death of Judge Ralph N. Smith opened a spot in the Second District of the Appellate Court of Indiana. Appointed to serve out the final year of Smith's term that ended in January 1937, Wiecking announced in the spring of 1936 that he would run for election to a full term. He would never appear on the ballot, however, after dying at the age of forty-three from a heart attack while playing golf with friends on July 28, 1936.

None of Wiecking's relatively few judicial opinions have been widely cited, relegating his greatest impact on the state to the few years prior to his death. Given the role he played in developing McNutt's plans to deal with the Great Depression through banking reform, and the state's response to the repeal of Prohibition—along with his prominent positions in the American Legion and in state government—that is still a long list of accomplishments at the front end of a promising career.

While his own legacy was cut short, it looked to be realized more completely through his son, Fred A. Wiecking Jr. But the younger Wiecking had a career path and early death that was eerily similar to his father. He also earned a law degree from Indiana University, served in the army during World War II, served as a deputy attorney general, had a brief flirtation with elective office (he lost a 1958 race for state representative), and died at the age of forty-one from a heart attack.

Selected Bibliography

Greencastle Daily Banner, July 11, 1934.
Greencastle Herald, August 29, 1928.
Indianapolis Star, October 12, 1928, October 29, 1928, November 5, 1935, April 12, April 18, 1931, April 19, 1931, December 26, 1932, April 18, 1958, July 15, 1963.
Indianapolis News, July 29, 1936.
In Memoriam. https://www.in.gov/judiciary/appeals/files/bios-hist-wiecking-fred.pdf.
Wiecking, Fred A. "High Lights of Indiana Economic Legislation in 1935."
Indiana Law Journal, 2, issue 1, Article 5 (1935).

INDIANA SUPREME COURT

PAUL E. LAYMON

September 11, 1936–January 1, 1941

GEORGE W. GEIB

Paul Laymon, who served five years on the Appellate Court of Indiana, was appointed in 1936 to complete an unexpected vacancy created by the death of Judge Fred A. Wiecking and then served an elective four-year term from 1937 to 1940. Laymon, who was born in Michigantown in Clinton County in 1899, used his 122-acre family farm in Jackson Township as a personal and political base for the next four decades. Laymon attended Indiana University but interrupted his studies for service in Europe in World War I. Upon his return he earned a degree and professional qualification of a law degree in 1921.

Energetic and personable, Laymon actively involved himself in local affairs and joined a roster of societies. His wartime service led him to the American Legion and its social affiliate the Forty and Eight (named for the numbering on French railroad boxcars that had carried forty men or eight horses to the front). In addition to his collegiate fraternity, Delta Tau Delta, he was also active in Gamma Eta Gamma law fraternity, Masonic Lodge, Elks Lodge, and Indiana Farm Bureau. He showed an early interest in public service, becoming county public prosecutor in 1923 and 1924. He was an avid golfer and almost all his surviving press photographs show him on the links, each time part of a foursome of influential men. In 1932 he was elected Clinton County judge on the Democratic ticket. His acquaintances included Governor Paul V. McNutt, with whom he campaigned in 1932, and by whom he was appointed to the appeals court vacancy four years later.

Laymon had the unusual distinction of presiding in a high-profile criminal trial in 1934. The case, which he tried as a special judge in Lebanon, concerned the contract killing of prominent Methodist minister M. K. Saunders, who had been active in the Ku Klux Klan. Those accused in the murder were a student at an Indianapolis embalming school and the battered wife of the deceased. Lawyers on both sides sought to sensationalize the case for the press. The defense, for example, provided the argument that because the victim had been active in the KKK many "witch burners" were trying to gain a seat on the jury to convict his client. Layton's conduct on the bench proved a model of judicial restraint. He allowed both sides to make their claims while denying either the opportunity to exclude opposing testimony. The jury found Norma Saunders was both guilty and insane.

No such furor surrounded Laymon's election in 1936 to the state bench. Already an incumbent by appointment, he was nominated without opposition by his party's state convention and rode the coattails of President Franklin D Roosevelt to an easy victory. He espoused ideas common within his party. He saw no reason to withdraw from politics, making an important public appearance in 1937 at an Indianapolis Democratic club where he defended Roosevelt's proposal to expand the membership of the U.S. Supreme Court to fifteen members.

On the bench Laymon's caseload included the range of issues set in motion by the Great Depression. Representative is *Hutton v. Gill.* The case featured a Michigan City classroom teacher whose salary had been reduced when she was placed by her cash-pressed school board into a non-job-related category titled "married women." Laymon dissented from the trial court by ruling that marital status was not a valid basis for determining professional credentials and categories.

In 1940 Laymon was renominated without opposition by at the party's convention. Like the rest of the Democratic ticket he encountered the remarkable Republican resurgence under presidential candidate Wendell Willkie and was defeated by Dan Flanagan by about 11,000 votes. Laymon briefly practiced law in Indianapolis with L. E. Slack, and then entered corporate practice with Standard Accident Life Insurance. His move to the company's headquarters in Detroit was followed by a move to California, first to head a company regional office and then to pursue the postwar real estate boom. He died in 1964 in Arcadia, California.

Selected Bibliography

Indianapolis Star, December 12, 1934, February 15, 1937, June 28, 1940, January 26, 1941.

CASE CITED

Hutton v. Gill, 7 N.E. 2d 1011 (Ind. App. 1937).

HADLEY FAMILY COLLECTION

A. JEWELL STEVENSON

October 14, 1938–January 1, 1943

CARL E. KRAMER

A. Jewell Stevenson's tenure on the Appellate Court of Indiana was a highlight of a legal, judicial, and administrative career that began during the 1920s and spanned the momentous administrations of governors Paul V. McNutt, his immediate successor, M. Clifford Townsend, and the first term of Henry F. Schricker. Stevenson's distinguished career also included service as a circuit court judge, director of the Indiana Department of Financial Institution, and private practice.

Stevenson, born in Hadley, Indiana, on January 10, 1894, attended the public schools of Hendricks County and then Central Normal College in Danville and Indiana State Normal College in Terre Haute. After military service during World War I, he attended Indiana University in Bloomington. He began his career as a teacher, serving for six years in elementary and high schools in Hendricks County while studying law. He married Josephine McCord in 1923, and they had two children.

After being admitted to the bar in 1920, he began practicing law with Danville attorney Edgar M. Blessing, who served on the appellate court from 1941 to 1945. After a decade in private practice, Stevenson, a Democrat, was elected judge of the Hendricks County Circuit Court. When Stevenson's six-year term ended in 1936, McNutt appointed him chief deputy attorney general of Indiana. In that position he played a major role in defending the administrative and social reforms initiated by McNutt during the Great Depression and President Franklin D. Roosevelt's New Deal.

Stevenson's service on the appeals court began on October 14, 1938, when he was appointed to fill the unexpired term of Judge Posey T. Kime, who had resigned to serve as a staff attorney with the Federal Power Commission. The following month, Stevenson was elected on the Democratic ticket to serve a full term on the court.

Stevenson displayed a talent for consensus building and loyalty to the progressive reforms of Roosevelt's New Deal and McNutt's Little New Deal. During his tenure, he wrote seven opinions, six of which reflected the unanimous view of the court. Several of his opinions, in a range of cases involving industrial accidents, a financial receivership, and an estate issue, demonstrated a sympathy for parties allegedly disadvantaged by those in positions of authority. For example, Stevenson's opinion in the case of *Wilson et al. v. La Porte Gas & Electric Co. et al.* reversed a decision by the state Industrial Board that had denied compensation to two minor stepchildren of a utility company employee killed in a job-related accident even though they had lived with their stepfather and were defined under state law as entitled to compensation.

A couple of Stevenson's opinions, including one in which an appeal was dismissed and another in which the trial court's judgment was reversed, reflected his insistence that attorneys in both trial and appellate courts follow proper procedure. He addressed this concern with respect to the appellate court level in "Common Mistakes in Appellate Procedure," a speech delivered at the August 1940 Law Institute in Fort Wayne.

Noting that more than one-fourth of cases that came before the court during the 1939–40 calendar year were disposed of because of mistakes made by attorneys, he chided lawyers for failing to take enough time to read and understand court rules and to prepare the record for appeal after the verdict or decision had been rendered. Adding that motions for new trials were often too long, he counseled that "fewer mistakes would be made if the attorneys were able and willing to select and present only such errors that are vital to the decision of the case in appeal."

After Stevenson's term on the appeals court expired in 1943, Schricker appointed him director of the Indiana Department of Financial Institutions, which had been created in 1933 to supervise banks, trust companies, building and loan associations, credit unions, and other Indiana-based financial organizations. When Schricker's first gubernatorial term ended, Stevenson returned to Danville, where he practiced law with John A. Kendall, another future appeals court judge. Stevenson's son, Allen Joe, joined them after his admission to the bar, creating the firm of Stevenson, Kendall, and Stevenson.

In addition to his legal practice, Stevenson served as a trustee of the Indiana Boys School and the Indiana Board of Education. He practiced law until his death on August 22, 1959. The appeals court marked his passing with a memorial tribute that read in part, "His opinions are his monument reflecting his legal sagacity and his adroit ability to apply his legal knowledge in the decisions of cases he was called upon to render."

Selected Bibliography

Stevenson, A. Jewell. "Common Mistakes in Appellate Procedure." *Indiana Law Journal* 16, Issue 1, Article 7. http//www.repository.law journal.edu/ilj/vol16/iss1/7.

———. Memorial Obituary. (/judiciary/appeals/files/bios-hist-stevenson-aj.pdf).

CASE CITED

Wilson et al. v. La Porte Gas & Electric Co. et. al., 22 N.E. 2d 882 (Ind. App 1939).

INDIANA SUPREME COURT

HUBER M. DeVOSS

January 1, 1939–January 1, 1943

MICHAEL J. DeBOER

During Huber M. DeVoss's four-year term on the Appellate Court of Indiana momentous events unfolded across the globe, including Adolf Hitler's invasion of Poland on September 1, 1939, and Japan's attack on Pearl Harbor on December 7, 1941, which was immediately followed by America's entry into World War II. These events became very personal for DeVoss when his only son was sent to fight in the European theater.

DeVoss, who was born in Farmland, Indiana, in Randolph County on October 16, 1879, was an infant when his parents, Lewis C. and Mary E. DeVoss, moved to Decatur, Indiana, which was the seat of government for Adams County. The handsome, Victorian-style county courthouse, built in 1872 and 1873, was less than a decade old when the family moved to Decatur. His father was a distinguished attorney who practiced law in Decatur for more than three decades, and DeVoss followed in his father's footsteps.

Admitted to the Adams County bar in 1902, DeVoss served as official court reporter from 1902 to 1917 and was elected city clerk of Decatur, serving two terms from 1909 to 1917. In 1912 and 1913, while he was serving in these positions, a large limestone Peace Monument—a war memorial uniquely devoted to peace—was designed, erected, and dedicated in the Adams County Courthouse square. DeVoss was elected mayor of Decatur in 1921 and was elected judge of the Adams Circuit Court in 1932, serving one six-year term.

In 1938 DeVoss was elected to the appeals court, which at that time was a statutory court. During his one term, he was able to draw upon three and a half decades of rich experience in the practice of law, the judiciary, and local government. During the court's November 1939 and November 1941 terms, he served as chief judge. As a member of the court, he authored twelve published opinions addressing a wide range of procedural and substantive issues. After his retirement from the court, he returned to private practice.

On June 2, 1944, nearly a year and a half after his term on the court ended, DeVoss died suddenly. He was survived by his wife, their only son, John L. DeVoss, and daughters Marjorie Townsend and L. Berniece Frisinger. John, a well-known attorney and community leader in Decatur, served in the U.S. Army during World War II with the glider infantry and participated in the Battle of the Bulge, which lasted from December 16, 1944 to January 25, 1945. Berniece served as a court reporter in the Adams Circuit Court. Until his retirement from the active practice of law in August 2013, Jay M. DeVoss, a grandson of Judge DeVoss, practiced law at the Decatur law firm in which his great-grandfather, grandfather, and father had practiced law and which continues to bear the DeVoss family name.

The affection and the respect for Judge DeVoss in the Adams County community, especially in the legal community, were conveyed in the heartfelt memorial that the Adams County Bar Association adopted following his unexpected passing. The association's resolution stated in part:

> Judge Huber M. DeVoss was an able lawyer, cordial friend, devoted father, intelligent, high-minded, and public-spirited citizen, in every sense a gentleman. Dignified in manner, voice, and bearing, possessed of a finely structured, keenly perceptive, exquisitely balanced, and delicately sympathetic mind, he enjoyed the highest respect of a community which for the whole of his adult life he served effectively in countless

> ways. He typified the traditional Good Advocate who disdains to plead a cause wherein his tongue must be confuted by his conscience.

The resolution, which was approved by his professional peers, also acknowledged his "lofty patriotism," his "surpassing statesmanship," and his "faithful service to humanity." The words crafted seven and a half decades ago, continue to pay tribute to a man who dedicated his adult life and his professional career to serving his clients, his community, his state, and his country in both private practice and public office.

Selected Bibliography

Historical Listing of Court of Appeals Judges. https://www.in.gov/judiciary/appeals/2401.htm.

Huber M. DeVoss obituary. https://www.in.gov/judiciary/appeals/files/bios-hist-devoss-huber.pdf.

Staton, Robert H., and Gina M. Hicklin. "The History of the Court of Appeals of Indiana," *Indiana Law Review* 30, no. 1 (1997): 203–31.

INDIANA SUPREME COURT

DAN C. FLANAGAN*

January 1, 1941–December 31, 1948

SCOTT M. BUSHNELL

Dan Collins Flanagan was an unsuccessful Republican candidate for judge of the Appellate Court of Indiana twice in the 1930s before winning election in November 1940 when GOP candidates statewide were aided by the presidential candidacy of Hoosier native Wendell Willkie. Once on the bench, Flanagan was elected chief judge of the appeals court by his five fellow judges in May 1943 and gained a full four-year term as chief judge after the November 1944 election.

The son of a lawyer, Flanagan was born on April 23, 1899, in Lafayette, Indiana. After graduating from the Frankfort public schools, he enlisted in the U.S. Army as the nation entered World War I and rose to the rank of sergeant in the field artillery. His tour of duty included seven months in France, where he served with distinction. Flanagan attended Butler University and the University of California before earning his law degree in 1921 from Benjamin Harrison Law School, which is now the Indiana University Robert H. McKinney School of Law, Indianapolis.

Flanagan opened a solo practice in Frankfort in 1921 and became deputy prosecutor in Clinton County the following year. He moved in 1924 to Fort Wayne, and in 1928, he became Allen County deputy prosecutor. In 1925 he married Mabelle Cass, and they had one son, Dan Jr. During the 1930s Flanagan rose to chairman of the Allen County Republican Central Committee, where he played a significant role in developing one of the strongest Republican organizations in the history of Allen County.

In 1949 Flanagan left the appeals court and returned to private practice. He also began lecturing at Valparaiso University and at the University of Notre Dame and wrote the two-volume *Indiana Trial and Appellate Practice* (1952) with F. Leroy Wiltrout and Frank Hamilton. Flanagan's earlier book, *Indiana Pleading and Procedure* (1947), was said to be "one of the most widely accepted legal works used by practicing attorneys in the state" according to an article in the *Fort Wayne Journal-Gazette* on October 8, 1952.

Flanagan's dedication to the practice of law did not diminish his love of politics. He played a pivotal role garnering Midwest support for the presidential candidacy of Dwight D. Eisenhower in 1952, serving as Indiana chairman of the candidate's advisory committee.

Flanagan was appointed to the Indiana Supreme Court by Governor George N. Craig in April 1953 to complete the term of Paul G. Jasper, who resigned to accept a post as counsel for a public utility. Jasper, also from Fort Wayne, had served as the Allen County Democratic chairman a decade after Flanagan had led the county's Republican Committee.

In his final year on the Supreme Court, Flanagan served as chief justice before his term ended on December 31, 1954. His opinions were well regarded for their clarity and conciseness. He was not without a "flowery" moment or two in his judgments, however. In one case, *Taylor v. State*, where he ruled in favor of an appellate who claimed to have been denied reasonable promptness in sentencing, Flanagan concluded his opinion: "An American citizen is entitled to live without a Damocles sword dangling over his head." The opinion prompted two other justices to write separate concurring opinions and two others to write separate dissenting opinions, one of whom observed, "that the legendary sword which the court has removed from over the heads of culprits now dangles over the heads of our trial judges."

In 1954 Flanagan decided not to seek another term on the Court. He returned to private practice and became well known in northeastern Indiana for his willingness to help young attorneys. Flanagan's "keen insight into the law" made him a valuable consultant, the Allen County Bar Association observed in its memorial tribute, adding that when Flanagan "appeared in court, the court was always well pleased to see him representing a client inasmuch as he knew that his client would have skilled representation, and that the legal points involved would remain clear-cut."

Flanagan died on February 28, 1960, in Fort Wayne. Although he had been ill for two months, the death of the fifty-nine-year-old was unexpected. He had announced he would seek the Republican nomination for judge on the Allen Circuit Court only a few weeks earlier. "He was a good trial lawyer, an excellent judge, an eloquent orator and a talented writer of clear, readable prose," the *Fort Wayne Journal-Gazette* wrote in its editorial on March 1, 1960.

Selected Bibliography

Adams, Wendy L., and Elizabeth R. Osborn, eds. *In Memoriam: Glimpses from Indiana's Legal Past*. Indianapolis: Indiana Supreme Court, 2006.

Fort Wayne Journal-Gazette, October 8, 1952, March 1, 1960.

CASE CITED

Taylor v. State, 233 Ind. 398 (1954).

*This profile is revised from one that appeared in *Justices of the Indiana Supreme Court* (2010).

INDIANA SUPREME COURT

EDGAR M. BLESSING

January 1, 1941–June 20, 1945

DAVID ROOT

Edgar M. Blessing was born on August 21, 1876, in the Benton County community of Wadena to George A. and Margaret J. Ladd Blessing. George was a Civil War veteran who fought for three years before returning to Indiana to take up farming. Edgar, who grew up on nearby farms and graduated from Oxford High School, taught school for two years while attending Indiana State Normal School in Terre Haute. After graduating in 1899, he served as principal of Plainfield High School for two years.

Blessing enrolled in the University of Michigan Law School in 1901 and graduated in 1904. The following year he began private practice in Hendricks County. Also, in 1905, he married Geraldine M. White. She committed suicide in 1933 and Blessing then married Elsie L. Currie Barnett in 1934.

Active in Republican politics, Blessing was elected Hendricks County Prosecutor in 1906 and served for two terms. The *Indianapolis Star* remarked that as prosecutor he possessed "unusual oratorical gifts." Nevertheless, such gifts proved insufficient in his bid for Congress in 1912. Instead, he became county attorney, a position in which he helped secure financing for the Hendricks County Courthouse. He also remained heavily involved in Republican politics, serving in 1920 as a delegate to the party's national convention in Chicago. Two years earlier he helped lead Hendricks Circuit Court Judge Solon A. Enloe's successful campaign for the appeals court. Enloe also served as dean of the law department at Central Normal College in Danville, where Blessing taught part time.

Blessing was appointed to the Indiana Public Service Commission in 1921 by Republican governor Warren McCray and served until 1923 when he was appointed solicitor for the Post Office Department by Postmaster General Harry S. New. Some controversy remains surrounding Blessing's decision to step down from the commission and take up the role of solicitor, with contemporary newspapers suggesting his appointment was to relieve McCray of the "embarrassment" Blessing brought to the commission because of several favorable rulings for utilities and against consumers regarding rates. That controversy can neither be confirmed nor denied, but he did take a 17 percent pay cut when changing posts ($6,000 to $5,000). He served as solicitor until 1925, when he returned to Danville to resume private practice with A. Jewell Stevenson, also a future judge of the appeals court.

Staying active in Republican politics throughout the 1930s, Blessing served as chairman of the party's sixth district and ran for the Indiana Supreme Court in 1938 but lost to Democrat H. Nathan Swaim in the general election. Two years later, in 1940, he rode the Republican wave of support for Hoosier native Wendell Willkie's bid for president and defeated William F. Dudine for judge on the Appellate Court of Indiana. Blessing assumed his seat on January 1, 1941, and served as chief judge in the May 1941 and November 1942 terms.

Blessing's legal and political career significantly exceeded his judicial one. Nevertheless, in the spirit of the progressive Republican Party that worked for passage of the Civil War Amendments to obtain racial equality and civil rights, as well as the Nineteenth Amendment procuring women's suffrage, he emulated these virtues in both his time as an attorney and judge. At the bar, in *Clark v. Bledsaw*, he successfully argued in the appeals court that compensation be paid to an illiterate African American woman who had been defrauded by a huckster out of property she owned. Shortly after his election to the bench he hired Ruth E. Maier as one of the first female law clerks to serve in the appeals court.

Outside his professional and political realms, Blessing led an active community life. He was a member of the American Bar Association, Indiana State Bar Association, Sons of Veterans, Scottish Rite, Masons, Knights of Pythias, and a Shriner of the Murat Temple.

Following the onset of a coronary illness in March 1943, one that slowly but steadily kept him away from the court, he died at home in Danville on June 20, 1945, at age sixty-eight. Recognized as a leader in politics and law, a memoriam from the Hendricks County Bar Association, citing his many accomplishments, concluded that his life "is an example of the heights to which industry, courage and close application to duty will lift an individual."

Selected Bibliography

Gulley, Otis E. *In Memoriam: Edgar M. Blessing.* Memorial of the Hendricks County Bar Association, 1945.

Hadley, Hon. John V. *History of Hendricks County, Indiana: Her People, Industries, and Institutions.* Indianapolis: B. F. Bowen and Company, 1914.

Indianapolis Star, January 7, February 9, 1912, May 27, 1920, August 25, September 16, 1923.

Hammond Times, November 14, 1940.

Kokomo Tribune, June 5, 1930, May 11, 1932.

Oakland Tribune, August 25, 1925.

Tucson (AZ) Daily Citizen, April 18, 1944.

Valparaiso Vidette-Messenger, November 12, 1938.

CASES CITED

Clark v. Bledsaw, 73 Ind. App. 282 (1920).

COURTESY OF DARTMOUTH COLLEGE LIBRARY

CHARLES H. BEDWELL

April 4, 1941–January 1, 1943

A. JAMES FULLER

Charles H. Bedwell's brief stint on the Appellate Court of Indiana was a sad twilight to a once-promising political career. A staunch Democrat and supporter of Progressive reform, Bedwell shot quickly to prominence in state politics and became Speaker of the Indiana House of Representatives. But he proved to be a shooting star, as he ran afoul of the party establishment dominated by Thomas Taggart. Banished to the political wilderness for nearly twenty years, he returned to office as a state senator in the 1930s and was later appointed to the court by Governor Henry F. Schricker to fill the vacancy due to the death of William H. Bridwell.

Born in Sullivan County, Indiana, on March 18, 1884, Bedwell graduated from Central Normal College in Danville and returned to his home county to teach school. He earned a law degree from Indiana University in 1907 and practiced as an attorney in Sullivan County, with most of his cases related to labor law. This fit well with the context of the area, as the rural county was deeply divided by politics and by class, with many of the working poor employed in coal mining.

As a county native and lifelong Democrat, Bedwell felt an affinity for the poor and working class, and his Progressive politics were a fitting outlet for his views on labor and justice. Early in his career, he served as a deputy prosecutor and in 1910 helped put down a local mob that came in response to the sheriff confiscating a large amount of illegal alcohol. When the authorities attempted to move barrels of beer, "a thirsty mob" attacked the wagons and recaptured the loot. Bedwell raced to the scene in a car, arriving just in time to help the sheriff and deputies disperse the crowd.

Bedwell, who won a seat in the legislature in 1912, aligned himself with the Progressive wing of the Democratic Party. He wrote a compulsory workman's compensation bill that set up a scale of rates and established an arbitration board to hear individual cases. He also introduced a bill to allow for county governments to tax coal mines, and further took on mining companies with safety regulations, introducing a bill requiring them to have trained fire bosses. His Progressive tendencies were also evident in a bill he introduced to make false advertising illegal. Despite being busy with politics, he did find time to marry Lulu Cain and they soon started a family, having two children.

It was no surprise when Bedwell won re-election in 1914, but it was shocking when he won the fight to be Speaker of the Indiana House of Representatives over the establishment candidates. Party boss Taggart at first opposed Bedwell, but when he saw that there was a groundswell of popular support for him, he changed his mind. This allowed Bedwell to become, at the time, the youngest Speaker in state history at age thirty and marked him as a rising star in Indiana politics. In his opening speech, he announced that he would not allow the passage of too many bills because it would cost the state too much money. He said that he would not allow a bill to go forward just because it came from the majority party. This immediately upset the party machine, as did his promise to prevent lobbying by interest groups—namely big business.

Within two days of taking the Speaker's chair, some wondered whether Bedwell was a "an anti-machine man" or a "triumph of the organization." Although some were already mentioning Bedwell as "the next candidate for governor," Taggart, already under investigation for his boss politics, had had enough. The party machine pulled its support and Bedwell was defeated for re-election in 1916.

After Taggart's death, Bedwell was able to return to politics, finally winning a seat in the state senate in 1934. He held that seat until 1941, when he was appointed to the appeals court. But he failed to win election to the court in 1943 and finished his disappointing career with an appointment to the state tax board in 1942. He died on March 19, 1948, an example of a bright young star who dared to buck the establishment, a move that cost him the potential to climb higher up the political ladder.

Selected Bibliography

Alexandria Times-Tribune, January 9, 1915.
Fort Wayne Daily News, January 7, 1915.
Indianapolis Star, November 7, 29, December 20, 1914, January 7, March 6, 1915.
Seymour Tribune, August 11, 1910.

COLLECTION OF THE WILLARD LIBRARY ARCHIVES

FLOYD S. DRAPER*

January 1, 1943–December 31, 1950

LORENZO ARREDONDO

Floyd Stanley Draper was first and foremost a public servant. He served continuously in public office from 1923, when he became chief deputy prosecutor for Lake County, until 1960, when he was appointed judge of the Lake County Criminal Court. Prior to this appointment, Draper had served two terms on the Appellate Court of Indiana and then four years on the Indiana Supreme Court.

Born October 17, 1893, in Fulton, New York, Draper was educated in public schools and graduated from Watertown High School. He received his law degree from Valparaiso University in 1915 and began private practice in Gary in 1917. Although he was a Republican in a highly Democratic area, he managed to thrive. He served two terms as chief deputy prosecutor in Lake County—from 1923 to 1924 and 1927 to 1931—and was city attorney for Gary in 1939.

Draper began his judicial career in 1942 when he was elected to the appeals court and reelected to a second term in 1946. Employers, in at least two cases, did not fare well before Draper. In *Calumet Paving Co. v. Butkins,* writing for the court, he affirmed a decision of the Industrial Board of Indiana that had awarded compensation to an employee injured by an accidental explosion of dynamite. In another case, *Chevrolet Muncie, Division of General Motors Corp. v. Hirst,* Draper again upheld a ruling of the Industrial Board that granted compensation to an employee who had suffered work-related illnesses from exposure to various chemical fumes.

In 1950 Draper handily won a seat on the Indiana Supreme Court. Republican candidates that year were aided by having the popular incumbent U.S. Senator Homer E. Capehart at the top of the ticket. Draper's former law clerk, Richard M. Givan, who later became chief justice of the Indiana Supreme Court, described him as being "on the conservative side. He took a harder line with criminals than some of the other justices." Draper's conservatism in criminal cases is evident in a dissenting opinion he wrote in *Taylor v. State*. The case involved lengthy judicial proceedings against a man who pleaded guilty to armed robbery, but whose sentencing was delayed for more than three years due to various hearings regarding his mental competency and his indefinite incarceration at either the Indiana Hospital for the Insane or the Village for Epileptics. He finally escaped from the epileptic center, and in his final appearance before the trial court was sentenced to ten to twenty years in prison, despite his plea for a new trial.

The majority opinion overturned the trial court's ruling with instructions to enter a judgment for the defendant. The majority opinion stated that there must be some "recognized legal purpose" for unusual delays in sentencing, and that even then the termination of the delay had to be fixed. Draper, perhaps drawing upon his experience as a prosecutor, wrote a strong dissent.

After four years, Draper decided not to complete his full term on the Court, resigning reportedly because of his brother's ill health. Following Draper's resignation in January 1955, Governor George N. Craig quickly appointed Isadore E. Levine to fill the vacancy.

Draper's role as a judge, however, did not end with his departure from the Supreme Court. For three years he was engaged in private practice in Gary before retiring, but fate intervened to bring him back to the bench. In

1960 Lake County Criminal Court Judge William J. Murray died in office. Governor Harold W. Handley tapped Draper to fill the vacant position.

Following his stint on the criminal court, Draper retired once again, this time for good. He moved to Bradenton, Florida, where he died on March 20, 1980. In its tribute, the Lake County Bar Association, remembering his willingness to give up retirement to serve as criminal court judge, said of him: "Whether he did it out of Republican loyalty . . . or out of a desire to restore faith to the Lake County judicial system . . . it was the action of a man possessed of a keen sense of duty."

Selected Bibliography

Adams, Wendy L., and Elizabeth R. Osborn, eds. *In Memoriam: Glimpses from Indiana's Legal Past*. Indianapolis: Indiana Supreme Court, 2006.
Indianapolis Star, March 22, 1980.
Indianapolis Times, April 21, 1952.

CASES CITED

Calumet Paving Co. v. Butkins, 47 N.E.2d 829 (Ind App. 1943).
Chevrolet Muncie, Div. of General Motors Corp. v. Hirst, 46 N.E.2d (Ind. App. 1943).
Taylor v. State of Indiana, 233 Ind. 398 (1954).

*This profile is revised from one that appeared in *Justices of the Indiana Supreme Court* (2010).

RUSH COUNTY COURTHOUSE

PAUL F. DOWELL

January 1, 1943–October 18, 1945

DAVID J. REMONDINI

Born the same year Appellate Court of Indiana was created in 1891, Paul F. Dowell rose from his southern Indiana roots to create a lifetime of public service before becoming one of the few court of appeals judges to die in office, at age fifty-four.

Dowell was born in Edinburgh, Indiana, on June 4, 1891, and attended school in both Columbus and in the Ohio River town of Madison, where he lived much of his life. Public service was already part of his upbringing. His father, a Pennsylvania Railroad superintendent, served on the Madison City Council.

Dowell, who graduated from Hanover College in 1913, was very engaged at Hanover as a singer, actor, and leader in many organizations. Likely due to these efforts, classmates seemed confident in his abilities, predicting that "relying on the ingenuity of Mr. Dowell," that the Pan Hellenic Dance would be a success.

A future interest in journalism may have been sparked at Hanover, where he served as president of the Indiana Intercollegiate Press Association. After graduation he attended law school at the University of Minnesota, where he specialized in international law. He remained in Minnesota for several years, writing editorials for the *Pioneer Press* in Saint Paul before returning to Madison. For a brief time he worked as a clerk for the Pennsylvania Railroad ticket office.

While in Madison, he married Anne Harper and opened a law practice. He also became involved in public service and was elected prosecutor for the judicial circuit for Jefferson and Switzerland Counties from 1929 to 1932. In addition, he was Madison city attorney from 1935 to 1939 and served on the Madison School Board. In 1940 he challenged the incumbent judge for the Jefferson and Switzerland Circuit but lost the election.

In Madison he was active in community enterprises and the Methodist Church and took a keen interest in young people and worked unselfishly to "alleviate the distress of the needy." Dowell also owned a pleasure boat, which he kept at his summer lodge on the Ohio River three miles east of Madison.

Described as an "ardent and lifelong Republican" Dowell was an active party member who was "naturally gifted as an orator and traveled the state to give speeches for his party's causes." On at least two occasions, he represented clients in court of appeals cases. One was *Quail v. Banta*, which was a family dispute over ownership of land, and the other, *State ex rel. Shepherd v. Nichols*, involved a wife who had been denied a change of venue in a divorce case.

Dowell won election to the appeals court in 1942 and took office on January 1, 1943, as one of six appellate judges. During his time on the appellate bench he authored thirty-two civil cases, including twelve as a presiding judge in the final year of his life.

His colleagues on the court found he had a "warm friendly nature" and "a keen sense of loyalty." In a tribute upon his death, three of his colleagues wrote, "He was devoted to his work and firm in the presentation of his views yet was at all times ready and willing to give respectful consideration to the views of his fellows."

During his lifetime he became involved in a host of organizations, including, Sigma Chi Fraternity, the Masonic Lodge, Order of the Eastern Star, the Shrine, Gatling Gun Club, the Elks and Moose lodges, the Knights of Pythias, the Columbia Club in Indianapolis, and the Indianapolis Press Club.

After a brief illness, he died suddenly of a heart attack on October 18, 1945, at Methodist Hospital in Indianapolis.

Selected Bibliography

Delphi Journal, October 22, 1942.
Madison Courier, October 18, 1945.
Staton, Robert H., and Gina M. Hicklin, "The History of the Court of Appeals of Indiana." *Indiana Law Review* 30, no. 1 (1997).

CASES CITED

Quail v. Banta, 48 N.E. 2d 841 (Ind. App. 1943).
Shepherd v. Nichols, 36 N.E. 2d 913 (Ind. App. 1941).

INDIANA SUPREME COURT

WILBUR A. ROYSE

January 1, 1943–December 31, 1958

DAVID J. REMONDINI

Wilbur Aliexis Royse, an Indianapolis native who studied to be a Catholic priest and lived as a strident anticommunist, served four terms on the Appellate Court of Indiana before losing his seat in 1958 when the entire statewide Republican ticket was defeated. In 1962 he campaigned to regain his seat on the bench, but the day before the nominating process by the Republican State Convention was to begin, he died of a heart attack in an Indianapolis hotel.

Royse, who was born in Indianapolis on July 7, 1896, attended Saint John Parochial and High School. An active Catholic, he was a member of Saint Joan of Arc Catholic Church near his Park Avenue home on the north side of Indianapolis. He was also editor of the *Indiana Catholic and Record*, the local archdiocesan publication later known as the *Criterion.*

After spending two years studying for the priesthood at Saint Meinrad Seminary in southern Indiana, Royse returned to Indianapolis and married Mayme Brown in 1916. He graduated from the American Central Law School in Indianapolis, a predecessor of the Indiana University Robert H. McKinney School of Law.

He practiced law with Thomas McGee for a few years and then began a solo practice in 1931. He also worked as a supervising deputy for the Marion County prosecutor and special corporation deputy in the secretary of state's office.

Royse served as a special judge in several cases in municipal and county courts. In one of his cases, he sentenced C. W. Hardwick, who opposed the right of women to smoke in public, to ten days in jail for slapping a cigarette from the mouth of Marjorie Pelecco as she sat in her husband's car on an Indianapolis street. Royse also gave the defendant a "stern lecture" about his behavior and called him "an outrageous rascal." As a judge, he ran a strict courtroom and even sentenced a lawyer to three days in jail for contempt after the lawyer kept interrupting him.

Later, Royse got a taste of his own medicine when he sparked the ire of a trial-court judge by sending his brother to request a continuance on the same day he was representing a defendant in a burglary trial. After delivering a stern lecture, the judge appointed a new attorney so the trial could begin.

Beside being widely known as an attorney, Royse also was active in Republican politics. He was named as an alternate delegate to the Republican National Convention in 1940 and two years later was elected as a Republican to his first term on the appellate court, beginning a sixteen-year tenure.

Royse most likely would have described himself as a "strict constructionist" as it relates to his legal views. In his 1958 campaign announcement he wrote that "courts must scrupulously avoid the oft-times alluring temptation to usurp the prerogatives of either the legislative or executive branches." A man of strong opinions, Royse, in his first campaign for the court in 1942, told a Greensburg audience that recent actions by President Franklin D. Roosevelt were a "deliberate effort to overturn our form of government" and he accused the president of seeking "to throttle public opinion and public expression which is adverse to his dictates."

In addition, Royse would frequently produce writings and often lecture about the dangers of communism, which he described as "as an enemy of religion and natural law" He also carried his religious convictions into his public life. While on the bench, he sent a telegraph to Secretary of State

Edward Stettinius urging him to start each session of the post–World War II meetings in San Francisco, which ultimately led to the creation of the United Nations, with a prayer. "Finite man cannot hope to attain the noble objectives of the peace process without the aid of God," he wrote.

During his time on the court, Royse was viewed as an active jurist who produced an average of twenty-nine opinions each year. He was well-regarded by his colleagues who elected him chief judge six times, the most of any appellate court judge. He and Mayme had one child, Rita Royse, who was the grandmother of the late Indianapolis activist and independent mayoral candidate Carl E. Moldthan. In his leisure time, his favorite hobby was said to be fishing with his six grandchildren.

After Royse lost his seat in 1958, he returned to practicing law. He appeared in several cases before his former court and was successful for a client who had sued his own attorney for overcharging him in a personal injury case.

SELECTED BIBLIOGRAPHY

Greencastle Daily Banner, July 31, 1931, October 29, 1942.
Indianapolis News, September 28, 1940.
Indianapolis Star, August 23, 1930, April 17, 1931, May 11, 1958, June 14, 1962.
Indianapolis Times, May 8, 1945.
Muncie Star-Press, July 27, 1931.
Tipton Daily Times, July 28, 1931.

CASES CITED

Justice v. Tripp, 158 N.E. 2d 809 (Ind. App. 1959).

INDIANA SUPREME COURT

HARRY L. CRUMPACKER

January 1, 1943–December 31, 1958

WILLIAM F. GULDE

Shortly after Christmas in 1926, Harry Lewis Crumpacker, judge of the La Porte-Porter County Superior Court, began receiving anonymous letters demanding that convicted murderer D. C. Stephenson, the former Grand Dragon of the Ku Klux Klan in Indiana who was in prison for murder, be released. Stephenson's lawyers were trying to get him out of the state penitentiary in Michigan City on a technicality, claiming that papers were not signed when his trial was moved from Marion County to Hamilton County. On December 29 Stephenson, dressed in a neatly pressed blue suit, testified in front of Crumpacker. However, Stephenson's vitriolic opening statement irritated the judge and he told the convicted murderer that his courtroom was not a forum for that kind of behavior. In the end, Crumpacker ruled against Stephenson and sent him back to prison.

While Crumpacker eventually rose to become a judge of the Appellate Court of Indiana, his early life was anything but stable. Born as the third child of Melvin and Eliza Crumpacker Lewis in 1881, young Harry never knew either of his biological parents. His mother died shortly after his birth of typhoid fever. His grieving father then farmed out all of the children and drifted south to New Orleans, where he was murdered on December 19, 1881. Harry was adopted by his Uncle John and Aunt Anna Crumpacker of La Porte while his siblings were raised by other relatives. His formative years were peaceful as he graduated from La Porte High School and eventually attended the University of Michigan, where he obtained his bachelor's degree in 1903 and his law degree in 1905.

After graduating from law school, Crumpacker moved to Michigan City, opened an office, and married Blanche Bosserman in the summer of 1907. The couple had three children before her death of scarlet fever in the summer of 1914. His wife's untimely death left the young attorney at a loss. Besides having three young children to raise, he was also in the middle of his first political campaign for the Republican Party, which he won by defeating a veteran judge for the La Porte-Porter County Superior Court.

For twenty years, Crumpacker was a fixture in Michigan City. Because its proximity to Lake County his court received many cases from its neighbors. In 1917, for example, he had to sort through an election controversy involving Gary's mayor. He presided over numerous murder trials, including some that involved Chicago gangsters. Years later, he told his grandson that he always tried to follow the law even in death penalty cases.

In 1934 Democratic landslides swept the country and, in that election, Crumpacker lost his bid for re-election to the superior court. He returned to private practice in Michigan City, but it would not be his last attempt at public office. In fact, he ran for the appeals court in 1936, the Indiana Supreme Court in 1938, the appeals court again in 1940, losing each time. Finally, in 1942, at the age of sixty-one, he was elected to the appeals court.

Crumpacker and his second wife, Harriett, moved into an apartment along Meridian Street in Indianapolis and remained in the capital for the next sixteen years. He wrote opinions for dozens of cases. In a 1950 decision he ruled that employers did not have to pay unemployment insurance for those employees who were chronically absent. The case involved Dorothy Merkle against the Daly Brothers Shoe Company of Marion. The judge noted that that she showed no regard for the interests of the employer and was not entitled to any insurance.

In a 1952 case Crumpacker ruled that a juvenile could not be punished without a hearing. The case concerned sixteen-year-old Lowell Green of South Bend, who was sentenced to the Indiana Boys School by the Saint Joseph Probate Court without a chance to defend himself. The appeals court reversed the local decision with Crumpacker writing that a juvenile's rights may not be disregarded.

Crumpacker clearly loved being a judge as he remained in service to the state until he was seventy-eight years old. He led as the chief judge of the appeals court five times. After leaving the bench, he and his wife returned to Michigan City, where he died in 1969.

Selected Bibliography

Chicago Tribune, December 21, 31, 1926.
Crumpacker, Harry L. III. Interview with author, December 6, 2019.
Huntington Herald, December 31, 1926.
Indianapolis News, December 25, 1917.
Logansport Pharos-Tribune, November 21, 1952.
Muncie Star-Press, December 26, 1926.
Munster Times, June 25, 1918, February 29, 1950.
New Orleans Times-Democrat, January 20, 1882.
South Bend Tribune, September 29, 1914.
Valparaiso Vidette-Messenger, November 8, 1934.

CASES CITED

In re Green, 108 N.E.2d 647 (Ind. App. 1952).
Merkle v. Review Board of Indiana Employment Security Division, 90 N.E.2d 524 (Ind. App. 1950).

INDIANA SUPREME COURT

FRANK HAMILTON

January 1, 1945–January 1, 1949

DORIA LYNCH

Frank Hamilton's election to the Appellate Court of Indiana in November 1944 was the pinnacle of a successful career in law and public service. From his time in private practice to his years on the court, Hamilton was highly regarded in life and lauded upon his death.

Born in Decatur County, Indiana, on April 2, 1883, Hamilton attended Butler University for one year before transferring to Indiana University. He remained in Bloomington for law school and graduated in 1905. That same year he was admitted to the Decatur County and Indiana Supreme Court bars.

Hamilton's career began in private practice, but in 1907 he became deputy prosecuting attorney for Decatur County, holding this position for two years before becoming county attorney for several terms. From 1919 until 1929, he served as Greensburg's city attorney. In 1930 Hamilton moved to Terre Haute, where he entered private practice with the firm of Hamill, Hickey and Hamilton, followed by a time as a solo practitioner.

While in Terre Haute, Hamilton remained active in public service and politics. He was appointed to the Republican Board of Election Commissioners for Vigo County and served as counsel for the school board of Terre Haute. In 1943 Attorney General James A. Emmert named Hamilton first assistant attorney general, putting him in an ideal position to run for election to the appeals court. After Judge Edgar M. Blessing decided not to run for re-election, Hamilton announced that he would seek the Republican nomination for the seat. The party named him as its candidate a few days later.

In the months between his nomination and election Hamilton crisscrossed the state campaigning for himself and fellow Republican candidates. One topic of debate was extending the polling hours in Indiana. In his position as first deputy attorney general, and apparently with concern about the effect such a move might have on his own chances of election, Hamilton questioned whether taverns would be allowed to open at 6:00 p.m. on election day, as they had in the past, if voting hours were extended. He noted "the evils which would result from having the taverns and the polls open at the same time."

Hamilton also revealed his Republican values during his campaign, stating, "The New Deal philosophy of regimentation and retardment of small business is not the American plan by which the nation became great. That same philosophy of penalizing the little fellow will not provide jobs in the post-war era. A return to stabilized economy can only be accomplished by a thorough house-cleaning in Washington and the election of Governors [Thomas] Dewey and [John] Bricker." This is an important reminder of the context in which Hamilton sought office; as World War II still raged in Europe and the Pacific, Hamilton, like other politicians, was already looking ahead to the political makeup of postwar America.

Hamilton won the 1944 election by 75,920 votes. While on the court, he wrote the opinion in a zoning case that allowed construction of a church to proceed because the project "will substantially serve the public convenience and welfare of the citizens of Indianapolis and that the erection of such a building will not substantially or permanently injure the appropriate use of the neighboring property." He also wrote the controlling opinion in a verbal contract case involving a life insurance policy for which neither a written receipt nor policy was ever issued. He served as chief judge of the court for the May 1946 term.

Hamilton ran for a second term in 1948 but lost to his Democratic opponent by nearly 60,000 votes. After leaving office, Hamilton returned to Greensburg and resumed private practice, but he remained interested in the activities and rulings by the appeals court. In fact, just weeks before his death on February 10, 1952, Hamilton submitted an amicus brief to the Indiana Supreme Court supporting the state superintendent of public education, Wilbur Young, in a dispute over the distribution of school tuition money. The Supreme Court, in overruling the appeals court, said that had distribution of funds proceeded on the basis of what the court ordered, some schools would get excessive payments while others would receive insufficient payments.

Upon his death, colleagues remembered him as "a capable lawyer of the old school, intensely devoted to the Constitution and the government it established. As a judge he was solely actuated by what was right and just."

Selected Bibliography

Greensburg Daily News, May 28, 1946.
Indianapolis News, May 29, 1944, November 2, 1944.
Indianapolis Star, November 3, 18, 1944, November 23, 1946, January 16, 1946, January 20, February 11, 1952.
Muncie Star-Press, November 5, 1948.

CASE CITED
Keeling v. Board of Zoning Appeals, 69 N.E.2d 613 (Ind. App. 1946).

INDIANA SUPREME COURT

DONALD E. BOWEN
October 23, 1945–December 31, 1958

DONALD B. KITE SR.

During his lengthy tenure as an appellate judge, Donald E. Bowen remained a staunch Republican who gave numerous speeches highly critical of the Democratic Party. In a speech in 1946, Bowen, one of his party's nominees for the Appellate Court of Indiana, criticized the Franklin D. Roosevelt administration's foreign policy and attacked the "false ideologies" of the New Deal and its "confused policies." Bowen observed in a subsequent speech that southern Senators who had broken with Harry Truman had "no more in common with the President and the present leaders of the Democratic Party when they meet than do two women who meet at a bridge party wearing identical hats." However, in 1958 Bowen, running for a fourth term on the court, noted he had repeatedly advocated to bar associations and others that the selection of judges "be less partisan."

Born on March 23, 1907, in Lebanon, Indiana, Bowen graduated from Lebanon High School and was a member of the High School Orators, who competed in the National Oratorical Contest. Bowen was president of his class at Indiana University, chairman of the Student Republican Club, and an "outstanding college debater." He was class valedictorian at IU law school and then taught banking law as a lecturer and served as acting director of IU's Institute of Criminal Administration. Bowen, who practiced law in Bloomington for more than sixteen years, also served as Monroe County attorney, Bloomington city attorney, and as attorney for the IU Board of Trustees, the Indiana Association of Township Trustees, and other organizations. Bowen was also a member of the Indiana State Police School faculty and he wrote two books.

After losing his race for judge of the Monroe-Owen Circuit Court, Bowen served as Monroe County Republican Chairman from 1934 to 1945 and was also Seventh District Republican chairman. He was appointed by Governor Ralph F. Gates on October 23, 1945, to finish the unexpired term of Appellate Court Judge Paul F. Dowell, who had died one week earlier. Bowen was elected to the court in 1946, following a campaign where he was described, or described himself, as a "friend of labor," and he was reelected in 1950 and 1954. Due in part to a Democratic landslide in 1958, Bowen was defeated for a fourth term on the court. He then returned to private practice.

During his service on the court, Bowen wrote a number of opinions that underscored his conservative philosophy but which also reveal that Bowen did not hesitate to carefully articulate his concerns regarding precedent, which he believed had led (or could lead) to unfair or illogical results. In 1955 Bowen wrote the decision in *Hunter v. Livingston*, where the court, sitting en banc, held that it was bound by the decisions of the Indiana Supreme Court, which at that time only gave the plaintiff's wife "the right to sue alone in cases involving her property[,]" which meant that she could not sue her husband for negligence.

While ruling against the wife, Bowen observed that "[t]o make such a distinction renders the person of the wife in a marriage completely subjugated to the will of her husband, as far as civil liability is concerned, for willful and wanton injuries inflicted upon her person either before or during marriage, and [suggests] that such injuries are of no concern or value when placed in the scales of justice alongside property rights."

Seventeen years later, when the Indiana Supreme Court rejected the doctrine of interspousal immunity in *Brooks v. Robinson,* it referenced Bowen "severely question[ing]" the doctrine in *Hunter v. Livingston.*

Bowen was particularly proud of his service as chairman of the executive committee of Indiana's bipartisan Lincoln Sesquicentennial Commission and his 1959 trip to Japan with members of Indiana's Lincoln Foundation, sponsored by the U.S. State Department "to tell youth groups about Abraham Lincoln." To this day the eldest of Bowen's nieces recall their uncle, who practiced law with their father (Justice Richard M. Givan) and who they remember as always in "high gear," as a lawyer who brought business into the firm, and as a "food enthusiast," teaching them a few Japanese words and bringing them beautiful silk dolls from his trip to Japan.

Bowen married his college classmate, Jennie Carpenter of Sullivan, Indiana, a schoolteacher who taught in Washington Township Schools in Indianapolis and in the Indianapolis Public Schools. Bowen died on January 28, 1972, at his home in Indianapolis. He is buried in Bloomington's Rose Hill Cemetery, as are his wife and their only child, William E. Bowen.

Selected Bibliography

Hammond Times, August 23, 1950.
Indianapolis News, October 25, 1945.
Indianapolis Star, October 26, 1945, September 19, 1957.
Kokomo Tribune, January 29, 1951.

FRANCIS L. WILTROUT

January 1, 1949–December 31, 1952

SHELLY K. McBRIDE

Francis LeRoy Wiltrout served just one term on the Appellate Court of Indiana, but his influence and legal approach helped shape the court long afterward. Known for being methodical, Wiltrout's legacy is systematic organization where disorder once existed.

He was born May 8, 1907, in Corunna, Indiana. After his mother Daisy's death, his father Francis Marion was left to raise a daughter Myrtle and eight-year-old LeRoy. By 1927 the elder Wiltrout had another son, Forrest, and three more marriages. He moved the family to Auburn, where Wiltrout graduated from high school, then worked as a court reporter and clerk. In 1928 when his family moved to Elkhart Wiltrout moved to Bloomington to study law at Indiana University, he also enrolled in the Reserve Officers' Traning Corps and was commissioned to serve in the U.S. Army Reserves.

While at IU he met fellow law student Margaret Williams. He graduated in 1933 and Margaret graduated in 1934. Wiltrout moved to Elkhart to practice law, married Margaret in 1937, and they had three children—Ann, Roy, and Margaret "Peggy."

Against the backdrop of Prohibition, the Great Depression, and evolving gender norms, Wiltrout spent the 1930s practicing in Elkhart's city court system. In 1934 he was appointed city court clerk, a new office created to address corrupt and incompetent police handling of money and evidence. In 1938 Wiltrout became deputy to newly elected Prosecutor Stanley Raymer. Local newspapers covered gambling and liquor raids, while the Great Depression was cited as justification for mercy in court.

A statewide tectonic shift occurred in 1935 when the Indiana Supreme Court held in *Walter v. State* that it was reversible error if women were excluded from jury pools. Indiana courts were forced to accommodate women in typically all-male jury rooms.

In 1941, with a wife and two-year-old child, Wiltrout was called to active duty as the United States was on the verge of entering World War II. He was stationed in Ohio at Patterson Field and Fairfield Air Depot, later named Wright-Patterson Air Force Base. He served in personnel, training, and the Judge Advocate General's Department of Fairfield Air Service Command. He received the Army Commendation Medal and rose to the rank of lieutenant colonel, receiving his discharge in 1946. Now with two children and a third on the way, the Wiltrouts moved back to Elkhart where he resumed his practice.

In 1948 Appellate Court of Indiana Judge Dan C. Flanagan, a Republican, decided not to run for re-election. Wiltrout was nominated by the Democratic Party. November election results surprised the nation when Democrat President Harry Truman prevailed over the favored Republican Thomas Dewey. Hoosier Democrats won every state race ensuring Wiltrout's victory over Muncie Judge Paul Lennington.

Wiltrout wrote twenty-two opinions his first year, on pace with veteran jurists of the appellate and supreme courts. Two other first-year colleagues wrote a combined twenty-one opinions that same year. Fellow judges elected Wiltrout twice as presiding judge for the district and once as chief judge presiding over the whole court. Unfortunately, political winds shifted in 1952 when Republican presidential candidate Dwight D. Eisenhower easily defeated Democrat Adlai Stevenson. Indiana voters handed back every state race to Republicans, including Wiltrout's loss to Dewey E. Kelley of Whiting, Indiana.

Wiltrout, with two former appellate court judges, Dan Flanagan and Frank Hamilton, coauthored the two-volume *Indiana Trial and Appellate Practice*, published in 1952 by West Publishing Company. Their work was designed to be a convenient reference for appellate rules, statutes, and case law too vast and prohibitive for lawyers who only occasionally handled appeals. Wiltrout later authored *Civil Procedure* in four volumes for West in 1967. He also served as editor and adviser for West's 1957 thirty-two-volume *Indiana Law Encyclopedia*.

These three works were cited by the Indiana Supreme and Appellate Courts in hundreds of cases over many years after Wiltrout's departure. In 1953, partnered with his former boss Raymer, Wiltrout resumed his Elkhart legal practice. From 1953 to 1972 he appeared in over thirty appeals, twelve to the Indiana Supreme Court.

His civic service included the Red Cross, Reserve Officers' Association, and Elkhart's Aviation Commission, which acquired the airport during his tenure. He became interested in amateur radio while learning Morse code with his son Roy for a Boy Scout project. He coauthored a book, *The Wiltrout Genealogy,* and gifted a copy to the public library in Auburn.

Wiltrout died on August 21, 1978, in Elkhart. He was survived by his wife and three children. A few months prior he told his family that he had become forgetful and decided he should retire. His daughter Peggy described him as a wonderful father who loved helping people.

Selected Bibliography

Garrett Clipper. Various issues, 1917 to 1948.
Indianapolis Star. Various issues, 1935 to 1952.
South Bend Tribune. Various issues, 1932 to 1978.
Wiltrout, F. Leroy, and Dan C. Flanagan. *Civil Procedure.* Saint Paul, MN: West Publishing Company, 1967.
———. Dan Flanagan, and Frank Hamilton. *Indiana Trial and Appellate Practice.* 2 vols. Saint Paul, MN: West Publishing Company, 1952.

CASE CITED
Walter v. State, 195 N.E. 2d 268 (Ind. 1935).

INDIANA SUPREME COURT

WARREN W. MARTIN

January 1, 1949–December 31, 1952; January 1, 1965–June 25, 1965

JAMES E. ST. CLAIR

The term public servant aptly describes the forty-one-year career of Warren W. Martin, who, in addition to military service in World War I, held numerous positions in city, county, and state governments and was twice elected to the Appellate Court of Indiana.

Martin, who was born on a farm in Warrick County in 1892, received his law degree from the Jefferson School of Law, which was later absorbed into the University of Louisville law school. He practiced law in Kentucky for a few years before returning to Indiana and winning elections as Warrick County Prosecutor and city attorney for Boonville during the ten-year period from 1924 to 1934.

Following his six-year tenure as a deputy attorney general for the state, Martin was appointed chairman of the Indiana Industrial Board in 1941 by Governor Henry F. Schricker, a position Martin held for the duration of World War II. The board, which was created in 1915, ruled on claims by injured employees for workers' compensation awards.

Martin was first elected to the appeals court in 1948 but lost his bid for re-election in 1952 and lost in elections to the court in 1954 and 1960. He was also unsuccessful in seeking a seat on the Indiana Supreme Court in 1956. Martin returned to the Industrial Board in 1957, serving until 1961 when he was appointed public counselor to the state Public Service Commission by Governor Matthew Welsh. In that position, Martin represented the public in transportation and public utility rate cases and other issues before the commission.

As public counselor, Martin's advocacy ranged widely, from opposing in one case a plan by Hoosier Co-Operative Energy Inc., a combination of sixteen Rural Electric Membership Corporations, to build a $60 million generating plant to supporting the installation of warning signals at a railroad crossing in eastern Hendricks County.

Interestingly, one of Martin's opinions during his first term on the appeals court involved his former agency, the state's industrial board. In *School City of Hammond v. Moriarity*, the school district sought review of a decision by a single board member to award worker's compensation to a widow after the death of her husband. The school district had sought a rehearing by the entire board, but Martin, in denying the appeal, noted the full board had already met to review the original finding.

In *Urban v. Reents*, a case on appeal from the White County Circuit Court, the driver of a car that struck a sixty-six-year-old man from behind at night claimed that the damages awarded were excessive and the trial court erred in denying a new trial. Both parties conceded that the headlights on the driver's car were out at the time. Martin denied the appeal, ruling that the award of $7,500 was appropriate, given the injured party's medical expenses and his ability to resume his work as a groundskeeper for a local golf course had been permanently impaired.

Martin was returned to the court of appeals in the election of 1964, but he served only six months, having suffered a fatal heart at his home on June 25, 1965. In one decision, *New York Central v. Knoll,* another personal injury case, Martin faulted the trial court in overruling the railroad's motion for a new trial and for giving erroneous instructions to the jury. He wrote that it is "fundamental that instructions to the jury must follow the evidence," adding, "plaintiffs cannot sue upon one set of facts and recover upon another."

Martin's first wife died in 1936 and he later remarried. His family of six sons and seven daughters included Warren W. Martin Jr., who served in the Indiana State Senate and as judge of the Clark County Superior Court. The senior Martin died in 1973.

Selected Bibliography

Indianapolis Star, October 12, 1961, February 9, 1962, June 26, 1965.

CASES CITED

School City of Hammond v. Moriarity, 93 N.E. 2d 367 (Ind. App. 1950).
Urban v. Reents, 106 N.E. 2d 399 (Ind. App. 1952).
New York C.R. Co. v. Knoll, 140 Ind. App. 264 (1965).

INDIANA SUPREME COURT

HAROLD E. ACHOR*

January 1, 1951–December 12, 1954

JOHN R. LEAL

Harold Edward Achor had a legal career that spanned thirty-five years, including ten years in private practice and nearly twenty-five years as a judge on three different courts. Ill health prevented him from serving longer.

Born in Coffeeville, Kansas, on November 16, 1907, Achor's parents moved to Kosciusko County, Indiana, while he was still an infant. He attended public schools in Atwood and graduated from Indiana Central College, now the University of Indianapolis, in 1928. Three years later he earned a law degree from Indiana University. In 1932 Achor entered private practice in Anderson, while also teaching speech and political science at Anderson College from 1932 to 1937.

In 1942 he was elected Madison Superior Court judge, a position he held for two terms. He was elected to the Appellate Court of Indiana in

1950 and served a four-year term. During that time, Achor wrote sixty-three majority opinions and seven dissents. His opinion writing on the court of appeals foreshadowed his approach to opinion writing on the Indiana Supreme Court. On both courts he stressed the importance of following court rules and examining evidence. A review of his opinions in cases before the appeals court pertaining to rulings by the Indiana Industrial Board in workmen's compensation cases illustrate how these two principles affected his decisions.

In *Stoner v. Howard Strober* a common-law wife claimed death benefits for her husband, which the Industrial Board denied, and she appealed. The court remanded the case back to the Industrial Board because, Achor wrote, "the finding of facts [is] seriously deficient" to sustain the board's decision." In *Slaubaugh v. Vore* the court upheld an award for workmen's compensation benefit for a widow who claimed her husband died of heart failure on the job as the result of strenuous work he was required to perform, which aggravated a previous heart condition. The employer appealed that decision. The board determined that there was enough evidence to link the worker's death to his work. In his majority opinion, Achor, citing "the rules of common law evidence," writing that the "findings of fact by the Industrial Board are supported by the evidence." He added that the Industrial Board was not a court, but an administrative body and therefore was not held to the same strict rules of evidence.

In 1954 Achor was elected to the Indiana Supreme Court and commuted from his home in Anderson. During the week, he usually stayed overnight in his private chambers to read briefs scheduled for oral argument. A workday of ten to twelve hours was not unusual for him or his law clerks. On cases assigned to him, he asked his law clerks to submit memoranda on the application of "rules of the court" and whether such were followed for the court to have proper jurisdiction. Achor required that all cases cited in the briefs be researched, to determine whether they had a bearing on the legal issues presented before the Court.

To Achor the rules and evidence went hand in hand. This is illustrated by his majority opinion in one case, which held that the trial court had erred in failing to determine that a defendant was no longer a minor whose parents were obligated to pay for a transcript of the court record for an appeal. The Court ruled that as an indigent adult he was entitled to have a transcript provided for him at public expense and ordered that one be provided. This resulted in the Court granting a rehearing of the case, *State ex rel. Butler v. Allen Superior Court*.

Achor was very particular with his written opinions. Court decisions at that time were typically unanimous, but a case that stirred much controversy and produced three separate concurring opinions and a partial dissent illustrates that this was not always true. The case, *State ex rel. Indiana State Bar Association v. Indiana State Real Estate Association*, was initiated by lawyers seeking an injunction against realtors to prevent them from "practicing law" in real estate transactions. The Court granted partial injunctive relief to the lawyers in ruling that only lawyers could execute certain legal documents such as deeds and mortgages. However, the Court also held that it was permissible for real-estate brokers and agents to complete certain forms generally used in standard real-estate transactions, even if the forms had been created by lawyers.

In his final year on the Court, Achor was frequently absent due to ill health. He worked at home a good deal of the time. He chose not to run for re-election and retired from the Court on December 12, 1966. He died on February 5, 1967, at the age of fifty-nine.

Selected Bibliography

Leal, John. Personal reminiscences based on his time as law clerk for Judge Achor during the time Achor was Chief Justice of the Indiana Supreme Court from 1961 to 1962.

Withered, Jerome L. *Hoosier Justice: A History of the Supreme Court of Indiana*. Indianapolis: Indiana Supreme Court, 1998.

CASES CITED

Slaubaugh v. Vore, 123 Ind. App. 497 (1953).

State ex rel. Butler v. Allen Superior Court, 241 Ind. 627 (1961).

State ex rel. Indiana State Bar Association v. Indiana State Real Estate Association, Inc. et al., 244 Ind. 214 (1963).

Stoner v. Howard Sober Inc., 124 Ind. App. 581 (1954).

*This profile is revised from one that appeared in *Justices of the Indiana Supreme Court* (2010).

INDIANA SUPREME COURT

JOHN A. KENDALL

January 1, 1953–December 31, 1956

JAMES R. WILLIAMS

In the twenty years prior to John Kendall's election to an appellate judgeship, he developed a reputation as a skilled advocate. Evidently his judicial colleagues felt this skill for persuasion could be effective in obtaining some basic comforts for them in their space at the Indiana Statehouse. In October 1953 Kendall was tasked by his colleagues to request that the State Budget Committee appropriate $5,000 to install showers for the court of appeals on the fourth floor of the statehouse. The Indiana Supreme Court already had showers on the third floor and the judges on Indiana's intermediate appeals court were reportedly envious; apparently, members of the Supreme Court "inherited their good fortune from horse and buggy days when most judges lived in their Statehouse offices during court terms." Despite Kendall's advocacy, the committee was noncommittal on additional showers.

Kendall was born in 1908 on a farm near Plainfield, Indiana, in Hendricks County. His father, John E. Kendall, was a farmer, prominent Mason, and member of the Friends Meeting as was his mother, Esther Jessup Kendall. Following his graduation from Plainfield schools, Kendall attended Indiana University, earning his bachelor of law degree in 1931. While at IU, he joined Phi Delta Theta and was active in Republican politics. He later received a doctor of jurisprudence from the university in 1951.

Following the completion of his law degree, Kendall moved to Danville, Indiana, where he set up his practice in 1932. Kendall, a lifelong Republican, was elected Hendricks County Prosecutor in November 1932 at the age of twenty-four. The following October he married Virginia Louise Mattern whom he had met at IU. The couple had a son, J. Richard, and a daughter, Ann.

Kendall, who assumed his duties as prosecutor in January 1933, served three two-year terms in addition to maintaining his private practice in Danville. Like many Hoosier lawyers of this era, Kendall mixed politics and his practice, serving both his clients and the community. Following his tenure as county prosecutor, he was elected as a state representative in 1940. After two terms in the Indiana General Assembly's lower chamber, he was elected to the Indiana Senate for the district covering Owen, Morgan and Hendricks Counties. During his senate tenure, Kendall chaired the powerful State Budget Committee for five years.

After two terms in the senate, he was elected to the Appellate Court of Indiana in November 1952, serving one term and was chief judge during the May 1953 and May 1956 terms. Kendall decided not to seek re-election and returned to the law firm of Stevenson and Kendall in Danville.

Kendall's service to Indiana did not end with his departure from the court. Subsequently, he served as chair of the Indiana Toll Road Commission and the Indiana State Police Board. However, his most consequential service may have been his term as president of the Indiana State Bar Association, which began in October 1970. It was in this position that Kendall took an active role in supporting the constitutional change providing for merit selection of candidates to the Indiana Supreme Court and the Court of Appeals.

The change would be a "real improvement," Kendall said, adding that running on a partisan ticket for his judicial seat was, at times, "both horrifying and humiliating." In part due to Kendall's leadership with the state bar, the constitutional amendment was approved by Indiana voters in November 1970.

Kendall retired in 1987 after practicing law for fifty-six years. He was named a Sagamore of the Wabash, an award that governors bestow to distinguished Hoosiers, and was an active member of the Danville Friends Meeting. He died on May 1, 1993, at the age of eighty-five survived by his wife of fifty-four years, Virginia, and their two children.

Selected Bibliography

Greenfield Daily Reporter, January 10, 1967.
Indianapolis News, September 9, 1930, May 3, 1993, October 25, 1993.
Indianapolis Star, April 1, 1939, March 4, 1944, March 8, 1956, December 4, 1968, October 25, 1970, July 31, 1975, May 3, 1993.
Richmond Palladium-Item, March 8, 1956.

LA PORTE COUNTY HISTORICAL SOCIETY MUSEUM

DEWEY E. KELLEY

January 1, 1953–December 31, 1964

ELIZABETH R. OSBORN

Like families all over the country, Dewey Kelley and his family were directly affected when America entered World War I in April 1917. At age seventeen, Kelley and five other local males enlisted at the Cambridge City, Indiana, recruiting station. He was eventually sent to the Naval Training School in Chicago, although his deployment to Europe was delayed when he was hospitalized with scarlet fever in 1918. He later served at an American Naval Air Station in Paullas, France, and stateside in New Jersey.

Both of Kelley's older brothers were already serving in the army. His oldest brother, assigned to the Fifty-Ninth Infantry Regiment, was killed in combat in July 1918. The Kelleys were one of nineteen Wayne County families with three or more sons in the military, a startling high number for a county with fewer than 50,000 residents.

Kelley, born June 10, 1898, in Memphis, near Jeffersonville, Indiana, was two years old when his father died. The family, after moves to New

Albany and Scottsburg, eventually settled in Cambridge City. During his years at Cambridge City High School, Kelley participated in school plays and musical events, represented his church at a statewide Sunday School conference, and participated in a local pageant celebrating Indiana's sesquicentennial in 1916.

Following his discharge from the navy, Kelley was back home by the fall of 1919. He held a series of odd jobs, including working on construction of a concrete highway from Richmond to Indianapolis and in the yards of the Pennsylvania Railroad. He eventually attended Valparaiso University Law School and graduated in 1922, first practicing law in Frankfort, where he met and married Roxie Yount in 1924. They moved to Kokomo but then on to Whiting after he lost his race for Howard County Prosecutor. In Whiting he worked for the firm of Fetterhoff and Ahlgren and served as the attorney for the Whiting School Board and as president of the Whiting Bar Association.

With America edging closer to and then entering World War II, Kelley's volunteer activities increased. He served on the advisory board of the U.S. Selective Service and during the war was appointed to the War Price Control and Rationing Program and was chairman of the Whiting Office of Price Administration. In 1942 he was elected judge of the Whiting City Court, a position he held until January 1, 1948. Running as a Republican, Kelley was elected to the Appellate Court of Indiana in 1952, wining re-election to the court in 1956 and 1960 before his defeat in 1964. He sought the party's nomination for the Indiana Supreme Court in 1966 but was defeated by Donald R. Mote.

During his tenure on the appeals court, one of Kelley's most consequential, and controversial, decisions was his 1959 opinion in *Meade Electric Co., etc. v. Hagberg, etc.*, in which he ruled that nonunion workers be required to pay the same fees as union members. He wrote that "Indiana's Right to Work Law is plain and unambiguous, and there is no prohibition against the requirement of the payment of fees or charges to a labor organization," adding that the law merely prohibits union membership as a condition of employment.

This contentious issue continued before Indiana courts well after Kelley's ruling. The Indiana Supreme Court in 2014, hearing an appeal of a decision by a Lake County judge, ruled 5–0 that the state's right-to-work law was constitutional because the state did not require unions to provide uncompensated services to nonmembers.

In another labor case, *Youngstown Sheet & Tube Co. v. Review Board of Indiana Employment Security Division, et al.*, Kelley supported the right of workers to picket and demonstrate against their layoffs at the same time they were receiving unemployment benefits. In his ruling upholding the decision of the state's employment agency to grant the workers compensation, Kelley wrote that "the general rule in Indiana that the decision of the Board on questions of fact . . . is conclusive and binding."

Kelley, both a Sagamore of the Wabash recipient and Kentucky Colonel, held memberships in national, state, and local bar associations, as well as a number of fraternal organizations, including the American Legion, Whiting Lodge of Masons, and the Scottish Rite. He died on March 21, 1987, at age eighty-eight.

SELECTED BIBLIOGRAPHY

Indianapolis Star, June 20, 1959, October 10, 1961, June 5, 1963, June 10, 1964, June 22, 1966.

CASES CITED

Meade Electric Co., etc. v Hagberg, etc., Ind. App. 631 (1959).
Youngstown Sheet & Tube Co. v Review Board of Indiana Employment Security Division, et al., 135 N.E. App. 461 (1963).

INDIANA SUPREME COURT

JOHN W. PFAFF

January 1, 1955–December 31, 1958; January 1, 1961–December 31, 1964; January 1, 1967–December 31, 1970

JEFFERY A. DUVALL

In addition to his distinguished career as jurist, Judge John W. Pfaff was active in a variety of civic groups and organizations including the Kiwanis Club, the Community Chest, the Red Cross, and the Tri-Valley Council of the Boy Scouts of America. He was also a past master of the Portage Lodge 675 Free and Accepted Masons, a 32nd Degree Mason, belonged to the United Fund, and was a longtime member of Ridgedale Presbyterian Church in South Bend, Indiana. Other organizations to which he belonged included the American Bar Association, the American Judicature Society, as well as the Indiana, Indianapolis, and Saint Joseph County bar associations. He also served as a judge on the Moot Court of Notre Dame's College of Law and was a member of the Beta Theta Pi fraternity.

Pfaff was born on February 26, 1901, in Marietta, Ohio, to Henry R. Pfaff, the son of German immigrants, and Bonnie Blagg. After spending his childhood in Ohio, Pfaff attended college in Indiana, graduating from

Hanover College in 1926. That same year he married Odessa Walker with whom he had two sons, John W. Pfaff Jr., who spent his career as a Federal Bureau of Investigation agent, and Robert A. Pfaff, who was an attorney. In 1929 Pfaff graduated from Indiana University School of Law in Bloomington. Later that same year he passed the Indiana bar and settled in South Bend, Indiana, where he first served as a staff member for Oliver M. Loomis, U.S. District Attorney, and later as an assistant to Superior Court Judge I. W. Hammond.

A lifelong Republican, Pfaff took a leave of absence from his firm Pfaff, Ettl and Mills in 1954 upon being elected to the first of his three terms of office on the Appellate Court of Indiana. Over the course of his years on the bench several of his opinions were published in *American Law Reports* a resource based on cases that represent emerging, unsettled, or changing areas of the law and legal issues. His ruling in *Merritt v. Economy Department Store* (1955), a case involving the statute of limitations, was the first of his opinions to be published in *ALR*. Other cases generated a somewhat unusual degree of public interest. For example, during his first term Pfaff's opinion in *Biedron v. Biedron* (1958), in which a resident of Poland appealed the superior court's decision granting her ex-husband's request to cease having to make court-ordered child support payments, was hailed by Indiana newspapers as a Cold War victory. In reality Pfaff's opinion reversed the lower court's decision, and sustained the appellant's motion for a new trial. The most controversial act of his first term, by far, was publicly criticizing, through a comment he made in a footnote to an otherwise routine Allen County damage suite, the state supreme court for its sudden insistence upon maintaining two divisions in the appellate court over fifty years after it first began sitting as a single body.

Pfaff was defeated in his bid for re-election in 1958 but was returned to the bench in 1960. Following another two-year break from the court, in 1966 he was once again reelected to what became his final term on the appellate court. Perhaps the most significant case of his third term was the "MTA" case, also known as the Inheritance Tax case, for which he authored one of the key opinions that ordered the Indiana State Auditor to pay the Mass Transportation Authority, and its attorney's, the sum of $12.7 million.

After failing in his bid for a fourth term on the court in 1970, Pfaff returned to South Bend. He died at his home in Edwardsburg, Michigan, on February 27, 1977.

Selected Bibliography

Greencastle Daily News, July 3, 1958.
Indianapolis Star, May 20, 1958, June 7, 1960, October 26, 1967, April 26, 1970, March 2, 1977.
"Obituaries." *Res Gestae* 21, no. 4 (1977): 180.

CASES CITED

Biedron v. Biedron, 148 N.E. 2d, 209 (1958) (Ind. App 105).
Merritt v. Economy Department Store, Inc., 128 N.E. 2d, 269 (1955) (Ind. App. 560).
State ex rel. Mass Transport Authority v. Indiana Revenue Board, 253 N.E.2d 725 (1969) 144 (Ind. App. 63).

INDIANA SUPREME COURT

JAMES C. COOPER

1957–1964, 1967–1970

RYAN T. SCHWIER

By the time Judge James Cooper ascended the Appellate Court of Indiana in 1957, the popular election of the Indiana judiciary—codified as fundamental law under the Indiana Constitution of 1851—had come under increasing scrutiny. Thirteen years later, Indiana amended its constitution to replace this partisan process with a merit-based system for selecting appellate judges and a democratic scheme with judicial retention. The story of Cooper is a notable chapter in the narrative of this constitutional transformation.

An Indianapolis native and a graduate of Arsenal Technical High School, Cooper attended the Benjamin Harrison Law School before his admission to the bar in 1927. After a stint in private practice, he ran successfully for Rush County Prosecutor in 1940. Seven years later, the Indiana Supreme Court appointed him to the office of State Public Defender, where he worked for nearly a decade assisting indigent prisoners in postconviction proceedings.

The author of more than two hundred judicial opinions during his tenure with the appellate court, Cooper penned the 1968 landmark decision in *State ex rel. Mass Transportation Authority of Greater Indianapolis v. Indiana Revenue Board*, popularly known as the Pocket Veto Case. On the last day of the 1967 legislative session, the Indiana General Assembly enacted legislation creating the Mass Transit Authority, an agency responsible for road maintenance and construction in Marion County. That same day, lawmakers adopted House Bill 1818 to finance the MTA through a redistribution of state inheritance taxes. Calling it a "foolhardy and dangerous" drain on the state budget, Governor Roger D. Branigin, a Democrat, exercised the "pocket veto," refusing to sign HB 1818 into law.

The constitution at the time barred the general assembly, "within two days" of its final adjournment, from presenting a bill to the governor. While Indiana courts recognized the executive authority to sign late bills into law, the constitution said nothing of the governor's failure to act on those bills. The pocket veto had simply become customary practice, a tool long used by the executive to dispose of unwanted legislation. In a 1931 decision, *State ex rel. Owen v. Fortieth Judicial Circuit*, the Indiana Supreme Court ostensibly approved the practice, finding no "obligation imposed upon [the governor] to act" on a bill presented late in the session. Still, the MTA sued, arguing that the state constitution prohibited the pocket veto. A favorable court ruling would revive HB 1818, entitling the MTA to around $5 million (close to $39 million today).

In a draft majority opinion, the court initially concluded that, under the *Owen* precedent, the governor's pocket veto rendered HB 1818 void. But after months of delay, Cooper circulated a dissent. With a reputation as one of the more partisan members on the court, Cooper may have used the case to help fellow local Republicans secure transportation funding for the new UNIGOV program, which merged the Indianapolis and Marion County governments. The three other Republican judges quickly fell in line, leaving a decision equally split along party lines. Judge Russell Smith soon offered the crucial Democratic vote, a quid pro quo for a postretirement administrative job with the court.

On December 31, 1968, the court ruled in a 5–3 decision that HB 1818 "became the law of the State of Indiana without the Governor's signature." With no discussion of the *Owen* precedent, the majority opinion effectively invalidated the pocket veto. As expected, the Indiana Supreme Court—with its Republican majority taking control of the bench on January 1—denied transfer, leaving Cooper's opinion undisturbed.

With its politics and judicial logrolling, the Pocket Veto Case embodied the less-than-dignifying influence of popular elections on Indiana's appellate courts. But to simply label the decision as a partisan product of this system takes a cynical view of the court and Cooper himself. While the majority opinion may have ignored binding precedent, it offered a more nuanced analysis of the pocket veto than *Owen*. More important the state ultimately vindicated Cooper's opinion three years later, ratifying a constitutional amendment to *expressly* abolish the pocket veto, a practice that, according to the Indiana Supreme Court "arguably directly contravened" the framers' intent.

Cooper died in office on September 13, 1970. Less than two months later, Indiana voters ratified the constitutional amendment replacing the partisan election of appellate judges with a merit-based system of judicial selection. While the Pocket Veto Case certainly propelled this reform, Cooper's career as a dedicated public servant would likely have made him a sound candidate for judicial retention.

Selected Bibliography

"Court Decision No Surprise." *Indianapolis News*, February 6, 1969.
Evans, Stan. "The Editor's Corner: How a Bill Becomes a Law." *Indianapolis News*, January 10, 1969.
"High Court Upholds Overturn of Vetoes." *Indianapolis News*, February 6, 1969.
Najam, Edward W., Jr. "Merit Selection in Indiana: The Foundation for a Fair and Impartial Appellate Judiciary." *Indiana. Law Review* 46 (2013): 15.
Nixon, William A., "The Pocket Veto Case." (Rusti L. Keen, ed.) (unpublished manuscript on file with the Indiana Court of Appeals).

CASES CITED

D & M Healthcare v. Kernan, 800 N.E. 2d 898, 904 (Ind. 2003).
State ex rel. Mass Transp. Auth. of Greater Indianapolis v. Indiana Revenue Bd., 144 Ind. App. 63, 242 N.E.2d 642 (1968).
State ex rel. Mass Transp. Auth. of Greater Indianapolis v. Indiana Revenue Bd., 146 Ind. App. 334, 255 N.E.2d 833, 834 (1970).
State ex rel. Owen v. Fortieth Judicial Circuit, 202 Ind. 354, 174 N.E. 423, 424 (1931).

MARTIN FAMILY COLLECTION

WALTER MYERS JR.*

January 1, 1959–December 31, 1962

THOMAS E. WHEELER II

Walter Myers Jr. was a Renaissance man. He was offered a scholarship to the Herron School of Art while in eighth grade. He enjoyed drawing charcoal sketches and painting in oils and was described by his brother as "quite an accomplished cartoonist." In addition to being an artist, Myers also enjoyed music, both classical and modern, and was actively involved with the Indianapolis Symphony.

Born on June 9, 1914, Myers was a lifelong resident of Indianapolis and joined a family of prominent attorneys devoted to public service. His father, a former Speaker of the Indiana House of Representatives and assistant U.S. Postmaster General, practiced law in Indianapolis for more than sixty years. His younger brother, Joseph, was a judge on the Marion County Municipal Court for thirty-five years, and his maternal grandfather was a judge in Virginia. Myers married Jane Weldon Kinghan on November 26, 1952, and had a son, Dennis, and a stepson, John R. Kinghan.

Myers attended public schools in Indianapolis and was the pitcher for the Shortridge High School city championship softball team. He graduated from Shortridge in 1931, after just three and a half years. He followed his father to Yale University, where he received an undergraduate degree in 1935 and law degree in 1938. During his junior year at Yale, Myers missed one-half of the school year due to a ruptured appendix. Despite this, he was able to graduate on time with his classmates and in the top 10 percent of his class. The numerous surgeries that Myers had as a result of his ruptured appendix precluded him from serving in the military during World War II, but he was active in bond drives and various other home-front activities.

After law school Myers returned to Indianapolis and began practicing with his father at the firm of Myers and Smith. Like his father, he was actively involved in Democratic politics, serving as precinct committeeman, ward chairman, and, eventually Marion County Chairman. Longtime Congressman Andrew Jacobs Jr. credits Myers, when he was party chair, with getting him his first job as a deputy at the Marion County Jail. Myers also served as deputy prosecuting attorney under Indianapolis mayor Al Feeney.

Myers lost in his bids for the Superior Court of Marion County in 1952 and four years later for the Marion County Circuit Court. Undeterred, he ran for and was elected to the Appellate Court of Indiana in 1958, serving as presiding judge for the May 1959 term and chief judge for the November 1959 term. He left the appellate court after his election to the Indiana Supreme Court in 1962.

Myers defeated incumbent Justice Arch N. Bobbitt, who was ousted in large part over his decision in a case regarding constitutional limitations on cities' power to let bonds for construction projects. The political defeat of Bobbitt based on a single decision was one of many factors that led the 1965 session of the Indiana General Assembly to create a Judicial Study Commission that ultimately recommended doing away with the election of appellate judges. This resulted in the 1970 amendment to Article 7 of the Indiana Constitution mandating the merit selection of appellate judges.

Although very active in partisan politics, Myers was nonpartisan in the discharge of his judicial duties and "demonstrated keenness of intellect, a sound understanding of the law, and an ability of expression which has been of great assistance" to his fellow judges and the attorneys who practiced before him. He maintained friendships with people from diverse backgrounds and cultivated these friendships during his tenure on the bench. As a judge he was focused on promoting efficiency in the courts through modernizing the way they did business.

Myers also had a keen interest in service to his community, acting as a member of the Pentalpha Masonic Lodge, Scottish Rite, Murat Shrine, and the Tau Kappa Epsilon fraternity. He was also a member and president of the Board of Managers for the Young Men's Christian Association Central Branch and served on the Board of the Marion County Tuberculosis Association. He took great pride in his service on the board of the Suemma Coleman Home and was very active in advocating the adoption of orphaned children. Myers and his wife were also heavily involved in the parish life at Second Presbyterian Church, where he served as an elder.

Following a six-week illness, Myers died on June 2, 1967, in Indianapolis, just four years into his six-year term on the Indiana Supreme Court.

Selected Bibliography

Adams, Wendy L., and Elizabeth R. Osborn, eds. *In Memoriam: Glimpses from Indiana's Legal Past*. Indianapolis: Indiana Supreme Court, 2006.

J. N. Myers to Chief Justice Richard M. Givan. October 19, 1978. On file in the Indiana Supreme Court Library.

*This profile is revised from one that appeared in *Justices of the Indiana Supreme Court* (2010).

1912 *ARBUTUS*, INDIANA UNIVERSITY ARCHIVES

G. REMY BIERLY

January 1, 1959–December 31, 1962; January 1, 1965–December 31, 1968
Chief Judge: May 1960, May 1965

DINA M. KELLAMS

At the time of his death in 1969, Hoosier educator, attorney, state representative, and judge of the Appellate Court of Indiana G. Remy Bierly was the oldest practicing attorney in Adams County. At age eight-two, as he explored a barn for a client, he either tripped or was kicked by an animal and sustained a head injury. He fell into a coma and died six weeks later.

Born George Remigius Bierly in Harrison County on July 6, 1887, "Remy" as he became known, was one of ten children born to Frederick and Louisa Bierly. He began what became a long career as a teacher and principal before completing his first bachelor's degree at Marion Normal College in 1911. He then attended Indiana State Normal School (today Indiana State University), completing course requirements in 1913. By year's end, he corresponded with officials at Indiana University about the number of credits IU would grant him for past course work and professional experience, and if he could start classes after the term had begun.

University officials offered Bierly two years credit toward his intended bachelor's in political science and suggested he work with individual faculty to arrange for his late entrance. With the two years credit, Bierly started at Indiana University in April 1913 and was able to graduate in June 1915. He then attended the University of Chicago, where he pursued but did not complete postgraduate studies in political science.

In 1910, while still teaching and attending college, Bierly sought election to the Indiana House of Representatives, but lost the nomination by nine votes. Two years later, he was elected to the House, representing Harrison County, his term coinciding in part with his studies at IU. His proposal that the state purchase the former statehouse in Corydon and convert it to a historical site failed.

Bierly served a second term in the house as the joint representative for Harrison and Crawford Counties in the 1922–24 term and represented Adams and Wells Counties in the 1950–52 session. It was during this term that he was part of a contentious scene at the statehouse in 1951. To avoid a vote on nine controversial Republican-backed "home rule" bills, thirty-six lawmakers from both parties staged a walkout to prevent a quorum. Police were called in to arrest or otherwise escort lawmakers to the statehouse, with Speaker W. O. Hughes calling for use of the "the whole damned force, if necessary." Bierly, who took part in the protest, returned to the statehouse once he heard of the police action that included the arrest of a representative. As others trickled back, a quorum was met and seven of the disputed bills, all focused on welfare and federal aid, passed.

Although he lacked a formal legal education, Bierly passed the bar in 1912 to practice before the Harrison Circuit Court, leading to a second lifelong career in law, which he practiced in tandem with his work as an educator until his retirement from teaching in 1936. Through the span of his long legal career, Bierly was admitted to the Adams County, Indianapolis, Indiana, and American bar associations, as well as admitted to practice before the U.S. Supreme Court.

In addition to his statehouse victories, Bierly was elected clerk of the Adams Circuit Court in 1936, elected prosecuting attorney of the Twenty-sixth Judicial Circuit (Adams and Jay Counties), as well as elections to the appeals court in 1958 and 1964.

Cases that came before the court during Bierly's two terms included issues such as employment and union grievances, divorce and death cases, and property disputes. One case that made headlines involved the American Legion Pulaski Post and its trust fund established in the 1940s for nearly 400 World War I veterans and heirs. Members of the post sued the fund's trustees, seeking to block payments from the fund to individuals, arguing that monies had been raised through general post activities. The lower court ruled in favor of the trustees, but Bierly, writing for the court in 1961, reversed the decision, citing Indiana's Not-For-Profit-Act, which said not-for-profits could not establish funds for distribution to its own members.

Bierly sought renomination to the court in 1968 at the Democratic state convention, but according to news reports, he was one of two incumbents who were asked to withdraw from the race. Bierly did so, reluctantly, and returned to private practice. He died the next year.

Selected Bibliography

Anderson Daily Bulletin, June 21, 1968.

Heller, Dick, ed. *The 1979 History of Adams County, Indiana*. Adams County Historical Society, 1980.

Terre Haute Tribune, October 6, 1951.

Yearbook of the State of Indiana, 1936. Indianapolis: State of Indiana.

CASES CITED

Bajdek v. Board of Trustees, 173 N.E.2d 61 (Ind. App. 1961).

INDIANA SUPREME COURT

JOHN S. GONAS

January 1, 1959–December 31, 1962

ELAINE B. BROWN

Passionate about improving the lives of his fellow citizens, Judge John S. Gonas authored *Delinquency: There Is an Answer* in 1968, encapsulating his work, views, and proposals on curbing juvenile delinquency, with a focus on prevention and rehabilitation. The book tells of his successful juvenile programs in South Bend, Indiana, and speaks to "his consuming interest" in youth. Gonas also had another passion in life—electoral politics. He served in both houses of the Indiana General Assembly, and sought other elective offices, such as U.S. senator, lieutenant governor, and governor.

Gonas was born May 14, 1907, in a log cabin in Cross Fork, Potter County, Pennsylvania. His father labored in the sawmills and coal mines, and hard work was part of his legacy. When he was young, Gonas worked his way through school as a coal miner, a factory worker, and a farmhand. In 1929 he earned a bachelor's degree in civil engineering from Tri-State

University in Angola, Indiana, and the following year obtained his law degree from the University of Chicago Law School. Subsequently he came to South Bend to practice law.

Gonas's political career began in 1936 when he was elected to the Indiana House of Representatives, a position he held until 1938. Four years later he was elected to the Indiana Senate and served until 1947. He claimed that during this time he "sponsored more labor legislation than anyone on the floor of the General Assembly." He served on the state budget committee during the tenure of both Governor M. Clifford Townsend and Governor Henry F. Schricker. During the 1945–47 session, which was the first postwar session, he introduced a bill providing for a "Veterans bonus" that was quickly dubbed the "Gonas Bonus." Although his bill did not pass, the legislature subsequently passed a bonus bill in 1949.

Gonas started his judicial career as judge of the juvenile court of South Bend. He was elected to that position in 1948 and remained on that court until 1958. Simultaneously he served as judge of the probate court. He was one of two U.S. judges selected to attend the International Congress of Juvenile Court Judges at Brussels, Belgium, in 1955, and was also a delegate to the United Nations Conference on Crime and Juvenile Delinquency in Switzerland. In 1956, while still on the lower court, Gonas made a run for governor along with eight other candidates seeking the Democratic nod, but he was unsuccessful. During his campaign he was known for wearing "sporty bow ties" and part of his campaign rhetoric was: "I just want people to judge me as I have judged others."

As his term on the juvenile court was ending in 1958, he sought the Democratic nomination for U.S. Senate, but withdrew on the eve of the Democratic State Convention after he failed to pay the required filing fee. However, running unopposed, he secured the party's nomination for the Second District of the Appellate Court of Indiana. He was successful in that bid and served one term from January 1, 1959 to December 31, 1962. He was chief judge in the May 1959 session. When his term ended he was denied the party's nomination for re-election to the court of appeals.

In 1960, when Gonas sought the nomination for the Saint Joseph County Circuit Court judgeship, he encountered strong opposition from some leaders of the local bar association. Gonas denied their charges and wondered why these same people who had endorsed him in the past were now turning against him. He suggested that "it is the political machine up there."

Gonas was defeated for the judgeship, but he was not done seeking public office. In 1961 he announced his candidacy for the U.S. Senate. "That's my way of life," he said, calling himself "Go Go Gonas," referring to his penchant for running for political office. In 1964 he announced his candidacy for lieutenant governor and then for governor. In 1967 he made an unsuccessful bid for the mayor of South Bend.

After a long life dedicated mostly to public service, Gonas died at the age of eighty-six in Fairhope, Alabama, survived by his sons, John Jr. and Roy.

Selected Bibliography

Gonas, John S. *Delinquency: There Is an Answer*. Np: Lex Legislatorum Publishing Company, 1968.

Indianapolis Star, June 25, 1958, April 21, 1960

Indianapolis Times, June 8, 22, 1956, January 2, 1962.

Shepard, Rebecca, ed. *A Biographical Directory of the Indiana General Assembly*. Vol. 2, *1900–1984*. Indianapolis: Select Committee on the Centennial History of the Indiana General Assembly in cooperation with the Indiana Historical Bureau, 1980.

INDIANA SUPREME COURT

JOHN R. AX

January 1, 1959–December 31, 1962

JAMES R. WILLIAMS

John R. Ax's career epitomized that of the small-town lawyer as a public servant so common in early- and mid-twentieth century Indiana. A native of Linton, Indiana, his professional life included service as school-board president in Huntingburg, city attorney for both Huntingburg and Linton, U.S. Commissioner at Crane Naval Depot, service as the Appellate Court of Indiana chief judge, businessman, and farmer.

He was born to Ora and Freda Schultz Ax on February 23, 1915, in Jasonville, where his father had a grocery store. Ora was a partner in the Ax and Fry Grocery Company, which had stores in Bloomington, Linton, and Jasonville. The Ax family maintained an active commercial and political presence in southwestern Indiana, as well as farming interests in Greene, Clay, and Knox Counties. Ax's father was active in Democratic politics and served on the Indiana Conservation Commission from 1949 to 1952. Ax followed his father's path into the Democratic Party, and, similarly, pursued a wide range of commercial interests throughout his career.

After graduating from Jasonville High School, Ax attended Indiana University, earning his bachelor's degree in business administration and graduating from IU law school. He married Kathryn M. Steinkamp of Huntingburg in 1938. She taught English and mathematics in area schools and helped manage the Ax farms. The couple eventually had five children. Following graduation from law school, Ax began practicing law in Linton and Huntingburg.

During his time in private practice from 1938 to 1959, Ax also served as city attorney for both Huntingburg and Linton, was elected president of the Huntingburg School Board, represented the Linton-Stockton School Corporation, and served as secretary of the Huntingburg Chamber of Commerce. It was also during this time that he and his wife undertook a wide range of business activities. These eventually included an ownership interest in radio stations in Jasper and Brazil, Indiana, and in Danville, Illinois; they also owned farms in Knox, Greene, Clay, and Sullivan Counties, and had interests in several coal mines in the region.

Although busy with his practice and many commercial pursuits, in 1958 Ax was elected as a Democrat to the appeals court in the First District. Ax's extensive law practice, along with his extensive business affairs, led many lawyers quickly to praise his judicial service. Reflecting the respect of his peers on the appeals court, he was selected as one of the two chief judges on the appeals court in November 1960. Arch N. Bobbitt was the other chief judge.

In June 1961 Ax had the distinction of interrupting a burglary at the Indiana Statehouse. Like many of Indiana's appellate judges and supreme court justices before and since, Ax was bunking in his chambers. He noticed that the court secretary's office was open and wandered in to check on it. He came upon a young man who insisted he was part of the cleaning crew and that he needed to find a sweeper. Upon further checking, Ax determined that the man's story was false and that there was evidence of a forced entry into the office. Fortunately, Ax's prowling around the cavernous halls of state government interrupted the burglar's attempt to pry open the secretary's desk in a search for money or other valuables. No matter, had he been able to get the desk opened, the would-be thief would have been disappointed; the secretary reported that her desk contained no money and little of tangible value.

Like his father before him, Ax had the political bug. As he neared the end of his term on the court of appeals, he entered the race for a seat on the Indiana Supreme Court in 1962, but was defeated by the Republican incumbent, Justice Norman Arterburn. Thereafter, Ax unsuccessfully sought his party's nomination for lieutenant governor in 1964. After that defeat, Ax never sought elected office again. However, in 1964 he was appointed U.S. Commissioner of the Crane Naval Ammunition Depot near Bloomington, now known as the Naval Surface Warfare Center, Crane Division, and was named to a four-year term on the Indiana Stream Pollution Control Board by Governor Roger D. Branigan. He also received a Sagamore of the Wabash.

Following his judicial service, Ax returned to Greene County, where he practiced law, tended to his business interests, and continued to be active in the community through a variety of philanthropic activities until his death on September 1, 1984, at the age of sixty-nine. His wife, Kathryn, survived him by nearly twenty-five years, dying at the age of ninety-two in May 2008.

Selected Bibliography

Greene County Daily World, May 20, 2008.
Indianapolis Star, June 23, 1962, September 2, 1984.
Jasper Herald, November 30, 1960, January 18, 1962, December 18, 1964, September 1, 1984.
Lafayette Journal and Courier, January 2, 1963.
Linton Daily Citizen, November 28, 1960.
Muncie Evening Press, June 8, 1961.
Terre Haute Tribune, June 1, 1961.
Vidette-Messenger of Porter County, February 5, 1964.
Vincennes Sun-Commercial, September 2, 1984.

INDIANA SUPREME COURT

RUSSELL W. SMITH

March 16, 1959–December 31, 1961; January 1, 1965–December 31, 1968

MICHELLE C. GOODMAN

Judge Russell W. Smith's diverse career, undoubtedly influenced by his father Judge Ralph N. Smith, who served on the Indiana Court of Appeals from January 1, 1933, to October 31, 1935, included service as a lawyer, legislator, superior court judge, appellate court judge, and court administrator, allowing him to leave his own mark on Indiana's legal landscape.

Born September 7, 1898, in Morrison, Illinois, Russell was raised by his father and mother, Olive McBride Smith. After the turn of the century, the Smiths moved to La Porte, Indiana, where Russell's father's ties to community organizations, such as the Masons and leadership roles within the Methodist church, helped frame Russell's life growing up. He graduated from La Porte High School then enrolled at Indiana University. He was inducted into the army on October 1, 1918, as part of the Student Army Training Corp during World War I. November 11, 1918, marked the end of the war, the dismantling of the Student Army Training Corp, and eventually Smith's service in the army. After completing his undergraduate and law degrees at the University of Michigan, he joined his father's law practice in 1923, working on personal injury, probate, real estate, and contract cases.

As a young lawyer, Smith, a Democrat, was elected to the Indiana House of Representatives for Starke and La Porte Counties, serving during 1927, 1931, and a special session in 1932. In 1931 Smith chaired the Organization of Courts Committee and passed legislation dividing the Porter–La Porte Superior Court into separate courts, which was signed into law that same year. This resulted in the existing superior court judge serving in La Porte Superior Court and the appointment of a new judge for Porter Superior Court. Smith was later elected judge of the La Porte Superior Court, serving from 1935 to 1943. This marked the first time in Indiana's legal history when a son and father simultaneously served as judges—Russell as a superior court judge and Ralph as an appellate court judge. This would be the last major milestone thirty-seven-year-old Russell would share with his father, who died on October 31, 1935. After leaving the superior court bench, Russell moved to Indianapolis and in 1953 married his wife LaVeta and gained a stepdaughter.

Experience as a legislator was certainly valuable when Smith began working as an attorney for the Indiana Legislative Bureau from 1951 to 1959. When the general assembly added two judgeships to the appellate court in 1959, Smith was appointed by Governor Harold W. Handley to fill one of the vacancies.

Near the beginning of his appellate court service, Smith concurred in *Meade Electric Co. v. Hagberg*, which reviewed portions of Indiana's first "Right to Work" law, later repealed in 1965. The appellate court held the law prohibited agreements conditioning employment on labor union membership but did not prohibit payment of required fair fees to the union for serving as the collective bargaining entity for all employees.

When Smith's campaign for another term on the bench was not successful, he returned to the legislature serving as attorney for the state senate Democrats in 1961 and 1963 and was appointed by Governor Matthew E. Welsh as director of the Legislative Bureau in 1963. Smith made a second run for the appellate bench in 1964 and secured his second term as appellate judge, eventually serving as chief judge, becoming the only father and son elected to serve this court.

During this term, Smith authored the *Brinkman v. Indianapolis* opinion allowing a wrongful death case to continue against the city, finding it could be held liable for the actions of police officers. He stated "[j]udicial consistency under the doctrine of stare decisis loses its virtue when it conflicts with common sense and present social needs. We, therefore, now recede from any prior decisions holding that a municipal corporation is immune from liability for the torts of police officers." This was the second case in a series where the appellate courts expanded liability for injuries caused by government actions, eventually replaced by Indiana's Tort Claim Act in 1974. Smith also concurred in the decision in *State ex rel Mass Transportation of Greater Indianapolis v. Indiana Revenue Board* that the governor did not possess authority to "pocket veto" legislation, which caused the general assembly to establish clearer procedures on time allowed for the assembly to address a governor's veto.

Smith's experience with the appellate court ran deep, from his days as appellate counsel through his service as the first court administrator from 1969 to 1970. Known as "conscientious, industrious, and energetic in discharge of his duties," Smith died on October 6, 1970, in Indianapolis.

Selected Bibliography

Indianapolis Star, October 8, 1970.
In Memoriam, December 10, 1970, https://www.in.gov/judiciary/appeals/files/bios-hist-smith-russell.pdf/.
Laramore, Jon. "Survey: Constitutional Law: Indiana Constitutional Developments." 38 *Indiana Law Review* (2005).
Meregaglia, Alesandro. *Blogging Hoosier History.* Indiana University Archives, https://blogs.libraries.indiana.edu/iubarchives/author/ameregag/page/2/.
Monks, Leander. *Courts and Lawyers of Indiana.* Indianapolis: Federal Publishing Company, 1916.
Walsh Justin. *A Biographical Directory of the Indiana General Assembly, 1816–1978.* Indianapolis: Select Committee on the Centennial History of the Indiana General Assembly, 1987.

CASES CITED

Brinkman v. Indianapolis, 231 N.E.2d 169 (Ind. Ct. App 1967).
Meade Electric Co. v. Hagberg, 159 N.E.2d 408 (Ind. Ct. App 1959).
State ex rel Mass Transportation of Greater Indianapolis v. Indiana Revenue Board, 249 N.E.2d 642 (Ind. Ct. App. 1968).

INDIANA SUPREME COURT

JOHN M. RYAN

March 16, 1959–December 21, 1964

MARK S. MASSA

John M. "Jack" Ryan was one of the most colorful, beloved, and influential public figures in Indiana during the second half of the twentieth century, serving in all three branches of government, running twice for statewide elective office, and collecting friends and admirers in both parties for six decades.

A diminutive Irishman of immense charm and wit, Ryan, born July 3, 1920, in Mahanoy City, Pennsylvania, grew up the son of a small-town lawyer in coal country and started college at Yale. But after a brief time in New Haven, he boarded a train for South Bend in 1937 and enrolled at Notre Dame, where his assigned roommate his freshman year was the son of Chicago gangster Al Capone. Ryan loved football but was too small to play, so he became the team manager and began a love affair with Notre Dame football that endured the rest of his life. So, too, did his devotion to Indiana begin to take root.

While at Notre Dame, he met Mary Ellen Kennedy of Indianapolis, a student at nearby Saint Mary's College. They were married sixty-one years and had a son and daughter and four grandchildren.

Ryan, who graduated from Notre Dame in 1941, joined the navy after America entered World War II, attaining the rank of lieutenant junior grade and was a pilot and flight instructor. After the war, he moved to Bloomington, earning a law degree from Indiana University in 1948.

A career in public service began a short time later in Indianapolis, first as a city prosecutor from 1951 to 1955, then as a Superior Court Judge for Marion County. In 1959 he was appointed to the Appellate Court of Indiana by Governor Harold W. Handley, then ran successfully in 1960 for a full four-year term.

While on the court, Ryan authored seventy-four opinions, only two of which ever drew a dissent. His opinions continue to influence Indiana law today, as the Indiana Supreme Court in 2019 cited Ryan's 1960 opinion in *Alumiwall Corp. v. Indiana Employment Security Board* in distinguishing employees from independent contractors.

Ryan's time on the appellate court was but prelude to his second act. In 1964 he sought the Republican nomination for lieutenant governor, telling the *Indianapolis Times* in a profile that "quite frankly, I like the political life. It's a little sedate up here." The *Times* noted Ryan "didn't get much challenge from fellow Republicans." His popularity as a witty, congenial judge plus solid backing from party leaders won him the convention nomination without opposition.

The Ristine-Ryan ticket lost in November in the Johnson-Goldwater landslide, but four years later, Ryan was elected to the state senate. Emblematic of his bipartisan friendships, his campaign enjoyed the support of Frank McKinney Sr., the former head of the Democratic National Committee. Ryan displayed the same bipartisan spirit years later when he wrote an op-ed piece in the *South Bend Tribune* supporting the candidacy of Democrat Terry A. Crone for the Saint Joseph County Circuit Court. Crone won the election and was later appointed to the court of appeals.

While serving in the senate, Ryan developed an even deeper friendship with Senator Robert D. Orr of Evansville. When Orr was elected lieutenant governor in 1972, Ryan became his special counsel and served as parliamentarian of the senate. When Orr was elected governor in 1980, Ryan continued to serve him as special counsel until Orr returned him to the bench in

1984, appointing him circuit court judge in Marion County, where he served until his retirement in 1992.

Ryan left a milelong list of professional achievements and community contributions. But he was most admired for his character and good cheer. The road rose up for those in his presence, and friends appreciated his mischievous wit. Later in his career, when he was not making it to many political events, people would see him having lunch at the Columbia Club in downtown Indianapolis and say, "hey Judge, I missed you the other night at that event." Ryan would ask in reply, "When were you there?" When the answer came, Ryan would say, "I must have left right before you got there!"

Or when people would say, "Good to see you, Judge," he'd say, "It's good to be seen." Former chief justice Randall T. Shepard, an early protégé and longtime friend and colleague, surmised it was meant to be understood, wryly, "as opposed to being viewed!"

Ryan died at the age of eighty-six on July 7, 2006. A scholarship in his name is awarded each year to an underprivileged law student at the Indiana University McKinney School of Law.

SELECTED BIBLIOGRAPHY

Indianapolis Star, December 8, 1951, December 27, 1956, September 10, 1967.
Indianapolis Times, June 24, 1964.
Interview. Kay Ryan Booth, May 8, 2019.
Interview. Terry Crone.
Interview. Randall T. Shepard, February 22, 2019.
Kleinberg, Eliot. "He Was Al Capone's Son." *South Florida History* 36, no. 2 (2008): 12, 13.

CASES CITED

Alumiwall Corp. v. Indiana Employment Security Board, 167 N.E.2d 60 (Ind. App. 1960).
Q.D.-A., Inc. v. Indiana Department of Workforce Development, 114 N.E.3d 840, 846 (Ind. 2019).

PHOTO COURTESY OF VINCENNES UNIVERSITY

DONALD H. HUNTER*

January 1, 1963–December 31, 1966

SARAH M. FRANK

Donald Herbert Hunter, who served on the Appellate Court of Indiana and the Indiana Supreme Court, was one of a few judges to serve on all levels of the judiciary, and he presided on the bench for thirty-seven years before he reached the mandatory retirement age. Hunter was a leading proponent of judicial reform and modernization of the Indiana courts. He strongly supported a proposal to the state's constitution that removed judges from partisan elections, and instead provided for appointment by the governor, subject to approval of retention votes every ten years. The amendment was approved by voters in 1970.

Hunter was a true Hoosier and a World War II hero, as well as an outstanding jurist. He was born in Anderson, Indiana, on October 21, 1911, and graduated from Anderson High School. He then worked his way through Lincoln Law School in Indianapolis and received his law degree in 1937. Hunter soon began his private practice in LaGrange and also was a deputy attorney general. From 1943 to 1944 he served one term in the Indiana House of Representatives.

Hunter joined the U.S. Army in 1943, was trained as a combat medic, and served on the front lines in Europe. He showed his courage during the battle for the bridge at Remagen, Germany, the only bridge remaining over the Rhine River in 1945. The American army was attempting to cross this bridge while the Germans were told to hold the bridge at all costs or to destroy it. Many soldiers did not make it across, but Hunter did. For his wartime valor, he was awarded the Combat Infantry Badge, the Combat Medical Badge, five Campaign Stars, the Bronze Star, and the Purple Heart. The Belgian government awarded him the Belgique Fourragere.

When Hunter returned to Indiana, he resumed his legal career. He was elected judge of the LaGrange Circuit Court, where he served from 1948 through 1962. He was elected to the appeals court in 1963 and served three years, including two terms as chief justice. One of his decisions on the appeals court, *Coleman v. Mitnick*, which reversed a ruling by the La Porte Superior Court, came during a period of increased civil rights activity. The owner of a Michigan City drugstore, being picketed by protesters over lack of minority employees, had one person arrested, an action that Hunter ruled unlawful. Hunter, elected to the Indiana Supreme Court in 1966, remained there until he reached the mandatory retirement age of seventy-five in 1985. He served three terms as chief justice of the supreme court, a position that rotated among the judges until 1972, when judicial reform created a permanent chief justiceship.

Hunter was always a strong advocate of judicial reform. From 1967 to 1971 he served on the Constitutional Revision Commission that initiated the judicial reform amendment. For his work on the commission he was awarded a Certificate of Commendation from Speaker of the House Otis R. Bowen. He wrote several law review articles about the need for judicial reform, explaining in one that the judiciary would have more respect if judges were appointed by an executive officer after receiving nominations from an independent screening panel. Hunter believed such a system would not only help ensure that judges were independent from political pressure, but also that the public would be afforded a voice in the ultimate composition of the courts.

Hunter served on numerous committees to improve the legal profession. In 1971 he was chairman of a special committee creating the Indiana Supreme Court Disciplinary Commission that strengthened the Code of Professional Responsibility for lawyers. In 1974 he served as a member of a commission to formulate and adopt codes of ethics for judges. He also worked for revision of the adoption laws and for upgrading judicial salaries. A lifelong scholar of Abraham Lincoln, he gave many speeches and addresses on the life of Lincoln.

Held in highest esteem by his colleagues, Hunter in May 1976 received a Sagamore of the Wabash honor from Bowen for his unselfish dedication and service to his fellow Hoosiers and the state. During his years on the appellate court and Supreme Court, Hunter and his wife lived in Anderson. They had two children and three grandchildren. Hunter died on October 27, 1991, in Lagrange. He left a legacy in his life and in his judicial opinions that reflects the values, bravery, and aspirations of his fellow Hoosiers.

Selected Bibliography

Hunter, Donald H. "Some Thoughts about Judicial Reform." *De Paul Law Review* 19, no. 3.

CASES CITED

Coleman v. Mitnick, etc. 202 N.E.2d 577 (Ind App. 1964).

*This profile is revised from one that appeared in *Justices of the Indiana Supreme Court* (2010).

DONALD R. MOTE*

January 1, 1963–December 31, 1966

DONALD J. "D.J" MOTE

Donald Roosevelt Mote was a small-town farm boy who rose from the fields of Randolph County to become a judge on the Appellate Court of Indiana and the Indiana Supreme Court.

Born in Crete, Indiana, on April 23, 1900, Mote was the son of Oliver P. and Emma A. Mote. He attended Spartanburg High School and began undergraduate studies at DePauw University in 1919. He graduated from Wabash College in Crawfordsville, Indiana, in 1924. A varsity letterman in football, Mote played left tackle for Wabash and was described as, "a bit light for the line, but makes up what he lacks in weight, with speed and fight."

Mote studied at the National Law School in Washington, DC (now the George Washington University Law School). During that time, he worked for Herbert Hoover, then the U.S. Secretary of Commerce, and was also a pardon deputy at the U.S. Department of Justice.

In 1926 Mote returned to Indianapolis and, on June 30, 1927, he was admitted to the practice of law in the Marion Circuit Court. During his time in Indianapolis he worked with Judge Milton B. Hottel, a former member of the appellate court. They later formed the firm Hottel, Mote and Smith that specialized in probate and insurance law. Mote's work with Hottel is said to have stimulated his interest in the appellate bench.

Active in Republican politics during his time in Indianapolis, Mote served as a Republican precinct committeeman, and for a time before entering private practice, was a deputy to Indiana attorney general Arthur Gilliam.

Mote married Flora Hunter on April 20, 1932. In 1937 they moved to Manchester, Indiana, where they had two children, Virginia and Thomas. He practiced law in Manchester for twenty-one years.

In 1958 Mote moved his practice to Wabash, Indiana, where he practiced law with Robert F. Gonderman and William H. Tallman. He remained politically active, serving as chair of the Wabash County Republican Finance Committee and in 1960 as an alternative delegate to the Republican National Convention. He also served as the Wabash County attorney from 1957 to 1962. Mote enjoyed spending his spare time at the Wabash Country Club or playing gin rummy at the Elks Club.

In June 1962 Mote was nominated for the appellate judgeship at the Republican State Convention. "It was a marvelous victory for me," he said. He began campaigning across the state, mostly by car, along the county fair circuit, and his campaign slogan was "Vote for Mote." On November 6, 1962, Mote won his bid for judge on the appellate court. He began his four-year term January 1, 1963.

During his time on the court, Mote was empaneled on more than three hundred cases and wrote seventy-five opinions for the majority. It was said of Mote, "As a member of the Appellate court of Indiana, he proved himself well qualified for the position. He was diligent in his work, aggressive in the presentation of his views, and his opinions were logical and well-written."

Mote served on the appellate court until he was elected to the Indiana Supreme Court in 1966, defeating incumbent Frederick E. Rakestraw by a margin of nearly 115,000 votes. The Wabash County Bar Association later described Mote as "a person of strong convictions and always fought vigorously for the principles in which he believed, even though the position he took was at the time an unpopular one."

On September 17, 1968, Mote lost his battle with cancer. A memorial service was held prior to Mote's funeral in the Wabash Circuit Courtroom. Dignitaries from the Indiana Supreme Court and appellate courts, the Indiana Bar Association, and several other bar associations were in attendance. Indiana Chief Justice David M. Lewis eulogized Mote as a "studious guardian of the law." Alluding to his cancer, Lewis said, "If you all knew the great effort Judge Mote made to serve as judge at the time of his suffering, it would be complete testimony to a fine gentleman."

Selected Bibliography

Adams, Wendy L., and Elizabeth R. Osborn, eds. *In Memoriam: Glimpses from Indiana's Legal Past*. Indianapolis: Indiana Supreme Court, 2006.
DePauw University Mirage, 1920.
Wabash College Bachelor, November 24, 1923.
Wabash Plain Dealer, June 20, August 3, 1962.

*This profile is revised from one that appeared in *Justices of the Indiana Supreme Court* (2010).

COURTESY NATIONAL ARCHIVES PHOTO NUMBER 238-OMT-V-T-8

JOSEPH O. CARSON II

January 1, 1963–December 31, 1970

DOUGLAS B. BATES

Born in Indianapolis on April 14, 1909, Joseph O. Carson II would go on to lead a life of service to his profession, his state, and his country. After receiving a bachelor's degree in chemistry from Indiana University in 1930, Carson, whose father was an attorney, attended IU law school, graduating in 1932. He was admitted to the bar that same year and moved back to Indianapolis to begin a career in private practice.

While practicing in Indianapolis, Carson became involved with important legal issues of the time. In 1941 he and his father joined a well-known New York attorney, Charles H. Tuttle, in briefing a case before the U.S. Supreme Court on behalf of certain union leaders. The officials had been charged with restraint of trade under the Sherman Act after they called for a strike against companies that had given work to members of a rival union. The trial court sided with the union members and dismissed the case, leading the government to appeal. Carson and the others were successful in arguing that the lower court's dismissal was proper on the grounds that the Sherman Act did not prevent such activities.

In August 1942 Carson enlisted in the U.S. Army Air Corps for service during World War II, remaining on active duty until his discharge in August 1946. He then relocated to North Vernon, Indiana, resuming his practice and becoming involved in politics as a Republican. Carson held various local offices before eventually being nominated by his party to run as a candidate for the Appellate Court of Indiana in the 1962 general election.

Carson won the election, thus beginning a career on the court that lasted from 1963 until 1970. During that time, he either authored or was part of the majority on several cases that helped shape Indiana evidentiary and procedural law. He was also called upon to decide politically sensitive issues of the time. In 1968 Carson and his colleagues on the appeals court were asked to decide an issue that would determine the political make-up of the Indiana Supreme Court for the 1968 term. At the time, justices were elected by popular vote in the general election after being nominated by their respective political parties. Leading up to the 1968 election, the Republicans held a 3–2 majority on the Court, with only two of the five seats being on the November ballot.

However, after the ballot had been printed, one of the Republican justices whose seat was not up for election died. The Republican State Committee nominated a candidate for the vacant position and attempted to mandate the State Election Board to place the position on the ballot. Governor Roger D. Branigin, declaring that it was "too late to certify a seat for the 1968 election," filled the position by appointing a Democrat. Just weeks before the election, the mandate action was moved to the appeals court, with Carson serving in the role of chief judge. Despite efforts to resolve the issue, the appeals court deadlocked 4–4 along party lines, forcing Carson to issue an order sending the matter to the Indiana Supreme Court, which eventually dismissed the case as moot because the election had taken place with the open position never making it on the ballot.

In 1970 Carson caused the "biggest excitement" of the state Republican convention when he "switched" from running for election to another term on the court of appeals to running as the Republican candidate for the Indiana Supreme Court, Southern Division. Carson won his party's nomination but lost in the general election. His attempt unsuccessful, Carson returned to Jennings County and in 1973 became the judge of the Jennings Circuit Court, which he presided over until 1978. After leaving the bench, Carson returned to private practice, eventually retiring in North Vernon.

Carson died from natural cause on November 14, 1998. Along with a reputation as a zealous advocate and thoughtful judge, Carson was known for his friendly manner and good nature.

Selected Bibliography

Anderson Daily Bulletin, December 27, 1968.
Greencastle Daily Banner, October 7, 1968.
Seymour Tribune, January 7, 1958.
Terre Haute Star, December 8, 1961.
Valparaiso Vidette Messenger, June 23, 1970

CASES CITED

Aldridge v. Aldridge, 233 N.E. 2d 781 (Ind. App. 1968).
Board of Commissioners v. Flowers, 201 N.E. 2d 571 (Ind. App. 1964).
N.Y.C.R. Co. v. Cavinder, 211 N.E. 2d 502 (Ind. App. 1965).
United States v. Hutcheson, 312 U.S. 219 (1941)

INDIANA SUPREME COURT

FRENCH CLEMENTS

January 1, 1963–December 16, 1963

HEATHER KIRKHAM COY*

Although Judge French Clements's time on the Appellate Court of Indiana was short, Governor Matthew E. Welsh, upon learning of Clements's death in 1963 said, "He was a fine gentleman and judge. He served his State and community well." Clements served his community and state through a forty-two-year career in law and politics.

Born August 4, 1894, in Cynthiana, Indiana, Clements came by his interest in law naturally. The son of Herdis F. Clements, Posey County Circuit Court judge from 1909 to 1946, Clements attended Indiana State Normal College, now Indiana State University, where he trained to be a teacher. After teaching school for two years and serving fifteen months in the U. S. Navy during World War I, Clements graduated from Northwestern University of Law in 1921 with bachelor of law degree and began his law practice in Evansville. He and his wife Ruth Costlow Clements of Kirklin, Indiana, were married in 1923 and had one child, a son, French Clements Jr. In addition to being a World War II veteran and member of the Indiana State Bar Association, Clements was a member of the Presbyterian Church, Elks and Masonic lodges, and Burdette American Legion Post where he served as Publicity Chairman

Clements began his law practice in Evansville in 1921 and his long political career in 1925 when he was elected to the Indiana House of Representatives where he served in the 1925 and 1927 sessions. In the 1925 session Clements proposed a bill "revising the procedure in selection of judges in cases where changes of venue are taken," and he coauthored a bill to permit the Indiana State Highway Commission to build a bridge over the Ohio River. The bill benefited Vanderburgh County by "providing that any money received from Kentucky for the construction of the bridge be used to retire any bonds issued by Vanderburgh County for the building of the bridge." By 1929 Clements was serving in the Indiana Senate where he introduced a resolution "calling for an appointment of a committee of six to study and approve a state sales tax revenue program" He continued to serve in the senate through the 1931 term and 1932 special session.

Following the special session Clements became involved in local politics, serving a four-year term as assistant Evansville city attorney and a four-year term on the Evansville Zoning Board until his election to probate court in 1952, a position he held for two consecutive terms. During his tenure as a probate court judge, Clements addressed important local issues such as Police Merit Commission rankings and the fluoridation of Evansville city water, although his decision in the latter issue was later reversed in the case of *Miller, et al. v. City of Evansville et al.* Superior Court Judge Benjamin E. Buente, who sat on the local bench at the same time as Clements, praised him for his "progressive ideas" and improvements to court filing systems, and as "an affable person . . . and a good judge."

Clements was elected to the Appellate Court of Indiana by a narrow margin of 9,226 votes over Democratic opponent Paul Tegart in the November 1962 election. He took his place on the appellate court on January 1, 1963. However, he became ill in November of 1963 and announced in December that "on the advice of my physician, I am hereby resigning as judge of the Appellate Court effective Dec. 16." After a forty-two-year career in the practice of law and political office, Clements died of lung cancer on December 19, 1963. At the time of Clements's death, Presiding Judge

Donald H. Hunter of the appellate court paid tribute to Clements: "His goal was to attain justice and to this aim he gave his entire faculty and vigor. We will long remember his kindness, his understanding, and his wholesome good fellowship"

*The author was assisted in the research for this essay by students in the Randall T. Shepard Leadership and Law Academy at William Henry Harrison High School in Evansville, Indiana.

Selected Bibliography

Evansville Courier and Press, August 7, 1962, November 8, 9, 1962, December 10, 20, 1963, January 4, 1964.
Greencastle Daily Banner, February 4, 1929.
Indianapolis Star, October 25, 1962.
Kokomo Tribune, January 29, 1925.

CASES CITED

Miller et al. v. City of Evansville et al. 189 N.E.2d 823 (1963 Ind. LEXIS 152).

YOUNG FAMILY COLLECTION

THOMAS J. FAULCONER III

December 23, 1963–December 31, 1968

JULIE C. S. McDONALD

The defendant was Connie Nicholas, a forty-five-year-old woman accused of shooting her lover, Forrest Teel, a wealthy Eli Lilly executive, in a fit of jealous rage, then attempting suicide by taking seventy-five sleeping pills mixed in pineapple juice. Reporters from throughout the country covered the five-week trial, and their reports were published on front pages around the world. Thomas Faulconer, who was the presiding judge, was in his first year on the bench. It was not only his first jury trial but also his first murder trial. In a bold move, Faulconer allowed reporters and photographers in court and radio stations to broadcast direct from the courtroom during trial.

Faulconer was elected to the Marion County Criminal Court in 1958 at the age of thirty-five but did not seek re-election in 1962 and returned to private practice. Governor Matthew E. Welsh appointed him to the

Appellate Court of Indiana in 1963 to finish the term of French Clements, who resigned due to lung cancer. During his tenure on the court he served as chief judge. Faulconer ran for re-election and won in 1964.

After starting his state judicial career with an open-door courtroom, it ended with a series of doors closing. In 1968 his party nominated him for a seat on the Indiana Supreme Court, but he lost in a Republican sweep. In 1968 Faulconer suffered another disappointment when Governor Roger D. Branigin selected another Democrat over Faulconer for a seat on the appellate court. In 1970, in the last round of elections before merit selection, Faulconer was defeated again when he lost to Republican Paul H. Buchanan Jr. for a seat on the appellate court. After a series of recount petitions, Buchanan was the certified winner by a margin of 476 votes in a race in which more than a million and a half people voted. Faulconer conceded in December, and a few weeks later the *Indianapolis Star* reported the expansion of the appellate court from eight to nine judges. The *Star* suggested that Faulconer had a "good crack" at the new ninth seat because he had dropped his challenge against Buchanan and received Buchanan's endorsement. Unfortunately for Faulconer, the general assembly directed that the ninth seat be placed in a district outside of Faulconer's area, and Governor Edgar D. Whitcomb selected Robert B. Lybrook.

After these disappointments, Faulconer continued his judicial career in 1971 as Indiana's first full-time federal magistrate and was the Chief Magistrate for the Southern District of Indiana from 1973 until his retirement in 1986. In all, he presided over more than 12,000 cases. Upon his retirement, Faulconer said, "It's about time I get away from the strain."

An example of the strain can be found in *State ex rel. Mass Transit Authority v. Indiana Review Board*, in which Faulconer's original draft of the majority opinion became the dissent. The case involved the status of a bill that changed the primary distribution of inheritance tax funds from the state to the transit authority. Faulconer opined that, because the bill was presented to the governor within two days of the general assembly's final adjournment, and because Indiana Supreme Court precedent and Article 5, section 14 of the Indiana Constitution prohibited presentation of bills within two days "next previous" to the final adjournment, the bill was effectively "pocket vetoed," consistent with practice in the state. A majority of the appellate court disagreed, holding that pocket vetoes were unconstitutional, and that the bill became law without the governor's signature. The

Indiana Supreme Court denied transfer, leaving the appellate court's decision in effect, forever changing both public transportation in Indianapolis and the practices of the general assembly and governor near the end of each legislative session.

Faulconer was born July 5, 1923, in Indianapolis, was educated at Indianapolis Public School Number 66 and Shortridge High School, graduated from Butler University, and received his doctor of law degree from Valparaiso School of Law. He received many honors throughout his life and career. He was especially proud that he earned the Eagle Scout award. He received the Distinguished Service Award from Butler University, was named Sagamore of the Wabash by the governor of Indiana, and a Kentucky Colonel by the governor of Kentucky.

Faulconer died on January 25, 2005, at the age of eighty-one. He was survived by his wife, two daughters, one son, and four grandchildren. His son Thomas wrote a book about his most famous jury trial entitled *In the Eyes of the Law*.

Selected Bibliography

Faulconer, Thomas. *In the Eyes of the Law: True Story of Love, Betrayal, Murder, Fame and Justice in 1950s America*. Bloomington, IN: AuthorHouse, 2002.
Franklin Journal, January 10, 1972.
Indianapolis News, Dec. 20, 1963.
Indianapolis Star, November 20, 1970, January 3, 1971, April 25, 1984, October 27, 1985, January 9, 2005.
Linton Daily Citizen, December 30, 1970.
Muncie Evening Press, December 18, 1968.
Tipton Daily Tribune, March 16, 1959.

CASE CITED

State ex rel. Mass Transit Auth. v. Indiana Review Bd., 242 N.E.2d 642 (Ind. App. 1968).

UNIVERSITY OF MICHIGAN LAW SCHOOL COLLECTION, BL 007031, BENTLEY HISTORICAL LIBRARY, UNIVERSITY OF MICHIGAN

GEORGE H. PRIME

January 1, 1965–December 31, 1968

BRADLEY S. BOSWELL

Judge George Henry Prime was a distinguished and devoted public servant. He honorably served in the Indiana General Assembly and on the Appellate Court of Indiana, all while working behind the scenes as a prominent Democratic political figure. After retiring from the court, Prime returned to his roots in southern Indiana and continued his career in the private sector.

Born in Chicago on January 5, 1905, Prime later moved to Indiana. He graduated from Hanover College in 1927 and the Indiana University School of Law in Indianapolis, now the Robert F. McKinney School of Law, in 1931. For many years, Prime was an attorney in private practice, mainly in Paoli, Scottsburg, and Seymour. He also served as an attorney for the Home Owners Loan Corporation, the Indiana Department of Financial Institutions, the U.S. Department of Agriculture, and the Office of Price Administration.

Prime served in the Indiana House of Representatives from November 4, 1936, to November 9, 1938, representing Orange and Washington Counties. He worked on many campaigns in his career, including serving as campaign manager in 1946 for the Democratic candidate in Indiana's Ninth Congressional District. Democratic governor Matthew E. Welsh awarded Prime with the prestigious Sagamore of the Wabash in 1964.

Prime was elected to the Appellate Court of Indiana during the 1964 general election. In his first year on the court, he served as the chief judge for the November 1965 term. Prime only served one term, choosing not to run for re-election in 1968. Despite his short time on the court he was involved in one of the most noteworthy cases in Indiana history—*State ex rel. Mass Transp. Authority of Greater Indianapolis v. Indiana Revenue Board,* commonly referred to as the MTA case.

The MTA case represents one of Indiana's most intriguing political disputes of the twentieth century. Governor Roger D. Branigan attempted to "pocket veto" a bill by not signing it after the legislature adjourned. That bill changed the distribution formula of the inheritance tax. The Metropolitan Transportation Authority, which stood to benefit from the changed formula, challenged the constitutionality of the pocket veto. The appellate court heard oral arguments on August 1, 1967, but the partisan-split judges, four Democrats and four Republicans, were slow to issue an opinion. Draft briefs were circulated, and it appeared that five votes—including Prime's—favored upholding Branigan's pocket veto. But the case took a partisan turn when Richard G. Lugar was elected mayor of Indianapolis in 1967 and needed the inheritance tax revenue to fund part of his new political agenda. On December 31, 1968, the Republican members of the court finally handed down a majority opinion that held the pocket veto was unconstitutional. They secured this majority by obtaining one Democrat's vote in exchange for a job offer. Prime concurred in the dissent, in favor of upholding the use of Branigan's pocket veto. The case later devolved even further, with the court holding the state auditor in contempt for not distributing the inheritance tax funds in accordance with the bill. However, Prime had left the court by that point.

As the MTA case indicates, Prime served on the court when nominees were chosen by political parties and ran on a partisan ballot. Partisan activity was more acceptable, and in some cases, even expected. That is no longer the case today, as the current judicial nominating process has greatly reduced partisan influence on the court. But during Prime's years on the court, his name could be found throughout newspaper articles indicating his attendance at Democratic fund-raisers, highlighting his speaking engagements at Democratic Party functions, and noting his close connections with prominent Democratic politicians, including Branigan. Ever part of the Indiana Democratic machine, Prime eschewed re-election and chose instead to work on Branigan's failed 1968 presidential primary bid, which was only run in Indiana and resulted in a loss to Senator Robert F. Kennedy of New York.

Prime returned to private life in Scottsburg, where he became a founder of the First Indiana National Bank of Scottsburg. He also served as the president of the Hanover College Alumni Association and in 1966 was awarded Hanover College's alumni achievement award, the highest honor that can be bestowed upon an alumnus of the college. Other recipients include Vice President Michael R. Pence and Governor Eric Holcomb.

Prime died in Scottsburg on January 23, 1990, at the age of eighty-five. He was laid to rest in the small Hanover Cemetery, next to his beloved alma mater.

Selected Bibliography

Foughty, Trevor. "*George Henry Prime.*" CapitolandWashington.com/. http://www.capitolandwashington.com/politicians/filter/7562/.
"How Bobby Kennedy Won the '68 Indiana Primary." *Newsweek*, May 19, 1968.
Indianapolis Recorder, October 29, 1966.
Indianapolis Star, October 3, 1946, February 27, 1968, January 25, 1990.
Nixon, William. "The Pocket Veto Case." Unedited draft chapter of 2001 book commemorating the Indiana Court of Appeals centennial (on file with the Court of Appeals of Indiana).
Seymour Daily Tribune, August 31, 1953, April 19, 1968.

CASES CITED

State ex rel. Mass Transp. Authority of Greater Indianapolis v. Indiana Revenue Board, 242 N.E.2d 642 (Ind. App. Ct. 1968).

HUBERT E. WICKENS

August 1, 1965–December 31, 1966

WILLIAM F. GULDE

On Tuesday evening, August 12, 1965, the Decatur County Bar Association gave a dinner in honor of Hubert E. Wickens for his recent appointment to the Appellate Court of Indiana by Governor Roger D. Branigan. Throughout the evening, local citizens told stories, some of them humorous, about their native son and their pride in him. The fifty-six-year-old attorney, who had spent many years serving the public, thanked the audience for their good wishes and faith in him.

Born to Hugh D. and Adele Gallagher Wickens on December 7, 1908, young Hubert grew up in Greensburg, Indiana, surrounded by several siblings and with a father who was a prominent local attorney. The family was very active with Saint Mary Catholic Church, an institution that Hubert remained a member of for his entire life. A graduate of Greensburg High School and later the Indiana University School of Law in Indianapolis (today the Robert H. McKinney School of Law), the new attorney returned to his hometown to practice law with his father.

Wickens successfully ran for Decatur County prosecuting attorney in 1930 at the age of twenty-two. He won re-election for the same post in 1932. At age twenty-six, he won a seat in the Indiana Senate as a member of the Democratic Party representing Decatur, Bartholomew, and Franklin Counties. The *Indianapolis News* noted that he was the youngest member of the chamber upon taking his position in 1935.

Wickens served in the state senate for one term championing many of President Franklin D. Roosevelt's New Deal policies for Indiana. While in the state senate he advocated for a merit system in the Indiana State Police and sponsored a bill to make the office of Court Reporter an appointed position rather than an elected one. His time as a senator was eclipsed in 1940 when Republicans won many offices as a result of the exciting presidential campaign of Wendell Willkie. After his defeat, Wickens returned to Greensburg to practice law with his father.

At age thirty-six the former legislator was not finished with public life. By 1944 Wickens was married and with three children and running as the Democratic nominee for Indiana Attorney General. In his campaign for that position, he tried to warn Hoosiers that a millionaire and chain-store lobbyist was the power behind the Republican Party. His efforts proved futile and he was soundly defeated for the office by James A. Emmert, who later served on the Indiana Supreme Court.

Wickens returned to Greensburg to practice law and once again immersed himself into local organizations, such as the Knights of Columbus and the Chamber of Commerce. In 1946 he suffered a great shock with the death of his thirty-one-year-old wife, Kathryn Hellmich Wickens. The young widower eventually met and married Bernice Glaze, a local widow.

Throughout the 1950s and into the 1960s Wickens continued to earn a reputation as an excellent attorney. In 1963 he began his tenure as the president of the Decatur County National Bank. Life seemed set for the respected attorney and then Governor Roger D. Branigan called in 1965 and asked him to fill the vacancy on the appellate court after the death of Judge Warren W. Martin Sr.

Wickens's tenure on the court, albeit brief, was extraordinarily busy. He authored forty majority opinions. In 1966 he wrote the opinion in *Fortson v. Iden* that ordered Alfred Iden, a Saint Joseph County resident, to pay for his wife's funeral even though they were separated. The court's decision reversed that of the Saint Joseph Circuit Court. He also wrote the opinion in *Yingst v. Pratt* that reversed a Grant County Circuit Court decision to award Merchie Pratt damages after the patron was shot in a bar altercation in Marion during a melee involving a robber and the owner of the establishment, Jennings Fudge. A broader case with wider implications came in 1966 in the case *State Board of Tax Comm'rs v. Wright*, which involved a Clay County campground owned by the Methodist Church that sought to remain tax exempt. Wickens noted in his opinion that "Property tax exemptions for religious purposes has its roots in antiquity."

In 1966 Wickens returned home to Greensburg to continue with his successful law practice and banking responsibilities. He died in 1979 at the age of seventy.

Selected Bibliography

Greensburg Daily News, August 13, 1965.
Indianapolis News, January 21, 1935, April 24, 1979, March 3, 1966.
Indianapolis Star, February 11, 1937, November 4, 1944, October 7, 1966.
Kokomo Morning Times, March 18, 1966.

CASES CITED

Fortson v. Iden, 138 Ind. App. 432 (1966).
State Board of Tax Comm'rs v. Wright, 139 Ind. App, 370 (1966).
Yingst v. Pratt, 139 Ind. App. 695 (1966).

PHOTO COURTESY OF SHELBY COUNTY HISTORICAL SOCIETY

CHARLES W. COOK

January 1, 1967–November 21, 1968

CARRIE STILLER

The year 1906 was a notable one, as it was the year President Theodore Roosevelt became the first American to win the Nobel Peace Prize for negotiating a settlement of the Russo-Japanese War. It was also the birth year of Judge Charles W. Cook Jr. of the Appellate Court of Indiana. Born January 26, 1906, in Indianapolis, Cook had an exemplary career in both the legal and judicial fields, working as an attorney for nearly thirty-eight years and eventually as a judge until his death on November 21, 1968.

Cook graduated from Indianapolis's Shortridge High School in 1923. Although it is unknown whether he served in the military, he was registered for the draft in Marion County. After high school he attended Indiana University Law School in Bloomington, Indiana. During law school, from 1927 to 1928, Cook served as a judicial law clerk for Judge Willis C. McMahan and Judge Charles Remy of the appellate court. Cook's law career began after receiving his bachelor of law degree in 1929 at the age of twenty-three. With his experience and his law degree, he landed his first job as an attorney at the firm of Bingham Mendenhall and Bingham, where he worked from 1929 to 1939. He became a member of Bingham Cook and Bingham in 1939 practicing there until 1949, when he became the senior partner at Cook and Mendenhall. Most of his work was in civil practice throughout his career

From 1957 until 1959 Cook served as the general counsel for the Indiana Toll Road Commission, appointed to that position by Governor Harold W. Hanley. Cook was executive director there until 1961. For several months before beginning his service on the court, Cook was an associate in the firm of Bose, Buchannan, McKinney and Evans.

Cook was elected to the appellate court in 1966. He took his seat on the court on January 1, 1967, and served until his death on November 21, 1968. His term would have expired January 1, 1970, the same year in which the state constitution was amended to reform the way that appellate judges were selected by instituting a merit-based system in which the governor selects the nominee from a list of recommended candidates. Judicial appointments last two years, and then the judge is subjected to a retention election through the ballot box, and if retained serves for another ten years, with no limit on the number of times a judge can be retained. Cook had benefited from the prior system which was more influenced by partisan politics at the state and national level. Judicial nominees were chosen by political parties and elected into office by voters. Though his time on the court was brief, Cook's name is associated with no less than twenty-seven published cases, including cases in the area of family law, estate, contract, civil procedure, employment, zoning, and tort.

Cook was survived by his wife Frances, whom he called Gene, and his two sons, James and Michael. He is buried at the Washington Park East Cemetery in Indianapolis. Cook was remembered by his colleagues for "his unique and penetrating grasp of legal principles as recorded in his written opinions" of the court. Acting Chief Justice Donald H. Hunter said in a memorial tribute that Cook had "an outstanding career as a lawyer" and that "his colleagues on the Appellate Court and his Judicial Colleagues on the Supreme Court have lost an outstanding jurist."

Selected bibliography

Greencastle Daily Banner, November 23, 1968.
Indianapolis Star, November 22, 1968.
Hunter, Donald, Acting Chief Justice. In Memoriam, November 21, 1968.
Res Gestae 12 (December 1968).

JASPER FAMILY COLLECTION

CHARLES S. WHITE

December 17, 1968–June 30, 1978

FRANK SULLIVAN JR.

The apex of Charles S. White's career directly intersected with both the U.S. Supreme Court, under the leadership of Chief Justice Earl Warren, constitutional law decisions and a new selection process for Indiana appellate judges.

Born in 1909 in Parke County, Indiana, White attended DePauw University and now-defunct Vorhees Law School in Terre Haute, and practiced in Parke and Vigo Counties following his admission to the bar in 1933. After World War II service in the U.S. Army Intelligence Corps, he enrolled in the Indianapolis Division of the Indiana University School of Law, believing he needed further legal education.

In 1965 Democratic Indiana Attorney General John J. Dillon appointed White as his chief counsel. He was part of Dillon's "dream team" that also included Virginia Dill McCarty, later U.S. Attorney for the Southern District of Indiana, and J. Patrick Endsley, later Marion Circuit Court and Federal Magistrate Judge.

In 1964 after the Warren Court issued the one person-one vote mandate, White was lead counsel defending new congressional boundaries drawn by a Democratic legislature against claims by the Republicans that they were unconstitutional.

When a vacancy on the Marion Criminal Court arose in 1966, Governor Roger D. Branigin appointed White to fill the unexpired term. Here White grappled with new Warren Court holdings on the due-process rights of the criminally accused. *Gideon v. Wainwright* was new on the books and *Miranda v. Arizona* was handed down on the very day of White's appointment. White came face-to-face with *Miranda* only two months later, dismissing a burglary charge on grounds that the suspect's advisements did not meet *Miranda*'s requirements. White's tenure on the criminal court did not survive the 1966 general election, in which he was defeated. He returned to serving as Dillon's chief counsel for the next two years, including representing the State in the famous *Metro-Transit* case that challenged the constitutionality of the state's long-standing practice of allowing the governor to "pocket veto" bills, and successfully defending a high-profile lawsuit by the Socialist Workers Party for a spot on the 1968 general election ballot in *State ex rel. Socialist Labor Party v. State Election Board.*

On December 17, 1968, Branigin appointed White, on Dillon's recommendation, to the Appellate Court of Indiana, filling a vacancy created by the death of Judge Charles W. Cook on November 21. The appointment demonstrated Branigin and Dillon's high regard for White, as other Democratic judges and lawyers (some rendered unemployed in the recent 1968 elections) coveted the appointment.

White was a lonely figure on the court during 1969 and 1970 as the only Democrat alongside seven Republicans. Change came with the 1970 election. White defeated future Supreme Court Justice Alfred J. Pivarnik and two other Democrats were also elected. In addition, a constitutional amendment was adopted that replaced partisan election with merit selection of appellate judges. Pursuant to the amendment's grandfather provisions, White became a member of a newly constituted, nine-member court of appeals on January 1, 1972. He was retained in office by the voters in 1974.

Under the court's new alignment, White was a judge of the Second District, along with Patrick D. Sullivan and Paul J. Buchanan Jr.. Although both

Sullivan and Buchanan had been elected to the appellate court as Republicans, White and Sullivan frequently were aligned in opposition to Buchanan.

As an appeals court judge, White reprised his criminal court judge experience applying Warren Court decisions in criminal cases. For example, in *Gibson v. State,* White set aside a guilty plea for failure to honor an accused's rights under *Boykin v. Alabama* that require a guilty plea be entered knowingly and voluntarily.

White participated in many other decisions. He was on the panel in a well-known landlord-tenant dispute, *Old Town Development Company v. Langford*, that recognized an implied warranty of habitability in residential leases, a holding subsequently vacated by the Indiana Supreme Court. In 1976 he wrote a significant tort law opinion, *O'Bryant v. Veteran's of Foreign Wars*, holding that members of an unincorporated association could sue for damages caused by the association's negligence. Ten years later, the Indiana Supreme Court expressly disapproved this holding, but overruled itself ten years after that; White's holding in *O'Bryant* returned to being Indiana law after a ten-year hiatus.

When White retired from the court effective June 30, 1978, he was replaced on the court by Vivian Sue Shields, the state's first female appellate court judge. White died on February 25, 1986, remembered by those who knew him as a cerebral lawyer and judge and a quiet and kind man.

Selected Bibliography

Indianapolis News, January 4, 1971.

Indianapolis Star, December 25, 1964, June 14, 1966, December 18, 1968, April 1, 1978, May 27, 2006.

Staton, Robert, and Gina Hicklin. "The History of the Court of Appeals on Indiana." *Indiana Law Review* 30, no.1 (1997): 203–31.

CASES CITED

Boykin v. Alabama, 395 U.S. 238 (1969).

Gideon v. Wainwright, 372 U.S. 335 (1963).

Gibson v. State, 162 Ind. App. 337, 319 N.E.2d 661 (1974).

Grills v. Branigin, 284 F. Supp. 176 (S.D. Ind.), aff'd sub nom. *Branigin v. Duddleston*, 391 U.S. 364 (1968).

Miranda v. Arizona, 384 U.S. 436 (1966).

O'Bryant v. Veterans of Foreign Wars, No. 1552, 176 Ind. App. 509, 376 N.E.2d 521 (1978).

Old Town Development Company v. Langford, 349 N.E.2d 744 (Ind. Ct. App. 1976).

State ex rel. Mass Transp. Auth. of Greater Indianapolis v. Indiana Revenue Bd., 144 Ind. App. 63, 242 N.E.2d 642 (1968).

State ex rel. Socialist Labor Party v. State Election Bd., 241 N.E.2d 69 (1968).

INDIANA SUPREME COURT

PATRICK D. SULLIVAN

January 1, 1969–July 31, 2007 • Senior Judge: August 1, 2007–
October 1, 2015

CALE J. BRADFORD

Judge Patrick Donnelly Sullivan, who has the distinction of being the longest-serving judge in Indiana Court of Appeals history, was described by a colleague at his 2007 retirement ceremony as a "sports nut, history addict, [and] political junkie." He is fondly remembered for having "vigor" and "passion" for the law and an unwavering commitment to justice. Sullivan was honest and genuine, had a good sense of humor, and showed empathy for all. A devoted public servant, Sullivan was on the appellate bench for 17,073 days.

Born on August 9, 1932, Sullivan served two years in the U.S. Navy during the Korean War. Sullivan was a proud alumnus of Washington and Lee University, earning both his undergraduate and law degrees from the university.

After law school Sullivan settled in Indianapolis, serving as a deputy attorney general before entering private practice. He also served as a senior commissioner with the Marion County Probate Court. In 1965 Sullivan moved to the bench full time, serving as a judge on the Marion County Superior Court until his election to the appeals court.

He was the last sitting member of the court to be popularly elected before the advent of the judicial selection and retention system that is currently used to select appellate judges in Indiana. First elected to the court in 1968, Sullivan was subsequently retained on the court by voters in 1972, 1982, 1992, and 2002. Having experienced both direct election of appellate judges and judicial selection and retention, Sullivan became a staunch supporter of the latter. Following his retirement from full-time service to the court on July 31, 2007, Sullivan continued to serve as a senior judge until his death on October 1, 2015.

Sullivan earned a reputation as a disciplined and incisive jurist. He is remembered as always being "supremely focused on the law and its nuances, always informed, always questioning, [and] never willing to leave one stone unturned." He had an ability to see the "whole picture" and to consider "even the remotest ramifications" of the court's rulings. Over the course of his career, Sullivan created a comprehensive self-curated legal digest that, even with the advent of computer-based legal research programs, was an invaluable resource.

Sullivan was a meticulous and prolific proofreader who took great care to give every case before him thorough consideration. He enjoyed the opportunity to "roll up his sleeves" and debate especially troubling cases. These debates, colleagues say, often led to stronger appellate decisions. When warranted, Sullivan was "particularly prepared to take on unpopular positions." For instance, Sullivan dissented from the majority's opinion affirming professional boxer Mike Tyson's well-publicized Indiana convictions for rape and sexual deviate conduct because he believed that Tyson "did not receive the requisite fairness which is essential to our system of criminal justice."

Sullivan went out of his way to welcome new colleagues when they joined the court and made them feel like integral and equal parts of the court. Given his willingness and ability to discuss complex legal matters, numerous colleagues considered him to be a confidant and mentor.

Sullivan shared his love of learning with lawyers, law students, and the public. During his tenure on the court, Sullivan was an adjunct professor at the Indiana University Robert H. McKinney School of Law, a lecturer on law and social policy at Indiana University-Purdue University at Indianapolis, and a lecturer on American diplomatic history at IU. He was also a faculty member at many appellate judges' seminars and lectured on "Law and the Layman" for adult education courses offered through the Indianapolis Public School System. In recognition of his judicial and public service, Sullivan received a Sagamore of the Wabash, a distinction awarded by Indiana's governor.

Sullivan's love of sports, especially baseball and golf, was widely recognized. For many years he particularly enjoyed serving on the board of directors for the Indianapolis Indians, the city's baseball franchise. Sullivan often shared his love of sports with others, discussing games and matches and offering his tickets to Indianapolis Indians and Butler University basketball games to colleagues, judicial clerks, and court staff.

Sullivan never lost sight of the fact that the cases brought before the court involved real persons facing real problems. He strove to treat all equally, no matter one's background, level of education, or financial position. His humor and demeanor put those around him at ease, and his passion for the law led him to continually seek justice. Over the course of his long tenure on the court, Sullivan spectacularly succeeded in upholding the trust placed in him by the citizens of Indiana.

Selected Bibliography

Baker, John G. Comments submitted to the author, February 13, 2019.
Ballard, Jonathan. Reflections submitted to the author, February 21, 2019.
Boyle, Heather. Reflections submitted to the author, March 20, 2019.
Carter, Caroline. Reflections submitted to the author, March 1, 2018.
Comments made by Senator Richard G. Lugar, the Honorable V. Sue Shields, the Honorable James S. Kirsch, John D. Profitt, and Jerry Garau. Webcast of Sullivan's July 20, 2007 Retirement Ceremony. https://www.youtube.com/watch?v=LRRVYIawOVg&feature=youtu.be (last visited March 26, 2019).
https://mycourts.in.gov/JR/Default.aspx?court=2 (last visited April 25, 2018).
http://obits.dignitymemorial.com/dignity-memorial/obituary.aspx?n=Patrick-Sullivan&lc=2531&pid=175988439&mid=6617562 (last accessed February 26, 2018).
http://www.in.gov/judiciary/appeals/2443.htm (last visited February 26, 2018).
Najam, Edward W. Comments submitted to the author. April 25, 2018.

CASE CITED

Tyson v. State, 619 N.E.2d 276, 301 (Ind. App. 1993), *trans. denied*.

INDIANA SUPREME COURT

ALLEN SHARP

January 1, 1969–November 1, 1973

GEOFFREY G. SLAUGHTER

Allen Sharp was a judge for more than forty years, but he served less than five years on the appellate bench. His brief tenure as a state judge began on the former Appellate Court of Indiana, to which he was elected in 1968, and ended on the newly created Court of Appeals of Indiana, from which he resigned 1973 to join the federal bench. He had a deserved reputation as a demanding and intimidating judge. He did not suffer fools or lawyers who were unprepared. He had a deep appreciation of history: he studied it, taught it, and wrote about it. He was an avid baseball fan but did not live to see his beloved Chicago Cubs win the 2016 World Series. He enjoyed a good story and told them well; not all of them were off-color. He did not like his middle name and never used it—not even his middle-name initial. And he said the great thing about law clerks was that you could count on someone to attend your funeral.

Sharp was born in Washington, DC, on February 11, 1932, and moved to Indiana as an infant with his family. His parents divorced when he was five years old. An only child, he lived with various friends and family for several years in Indiana, Oklahoma, and Texas. He returned to Indiana to attend high school in Brown County, and graduated in 1950.

He received a scholarship to attend Indiana State Teachers College, now Indiana State University, where he was student-body president and president of Young Republicans. He finished his degree at George Washington University in 1954 and applied to law school. He received a Root-Tilden scholarship to attend New York University. Before classes began, he spent a weekend there meeting other Root-Tilden scholars and found Greenwich Village such a culture shock that he declined the scholarship and returned to Indiana.

In 1957, after graduating from Indiana University's law school in Bloomington, he joined the U.S. Air Force and later enrolled in the Judge Advocate General program. He remained in the Air Force Reserves for nearly thirty years and attained the rank of lieutenant colonel. He moved to Williamsport to begin a county-seat law practice, and in 1964 he married a local woman. They had two daughters. He ran unsuccessfully for the state senate that year.

In 1968, at age thirty-six, he won the only case he argued before the U.S. Supreme Court—*Hopkins v. Cohen*, which was about attorneys' fees in a Social Security case. Also, that year, Sharp rode Richard Nixon's coattails and won a seat on the state appellate bench. He was a highly productive judge: "I never pretended to be a great . . . scholar. I just ground out opinions. . . . [S]tatistically I was writing more opinions than anybody else, and became known for that more than any particular area in which I was interested."

Nixon appointed Sharp to the Northern District of Indiana in 1973 during a tumultuous time in his administration. Just forty-one years old, Sharp was confirmed on October 4. On October 10, Vice President Spiro Agnew resigned from office. The next day the president signed Sharp's commission. October 20 was the infamous Saturday Night Massacre, when the Justice Department's two top officials resigned after refusing to carry out the president's order to fire special prosecutor Archibald Cox. The third-ranking official, Solicitor General Robert Bork, carried out the order and fired Cox. On November 1, Bork appointed Leon Jaworski as Cox's successor—the same day Sharp was sworn in as a U.S. District Judge. Later that month, an eighteen-plus-minute portion of one of Nixon's White House tapes was found to have been erased. Sharp later joked that the missing minutes of tape would have revealed Nixon's embarrassment at having appointed Sharp to the bench.

Sharp served on the federal bench for more than thirty-five years. He earned a master's in history from Butler University in 1986. And he is the author of several essays, including "Presidents as Supreme Court Advocates: Before and After the White House," published in the *Journal of Supreme Court History*.

He died on July 10, 2009, at his home in Granger, Indiana. Among those attending his memorial service were many past and present law clerks.

Selected Bibliography

A Ceremony in Memory of the Honorable Allen Sharp (Sept. 4, 2009). (Remarks of District Judge Robert L. Miller Jr.) (Appears in 733 F. Supp. 2d).

Federal Judicial Center online biography. https://www.fjc.gov/history/judges/sharp-allen/.

The Oral History of Judge Allen Sharp–As Told to Collins Fitzpatrick, Circuit Executive of the Seventh Circuit (Sept. 6, 2007). http://www.google.com/url?sa=t&rct=j&q=&esrc=s&source=web&cd=2&ved=2ahUKEwjO9fn4x5HjAhVPHs0KHRLlDdIQFjABegQIARAC&url=http%3A%2F%2Fwww.lb7.uscourts.gov%.

Sharp, Allen, "Benjamin Harrison: High-Priced Counsel." In *America's Lawyer-Presidents: From Law Office to Oval Office*. Edited by Norman Cross. Evanston, IL: Northwestern University Press, 2004.

———. "Presidents as Supreme Court Advocates: Before and After the White House." *Journal of Supreme Court History* 28 (June 18, 2003): 116–44.

———. "The U.S. Supreme Court on Circuit in Indiana, 1837–1891." In *The History of Indiana Law*. Edited by David J. Bodenhamer and Randall T. Shepard. Athens: Ohio University Press, 2006.

CASE CITED

Hopkins v. Cohen, 390 U.S. 530 (1968).

INDIANA SUPREME COURT

JOE W. LOWDERMILK

January 1, 1969–December 31, 1979

SCOTT L. TYLER

From humble beginnings on a farm in Sullivan County, Joe W. Lowdermilk, who was born 1910, cultivated values rooted in hard work, integrity, and compassion, which yielded a bountiful legal career and service on the Court of Appeals of Indiana. He began his law practice in 1934 and was elected to his first of two terms as Sullivan County Prosecutor in 1943.

In 1952 Lowdermilk, a Republican, was elected judge of the Sullivan County Circuit Court despite the county's reputation as reliably Democratic. His election was an even bigger achievement considering that Dwight Eisenhower, the GOP presidential candidate, won every county in Indiana that year except Lake and Sullivan. Four years later Lowdermilk won re-election, a year in which Eisenhower won every county in the state except Sullivan, which led many people to remark that he was even more popular than the president.

Lowdermilk's popularity and reputation grew further during his two terms as circuit court judge. Due to Indiana's former civil rule that permitted an automatic change of venue, lawsuits filed in more populous counties were frequently transferred to more rural counties, including Sullivan. Over time, Lowdermilk came to be recognized well beyond Sullivan County as a fair and capable trial judge. He also drew the attention of several court of appeals judges who encouraged him to run for a seat on the appeals court in 1968. He did and was elected, beginning his service in January 1969.

In 1970 Lowdermilk played a prominent role in a rare constitutional battle over the separation of powers that culminated in the arrest of the state auditor for contempt. The controversy arose from legislation that afforded counties a greater share of inheritance taxes. Roger D. Branigan, governor at the time, exercised a pocket veto of the measure, but his action was later deemed unconstitutional. The predecessor to the Indianapolis Transportation Department subsequently was awarded a judgment for $12.7 million, which represented the city's share of the inheritance taxes for the years 1967–68. State Auditor Trudy S. Etherton, however, refused to issue payment to satisfy the judgment.

Relying on advice from Indiana's attorney general, Etherton asserted that state law required an appropriation before the issuance of any warrants for state funds. Since no such appropriation had been made, she claimed she would violate her oath of office by issuing payment. Etherton, a Republican, was supported in her position by fellow Republican, Governor Edgar D. Whitcomb.

Etherton's refusal to authorize the funds to pay the judgment ultimately led to a finding of contempt and an appeal. The appeals court, presiding over the case, composed of seven Republicans, upheld the finding of contempt. Writing for the court, Lowdermilk declared that Etherton had not only refused to comply with the court's order but had also "continued to question our right to interpret the law," according to an account in the *Evansville Courier-Press.* He then asked, "what check is there on the executive if it is not bound by the law as the law is determined by the courts, pursuant to the duty prescribed for them by the constitution?" The appeals court, led by Lowdermilk, displayed remarkable courage and played a pivotal role in preserving a bedrock constitutional principle.

In 1972 Lowdermilk won a retention election for a ten-year term. He retired in 1979 and operated a farm in his native Sullivan County. He died in a farming accident in 1982.

Selected Bibliography

Evansville Courier-Press, February 27, 1970.

CASE CITED

State Ex Rel Mass Transportation Authority v. Indiana Revenue Board, et al., 255 N.E.2d 833 (Ind. App. 1970).

INDIANA SUPREME COURT

GEORGE B. HOFFMAN JR.

January 1, 1969–October 3, 1998 • Senior Judge: October 3, 1998–December 25, 2006

DAVID A. ROOT

The eighty-third judge on the Court of Appeals of Indiana, George B. Hoffman Jr. was born on March 6, 1924, in Sunbury, Pennsylvania, to George B. and Mary Ditzler Hoffman Sr. The senior Hoffman engaged in several working-class occupations while George Jr. graduated from Hammond High School in northwest Indiana in 1942. While in school Hoffman served in student government, wrote for the newspaper, acted in school plays, and worked as a manager at the Holman Theatre.

Following graduation, Hoffman served in the 102nd Infantry Division of the U.S. Army during World War II. Entering as a private, he advanced to corporal, earning a Bronze Star for heroic service in combat and a Purple Heart for injuries suffered in November 1944 near Immendorf, Germany. Upon returning stateside in September 1945, he married Margaret A. Cross, who was an educator. Together they had five sons. She preceded him in death in 1994, after which he married Louise (Gibbs) Scudder in 1997.

Hoffman graduated from Muskingum College in 1948 and Valparaiso University School of Law in 1951. Following law school, he engaged in private practice in Hammond until 1969. Alongside his practice, Hoffman was active in community and political affairs, serving as the president of the Hammond Bar Association in 1968 and helping to organize the Hammond Legal Aid Organization. He also served as a scoutmaster in Boy Scouts, participated in the American Red Cross and Young Men's Christian Association, coached youth football and basketball, and was a member of the United Methodist Church. These community efforts made him the recipient of numerous awards from the Hammond Chamber of Commerce.

Hoffman also was an active participant in local politics. In 1959 he served as chairman of the Lake County Republican Central Committee and ran for Hammond city judge, losing to incumbent Frank A. J. Stodola. In 1963–64, as Hammond city chairman for the GOP, he became embroiled in an intraparty dispute over a perceived lack of leadership, seeking to oust Lake County Republican Chairman Theodore L. Sendak, who Hoffman publicly stated was "trying to make a country club out of the Republican Party in Lake County." The state party sided with Sendak and the dispute dissipated.

Riding the wave of Richard Nixon's presidential campaign in 1968, Hoffman won election to the Appellate Court of Indiana and won retention elections in 1972, 1982, and 1992. He served as the first chief judge after a 1970 amendment to the Indiana Constitution reorganized and renamed the Court of Appeals of Indiana. In this capacity he initiated the court's program of "Appeals on Wheels," taking oral arguments to various venues around the state, including law schools, colleges and universities, high schools, and county courts. Meanwhile, on the bench, he was the first judge to write 2,000 opinions, which covered the gamut from criminal cases to contract disputes to constitutional questions to family law to tax claims. Moreover, his opinions have been cited by the Indiana Supreme Court and courts all over the country on every level, including the U.S. Supreme Court.

Of his numerous opinions, one highlight concerned the rights of the criminally accused. In *State v. Heltzel*, Hoffman held that the importance of secrecy in grand jury proceedings outweighed freedom of the press claims as to what reporters could discover and publish. He ruled that protections for the criminally accused were imperative and superior to civil protections of media and journalists. Although the Indiana Supreme Court ultimately vacated his decision on other grounds, it sided with him in noting the importance such secrecy affords in protecting the rights of those under criminal investigation.

Nearing the statutorily mandated retirement age of seventy-five, Hoffman left the bench in 1998 and became a senior judge until his death from sepsis on Christmas Day 2009 at age eighty-five. During his tenure, he sat in more than 9,000 cases and held posts such as chairman of the board of trustees of the Judges Retirement System and a member of the executive committee of the Indiana Judicial Center. He was also a member of the Indiana Judges Association and a six-time recipient of the Sagamore of the Wabash Award. Amassing a lengthy tenure in the Indiana bar—both as a lawyer and judge—Hoffman left his most notable mark through his judicial contributions and, in so doing, set an estimable example to be followed by all who have and continue to serve after him.

Selected Bibliography

Graf, Jeffrey. "Sagamore of the Wabash." Reference Services Department, Herman B Wells Library, Indiana University Libraries, Bloomington (2017)
Kokomo Tribune, January 12, 14, 1964.
Indianapolis Star, January 6, 2010.
Staton, Robert H., and Gina M. Hicklin. "The History of the Court of Appeals of Indiana." *Indiana Law Review* 30, no. 1 (1997): 203–31.
Turner Publishing, comp. *102nd Infantry Division: "The Ozarks."* (Nashville: Turner Publishing Company, 2000).
Valparaiso Vidette-Messenger, January 19, 1972.

CASE CITED
State v. Hetzel, 535 N.E.2d 1221 (1989).

BRETZMAN COLLECTION, INDIANA HISTORICAL SOCIETY

ROBERT B. LYBROOK

September 17, 1970–December 31, 1970; January 1, 1972–September 30, 1979

DAVID J. REMONDINI

Judge Robert B. Lybrook was one of the few judges in the history of the Court of Appeals of Indiana to serve two separate terms on the bench. His tenure bridged the modern era of the court, which was transitioning from an elected, statute-based institution to one created by the Indiana Constitution and grounded on merit selection.

Born in Gary, Indiana, Lybrook also lived in Ohio and in Kokomo and Indianapolis. He graduated from Indianapolis's Arsenal Technical High School in 1932. He next earned a journalism degree and then a law degree from Indiana University in Bloomington. He became a member of the Indiana Bar in 1937 and started a law practice in Franklin, interrupted by his service in the U.S. Navy during World War II. After the war, he returned to his practice in Franklin, but he soon entered public service and established a solid legal pedigree. He served as prosecutor from 1946 to 1950 in the

Eighth Judicial Circuit, which included Johnson and Brown Counties. In 1954 he was appointed judge of the same circuit and served two terms. In 1967 he moved to Nashville and practiced law under the name Lybrook and Bradley and served as county attorney until he was appointed to the appellate court. He and his family lived in the area his entire married life. One son, Robert Lybrook, also became a judicial officer, serving as a longtime magistrate in Morgan County.

At the state GOP convention in the summer of 1970, with just minutes to go before the filing deadline, Lybrook placed his name on the convention ballot. He became an unopposed candidate for one of the two Republican openings for the appellate court's first district seat. He filled what would be an upcoming vacancy in that district that was prompted by incumbent Judge James C. Cooper's decision to retire at the end of his term. Citing health reasons, Cooper opted not to seek a fourth term. However, Cooper died in September of 1970 just months before the November general election. Governor Edgar D. Whitcomb selected Lybrook to fill the vacant seat and serve out the remainder of Cooper's term.

During his campaign Lybrook advocated for changes to speed up the judicial process, according to a brief newspaper account. But he said that even if the pace is accelerated, the system must retain "fairness and justice." But Indiana trended strongly Democratic in 1970 and most top statewide offices were captured by Democrats. Lybrook was one of several unsuccessful Republican candidates in the November election. It was the same election that gave voters the opportunity to create a merit-based court of appeals and potentially represented the final time voters would elect appellate judges in Indiana.

After final approval from the voters to amend the Indiana Constitution in November 1970, the newly constituted Court of Appeals of Indiana was expanded from eight seats to nine seats. Whitcomb tapped Lybrook to fill that ninth seat. He took office January 1, 1972, and was retained in the November election in 1974 for a ten-year term.

It does not appear that Lybrook worked on any cases during his brief first term. During his second tenure, however, he participated in more than 400 cases and dissented in just one, *Rayburn v. Eisen* in 1975. In that case he disagreed with his "learned colleagues" decision to uphold a change of venue motion.

Lybrook retired on September 30, 1979, several years short of a full term. Then sixty-five he could have served until he was seventy-five but said "it's time for retirement now." As for his reasons, he said simply, "I live on a lake near a golf course. I will read a lot and go to Florida in the winter."

Lybrook died August 3, 1981, at age sixty-seven. He had been ill since April and been at Methodist Hospital in Indianapolis for the prior three weeks. In his memorial obituary, his colleagues described him as a "patient, quiet, courteous, unassuming man who daily demonstrated his innate sense of fairness, coupled with a great and good sense of humor and a warm and friendly personality." A newspaper editorial noted that "Judge Lybrook had such a gracious personality that it was a pleasure to talk to him, even when he disagreed with you. You found yourself welcoming a word from him, though it might be a rebuke."

Selected Bibliography

Anderson Herald, November 1, 1970.
Columbus Republic, July 2, 1979; August 5, 1981.
Franklin Daily Journal, June 18, September 17, 1970.
In Memoriam. https://www.in.gov/judiciary/appeals/files/bios-hist-lybrook-robert.pdf.
Indianapolis News, November 5, 1970, August 4, 1981, September 1, 1979.
Nashville Brown County Democrat, June 18, 1970.
Remondini, Dave. E-mail exchange with Robert Lybrook (son of Judge Lybrook), August 23, 2019.
Reporter-Times, August 5, 1981.

CASE CITED
Rayburn v. Eisen, 336 N.E.2d 392 (1975).

INDIANA SUPREME COURT

JONATHAN J. ROBERTSON

January 1, 1971–December 31, 1997 • Senior Judge: January 1, 1998–October 13, 2008

JOHN G. BAKER

Jonathan J. Robertson II, who served on the Court of Appeals of Indiana from 1971 through 2008, approached life and law with a twinkle in his eye. A self-described "lovable curmudgeon," he dedicated his career to public service, viewed his work through a lens of fairness, and remained firmly rooted in his southern Indiana community.

In 1954 Robertson received a bachelor of science degree from Indiana University and shortly thereafter he joined the U.S. Army. After leaving the army in 1956, Robertson returned home to Seymour and worked on the family farm. When a nearby river flooded so badly that it ruined all of their crops, Robertson took it as a sign to make a new life for himself. He moved to Nashville, Tennessee, and attended law school at Vanderbilt University, graduating in 1961.

Robertson returned to Seymour with his new law degree. He entered private practice, served as county prosecutor for two years, and served as attorney for the Indiana House of Representatives. In 1965 Robertson was elected Jackson County circuit court judge. He disliked the campaigning process, noting that he had "knocked on every door in the county" and had to have his shoes resoled twice.

Realizing that he did not enjoy being a trial judge, in 1970 he once again prepared to make a major change. He decided to move to Florida, going so far as to take the Florida bar examination. Before he made the move, however, the Indiana Democratic State Chairman contacted Robertson and suggested that he run for the appellate court. He decided to enter the race in what would be the last year the Appellate Court of Indiana, as it was then known, was open to partisan elections.

Robertson still firmly disliked campaigning, musing that the statewide campaign "was about as bad a thing as I ever got into," and estimating that he drove about 8,000 or 9,000 miles in a three-month period as part of the campaign. He won the election and was glad to have succeeded, but "sometimes when the snow is about knee-deep around here," he would think, "man, I like Florida." He was retained on the court by retention elections in 1974, 1984, and 1994.

Robertson began his Court of Appeals of Indiana tenure in 1971. He never moved to Indianapolis, believing that because he was elected from Seymour, he should live in Seymour. Three to four days a week, he would leave his home around 6:00 a.m. and arrive in Indianapolis by 8:00 a.m. From 1975 to 1978, when Robertson was chief judge, he tried to make the trip to Indianapolis every day because he "was worried that something would happen and I wouldn't be there." He used the driving time to mull over cases, frequently arriving at his destination prepared to make notes on a nearby legal pad.

Early in his tenure, the caseload was light and the cases were easy. Nevertheless, Robertson wryly observed that because their drafts required nine copies using carbon paper and manual typewriters, the typists "had arms on them like the Green Bay Packers" because they had to strike the keys so forcefully.

He noted with regret that there was a significant partisan divide on the court of appeals, complicated by big personalities and clashing egos. According to Robertson, "I think I am the only guy that can truthfully say that

I've been friends with every judge I have worked with." When the court of appeals redistricted to have three districts of three judges each, he was on a panel with Joe W. Lowdermilk and Robert B. Lybrook. The three became lifelong friends and met each afternoon for coffee, which both solidified their friendship and improved their efficiency at work.

At one time the most prolific judge in Court of Appeals of Indiana history, he approached every case seeking to achieve fairness. He credited his drive for fairness to the community he was from, the way he was raised, and the people in his life, using the "sum total of life's experiences" to work through every appellate case he encountered.

Deciding to leave when he was still at the top of his game, Robertson retired from the court in November 1997. He continued to serve as a senior judge for the court of appeals and as a senior trial court judge for ten years. Looking back, Robertson was grateful that he became a court of appeals judge rather than move to Florida, feeling a sense of pride in his "productive public service."

Robertson died on October 13, 2008, survived by his wife, Virginia, children, Joseph, Jonathan J. III, and Jill, and grandchildren. He is remembered for his easy laugh, his commonsense, and his quiet decades of public service.

Selected Bibliography

Nixon, William. Interview with Judge Robertson, October 6, 2000 (on file with the Court of Appeals of Indiana).

PHOTO FROM COURT OF INTERNATIONAL TRADE

ROBERT H. STATON

January 1, 1971–March 15, 2000 • Senior Judge: March 16, 2000–January 25, 2006

MARGRET G. ROBB

Calligraphy, the art of beautiful writing "in an expressive, harmonious and skillful manner," is not a form of communication that receives much attention or respect in our e-mail, text-messaging, 280-character tweeting obsessed age. Let it be noted that Judge Robert H. Staton was, perhaps, one of the last dedicated practitioners and a fervent devotee of this ancient art that provides a clue into the character and personality that illuminated his professional life. Calligraphy, in many respects, was illustrative of the carefully chosen words he employed to communicate his strongly held beliefs throughout his distinguished career.

Calligraphy is an apt metaphor for the care and precision Staton brought to his work, and more important to his life. He was an exemplar of the knowledgeable man of strong convictions whom Henry David Thoreau memorialized in *Walden*, as one who "does not keep pace with his companion . . . because he hears a different drummer."

Staton marched to a different drummer, but he was by no means an iconoclast, as his more than 3,000 appellate decisions testify. Like his calligraphy they are purposefully written, beautifully crafted models of forensic logic and rhetoric that reflect a love of language, clear thinking, and eloquence. However, the judge was also a practical man whose different drummer knew the value of law and public service for the benefit of society.

In many ways Staton's judgment and strongly held opinions were defined by his lifelong study of the classics, his intellectual curiosity, his respect for reason, and his strongly held belief that a reputation takes years to earn but can be lost in a moment of carelessness. He was not a man who closeted himself in an ivory tower but was fully engaged with the world.

Born in Indianapolis in 1925, Staton joined the military at eighteen and served with distinction in the U.S. Army during World War II, achieving the rank of major. A modest man, few people knew that he was awarded the Silver Star, the Distinguished Flying Cross, and two Bronze Stars. He was a participant in the Battle of Anzio, an experience that never left him. On his return to civilian life, he earned an undergraduate degree from Indiana University in Bloomington in 1952, and a law degree from Indiana University at Indianapolis in 1955. After serving as Marion County deputy prosecuting attorney and then chief trial deputy, he entered private practice and continued to look for other ways to serve.

In 1966 he ran for the congressional seat from Indiana's Tenth District, and although he lost the election, it did lead to his subsequent election in November 1970 to the Appellate Court of Indiana. This was the last year in which appellate judges were elected by popular vote. He campaigned by walking across the state meeting with prospective voters in every county—not all of whom were welcoming. Subsequently, Staton was retained for three terms and served until his retirement in 2000.

In addition to serving as judge, he immersed himself in professional matters. Over the years he served as the first editor of *Res Gestae*, the Indiana Bar Association journal, and authored several state legal histories. A believer in the importance of lifelong learning, Staton was a driving force in making Continuing Legal Education for lawyers mandatory and in 1986, with the approval of the Indiana Supreme Court, he was named First Chairman of Indiana's Commission of Continuing Legal Education.

After retirement, he served as president of the IU Alumni Association and completed a term on the Executive Council from 2004 to 2007. In a fitting tribute, the IU Robert H. McKinney School of Law Moot Court competition was named in his honor. He was also designated a Life Honorary Editor of the *Indiana Law Review* and was a twice recognized as a Sagamore of the Wabash.

Held in high esteem by scores of clerks he has mentored over the years, it is worth remembering that at a time when women law clerks simply did not exist, the judge not only hired the court of appeals first female law clerk, but selected a second female clerk for his chambers before any other appeals judge hired a first. It should not come as a surprise that his two daughters chose to follow their father's lead and become attorneys themselves. Staton lived what Socrates described as a full and meaningful life. He was devoted to his family, his profession, and his service to others. Not a bad legacy.

Selected Bibliography

Montgomery, Jenny. "Former Appellate Court Judge Dies." *Indiana Lawyer*, July 21, 2011.

———. "Former Clerks Recall a Judge Who Gave Support and Kindness." *Indiana Lawyer*, August 3, 2011.

Robert H. Staton obituary, https://www.legacy.com/obituaries/indystar/obituary.aspx?n=robert-h-staton&pid=152674563.

Staton, Robert H., and Gina M. Hicklin. "The History of the Court of Appeals of Indiana." *Indiana Law Review* 30, no. 1 (1997): 203–31

Much of this essay is based on firsthand knowledge of Judge Staton, who was a mentor and friend for more than twenty years, and by his many close friends who knew him personally and professionally over the course of his life and cherished his friendship.

PAUL H. BUCHANAN JR.

January 1, 1971–January 6, 1993

JAMES S. KIRSCH

Paul H. Buchanan Jr. served as Judge of the Court of Appeals of Indiana for twenty-two years, from 1971 to 1993, and as Chief Judge of the Court of Appeals for nine of those years. He left the bench upon reaching the mandatory retirement age of seventy-five, the first appellate judge in Indiana to retire by statute.

During his tenure, Buchanan authored more than 2,000 opinions. In his opinion writing he was committed to "brevity, clarity, and forcefulness" and was known for the format he developed for writing opinions that divided them into four main parts: Case Summary, Statement of Facts, Legal Issues, and Decision. He wrote an article in the *Journal of the American Bar Association* in 1976 advocating this structure as the best way to write an opinion, and his approach was referenced in other legal journals.

Born in Indianapolis on January 6, 1918, to Paul H. Sr., and Ruth Geiger Buchanan, he was a graduate of Park School, Swarthmore College, and the

University of Denver Law School. Prior to the United States' entry into World War II, he joined the navy and served three years in the Pacific theater, finishing his service with the rank of lieutenant, junior grade.

From 1949 to 1955 Buchanan was a sole practitioner in Indianapolis specializing in the areas of tax law and real estate transactions. In 1955 he and Lewis Bose, a former classmate at Swarthmore, founded Cook Bose and Buchanan. In 1969 Buchanan was elected president of the Indianapolis Bar Association, and, a year later, he founded and became president of the Indianapolis Bar Foundation.

Buchanan ran for the Court of Appeals of Indiana in 1970, the last year that partisan elections were held for Indiana's appellate courts. He was the only Republican to be elected that year to a statewide office.

Buchanan was a lecturer at the distinguished lecturer program at the Indiana University School of Law-Indianapolis, now the McKinney School of Law, and received Citations of Merit from the American Bar Association and the Indiana State Bar Association. He was a member of the board of directors of the American Judicature Society, the House of Delegates of the American Bar Association, the board of managers of the Indiana State Bar Association, and the Indiana Supreme Court Disciplinary Commission. He also was counsel to and member of the board of directors of the Washington Park Cemetery Association and Flanner and Buchanan.

Beginning in 1969, for three decades Buchanan wrote "Ex Parte Line," a monthly column about lawyers and courts that appeared in *Res Gestae* magazine, the monthly publication of the Indiana State Bar Association. He also published in the *National Law Review* and numerous state bar publications.

A frequent guest speaker across the state he served on several boards of directors, including the Indianapolis Junior Chamber of Commerce (Jaycees), Meridian Street United Methodist Church, Methodist Hospital, Contemporary Club of Indianapolis, Indiana State Symphony Society, Wabash College, Greater Indianapolis Progress Committee, Columbia Club, and the Columbia Club Foundation. He was also a lifetime trustee of the Indianapolis Museum of Art.

Buchanan was honored as a Sagamore of the Wabash by Governors Otis R. Bowen and Mitchell E. Daniels. He was awarded an honorary doctor of laws degree from Wabash College and also the David Warner Peck Award for eminence in the law.

Other honors include the distinguished service award of the Disciplinary Commission of the Indiana Supreme Court, the extraordinary service award from the Indiana State Bar Association for "Ex Parte Line," the Award of Past Presidents of the Downtown Kiwanis Club of Indianapolis, and the Benjamin Harrison Medallion from the Columbia Club.

Buchanan inherited a love of art from his mother and collected paintings, primarily from the Hudson River School, Brown County artists, and many works of Asian origin. He was also the proud owner of portraits of George and Martha Washington painted by Rembrandt Peale.

Buchanan was the father of three children: Brian, Bruce, and Lucinda Buchanan Pfeifer and was the stepfather of Melissa Mau and Mark Flint, the children of his wife, Ruth. He was a grandson of the founder of Flanner and Buchanan Funeral Centers, a family-owned business since its founding in downtown Indianapolis in 1881. His father, Paul Buchanan Sr., followed the family tradition into the funeral business, and his two sons are the fourth generation of their family to be involved in the ownership of Flanner and Buchanan.

A gentleman, scholar, prolific author, respected lawyer, distinguished judge, and noted art collector, Paul H. Buchanan Jr. passed away on November 6, 2008.

Selected Bibliography

Buchanan, Paul H. "For structure, Digestible, Streamlined Judicial Opinions." *Journal of the American Bar Association* 60 (October 1974): 1249–51.

Paul H. Buchanan Obituary. Flanner & Buchanan Mortuary, Indianapolis, IN. https://www.legacy.com/obituaries/name/paul-buchanan-obituary?pid=178440773.

INDIANA SUPREME COURT

WILLIAM I. GARRARD

January 24, 1974–January 24, 2000 • Senior Judge: January 24, 2000–December 31, 2016

PAUL D. MATHIAS

William I. Garrard was born in Indianapolis on October 16, 1932, and raised in Frankfort, Indiana, graduating from Frankfort High School in 1950. He was an Eagle Scout and a 1954 graduate of Wabash College. He served as an enlisted soldier in the U.S. Army and was honorably discharged. After his army service he enrolled at the Indiana University School of Law in Bloomington. He distinguished himself by election to the Order of the Coif and graduated in 1959, with distinction.

Garrard's first and only position in the private practice of law began in 1959 when he joined the Warsaw, Indiana, law firm of Graham, Rasor, Eschbach and Harris. There he practiced employment law and handled the firm's appellate work. He also added to his responsibilities the role of deputy prosecutor and continued in that capacity for the next ten years. During his fifteen-year career in private practice Garrard took two cases to the appellate courts in behalf of clients that resulted in modifications of Indiana law. One dealt with a quadriplegic who was injured in a diving accident. Initially denied compensation by the trial court that verdict was overturned by the Court of Appeals of Indiana. He was later awarded compensation in a second trial after a change in Indiana law.

In the second case the state's laws on workmen's compensation were changed when Garrard's client, a widow whose husband was killed when hit by a Penn Central train was denied benefits. Although the court of appeals agreed with the lower court's ruling, the Indiana Supreme Court upheld the widow's claim and state law changed allowing her to recover benefits for herself and her children.

Away from his practice, Garrard was the extremely happy father of two daughters and one son. He was an avid outdoorsman who hunted and fished throughout the country. Many of his hunting and fishing trophies decorated the walls of his office in the Indiana Statehouse.

When Garrard was appointed to the Court of Appeals of Indiana by Governor Otis R. Bowen in 1974, he was one of the earliest appointees after the 1970 amendment to Indiana's Constitution that ended the partisan election of judges to the appeals court and Supreme Court. His opinions became known as "Garrard Opinions" because of their directness, lucidity, and brevity. He authored several opinions of note. Among them is the 1976 case *Wilson v. State*, which adopted the procedure and law of the federal courts concerning the proper use in Indiana trial courts of machine-made document copies. He also authored the 1985 opinion in *Cassellman v. State* establishing Indiana's "Castle Doctrine," thereby providing a measure of legal protection for homeowners who resist unlawful entry to their homes by law enforcement officers. Garrard's work was also mentioned in or the subject of several articles in the multivolume *American Law Reports*, a well-respected resource used by attorneys and judges to learn about the history and public policy behind current law. During his time on the court he was an adjunct professor at the Maurer School of law for ten years.

Garrard was a leader and an example to his colleagues. According to Judge James S. Kirsch he was known on the court for his "bright and open mind and for his thoughtfulness." Kirsch said Garrard was admired by colleagues both for his work and for his work ethic. Judge John G. Baker recalls that Garrard was known as an "intellect" and "Renaissance Man" who was extremely well-read, especially in history and jurisprudence. Baker and other judges enjoyed many instructive discussions with him about the law and the philosophy behind it.

Garrard also expanded the role of court of appeals judges beyond decision making. He was the first to become involved with the Indiana Continuing Legal Education Forum and presented there many times. He was also the court's first judge to obtain a master of laws degree from the University of Virginia. His example led several more judges and one justice to Virginia's preeminent legal studies program.

Among the many distinctions Garrard earned during his career are the David W. Peck Award for Eminence in the Law and the Frederick Urbaska Award for Civil Service, both awarded by his alma mater, Wabash College. He was also awarded the Sagamore of the Wabash, Indiana's highest award, by three Indiana governors. In addition, Garrard was inducted into the Indiana University School of Law Academy of Law Alumni Fellows in 2000.

Garrard proudly served his fellow Hoosiers on the court of appeals for twenty-six years before his retirement in 2000, as well as for an additional sixteen years as a senior judge on the court. He is married to retired Court of Appeals Judge Linda L. Chezem.

Selected Bibliography

Baker, John G. Telephone interview with author, Indiana, June 19, 2019.
Garrard, William I. Telephone interview with author, June 12, 2018.
Kirsch, James S. Telephone interview with author, June 20, 2019.
Lemon, Thomas R. Telephone interview with author, May 18, 2019.
"Name Local Attorney Garrard Indiana Appeals Court Judge. *Wabash Times Union*, December 27, 1993.
Wabash College 2018–2019 Academic Bulletin, Prizes and Awards. (June 19, 2019), http://bulletin.wabash.edu/scholarships/prizes-awards/.

CASES CITED

Cassellman v. State, 472 N.E. 2d 1310 (Ind. App. 1985).
Wilson v. State, 348 N.E. 2d 90 (Ind. App. 1976).

INDIANA SUPREME COURT

VIVIAN SUE SHIELDS

July 1, 1978–January 27, 1994

DORIA LYNCH

A legend in Indiana's legal profession, Vivian Sue Shields was the lone female graduate in her law school class (1961), Indiana's first female trial court judge (1964), the first woman to serve on the Court of Appeals of Indiana (1978), and the first woman to be appointed as a federal magistrate judge in Indiana (1994). Throughout the course of her legal career, she went where no other woman had gone before and laid a path that many female attorneys have since trodden.

Vivian Sue Blodgett was born in Wilmore, Kentucky, on January 17, 1939. She graduated from high school in 1955 and enrolled at Ball State University in August of that year, at the age of sixteen. While she had originally intended to study nursing, Shields pursued a degree in government and history instead. She enrolled at the Indiana University School of Law in the fall of 1958 and graduated three years later as a member of the Order of the Coif.

After marrying fellow law student William Shields in September 1961, Vivian sought employment in a profession that was not accommodating of women. Following an interview with a law firm in Chicago, she was told, "that I was very well qualified but, unfortunately, I could not be considered as an associate because they did not have appropriate restroom facilities for a female associate." Following a brief stint with the Internal Revenue Service in Cincinnati, Shields began working at the Indiana Attorney General's Office in January 1962. Concerned that Attorney General Ed Steers would be voted out of office in the 1964 elections and that she would lose her job as a result, she decided that the best way to secure employment would be to run for a new judgeship on the Hamilton County Superior Court. At the age of twenty-five she defeated a heavily favored opponent in the Republican primary and ran unopposed in November; when she took office on January 1, 1965, she was the first female trial court judge in Indiana.

While on the Hamilton County bench, Shields had two sons, one in 1969 and one in 1971. In 1977 she applied for a justiceship on the Indiana Supreme Court, one of two unsuccessful attempts to become the first woman to serve that institution. In 1978 she applied for and was appointed by Governor Otis R. Bowen to the Court of Appeals of Indiana. When asked about her decision to pursue an elevation to the appeals court bench, Shields said, "One, I was disappointed I didn't get the Supreme Court, and I felt like I had to try again. That wasn't nearly as important as the fact that the kids were getting older and getting in more activities, and I wanted to be able to control my schedule." While on the court of appeals, Shields authored numerous opinions and was widely recognized for her contributions to family law cases. In *Stout v. Tippecanoe County Department of Public Welfare* Shields wrote that the final responsibility in granting an adoption rests with the trial court based upon the best interests of the child. In *In re Adoption of Infant Hewitt*, Shields's opinion held that the Indiana statute that permitted but did not require consent of a birth parent to an adoption was not an unconstitutional interference with parental rights.

On October 13, 1993, then-Chief Judge Gene E. Brooks of the U.S. District Court for the Southern District of Indiana announced that the court had selected Shields to replace retiring Magistrate Judge J. Patrick Endsley. Continuing with the trend that she had established for herself in law school, Shields became the first woman to take on this position. In her new position, Shields found that she enjoyed working directly with lawyers and their clients, spending much of her time in settlement conferences and in the discovery stages of federal lawsuits. In the multidistrict litigation case involving Bridgestone/Firestone Inc. tires and Ford Motor Company, Shields successfully negotiated numerous settlements among the parties and organized complex discovery issues among plaintiffs from multiple countries and across the United States. She did the same in thousands of other cases during her time as a magistrate judge.

Shields retired in January 2007, wrapping up a career of forty-two years on the bench. She currently resides in Texas.

Selected Bibliography

DeLaney, Kathleen. "Highly Decorated 'Traffic Cop' to Retire from Federal Bench." *Res Gestae* 50, no. 2 (2006): 11–12.

"In the Matter of the Installation of Judge V. Sue Shields as United States Magistrate Judge." Transcript by D. R. Oesterreich, January 28, 1994. U.S. District Court for the Southern District of Indiana.

Shields, Vivian Sue. "Challenges: Past, Present & Future." Antoinette Dakin Leach Award Acceptance Speech, Indianapolis, IN, January 12, 1990. *Res Gestae* (June 1990).

Vivian Sue Shields. Interviews by Doria M. Lynch, July 14, 18, 21, 2006. Transcript, Indiana Historical Society William Henry Smith Memorial Library, Indianapolis.

Vivian Sue Shields. Interview by Douglas J. Hill, 2006. Transcript and video, Indiana Historical Society William Henry Smith Memorial Library, Indianapolis.

CASES CITED

Stout v. Tippecanoe County Department of Public Welfare, 395 N.E.2d 444 (Ind. Ct. App. 1979).

In re Adoption of Infant Hewitt, 396 N.E.2d 938 (Ind. Ct. App. 1979).

RAKESTRAW FAMILY COLLECTION

EUGENE N. CHIPMAN SR.

August 1, 1978–October 26, 1981

MARK A. BATES

Governor Otis R. Bowen said it was "not hard" to appoint Eugene Nelson Chipman Sr. to the newly created Fourth District Court of Appeals of Indiana. And it was "not hard" for Chipman to leave the court and return to his hometown to the trial career and people he loved. Still enjoying life in Plymouth, Indiana, Chipman retired where his legal career began many years ago.

Chipman was born on December 1, 1927, in Plymouth. His father, Albert, was a lawyer who became the circuit court judge that same year. Eugene went to Plymouth High School for two years, but transferred to Culver Military Academy when his parents moved to Washington, DC. The elder Chipman wanted to serve in the military after America entered World War II, but he was considered too old. Instead, he became a military lawyer in the court of claims. Culver was an ideal solution to the problem caused by the move: the younger Chipman could finish high school and board there as well. He attended Culver for two years and graduated in 1945. He excelled at track and rowing and Culver named him to its inaugural Athletic Hall of Fame.

Chipman attended the University of Michigan for one year and studied engineering. He was appointed to the U.S. Naval Academy, where he received honorable mention as All American for rowing. He graduated in 1950 and was stationed in Norfolk, Virginia, with his young family. Chipman flew planes in the Atlantic Squadron's antisubmarine unit for six years.

There was a push to get servicemen into law school and the Indiana University School of Law in Bloomington (today the Maurer School of Law) recruited Chipman. He graduated in 1959 and returned to Plymouth to practice law with his father. The escalating tension during the Cold War saw Chipman recalled to active duty in Seattle, Washington. He piloted planes along the West Coast while spotters kept a lookout for Soviet submarines. A mysterious shadow that was spotted one day turned out to be a whale. According to Chipman, there was "no engagement with that enemy."

Chipman returned to Plymouth after he successfully ran for prosecutor while still serving in Washington. His two-year term began in 1963 and he was reelected twice. The part-time prosecutor's position allowed Chipman to continue practicing law with his father. Chipman and his wife, Ida, were involved in local politics and Ida served as campaign manager for Bowen's first run as governor. They had a close relationship with Bowen, who appointed Albert Chipman as the first judge on the Marshall Superior Court.

Due to the huge backlog of cases, the legislature created a Fourth District Court of Appeals of Indiana and Chipman, James B. Young, and Stanley B. Miller were the first appointees. They began on August 1, 1978, and their district encompassed all of Indiana. Chipman enjoyed oral arguments and was instrumental in holding them throughout the state, not just in Indianapolis. It continues today as "Appeals on Wheels." He also promoted the use of visual aids in the courtroom. This was best reflected in Chipman's decision whereby Indiana adopted the "silent witness" theory for the admission of photographic evidence at trial.

Chipman tired of sleeping on a cot in his office during the week and driving home to Plymouth each weekend. After three years of reading transcripts, Chipman realized he missed the excitement and challenge of trial work. As his law clerk described it, "Chip" (he urged his clerks to call him that) preferred to make law in the courtroom and not from the bench.

After retiring, Chipman returned to Plymouth on October 26, 1981, and went into practice with his namesake, who had graduated from Valparaiso Law School. Three generations of Chipmans could now boast of a law practice in the community. Chipman ran and served for one term as judge of the Marshall Superior Court and sat as a county commissioner twice. Marshall County was growing in population and much of Chipman's work as a commissioner involved the construction of new roads.

An avid golfer and bridge player, Chipman also enjoyed flying private planes, woodworking, and leatherworking. Although age limits his activities, Chipman still enjoys spending time with his family and friends in Plymouth. His life and career have truly come full circle.

Selected bibliography

Chipman, Eugene Nelson Sr. Interview with the author, June 5, 2019.
Dilts, Jon P. Interview with the author, May 29, 2019.
Franklin Daily Journal, June 9, 1978.
South Bend Tribune, May 24, 1973.
Website, Culver Academies Athletic Hall of Fame 1994 Inductees.

CASES CITED

Bergner v. State, 397 N.E.2d 1012 (Ind. Ct. App. 1979).

INDIANA SUPREME COURT

STANLEY B. MILLER

August 1, 1978–June 20, 1994

RUTH D. REICHARD

Judge Stanley B. Miller lived a life distinguished by community engagement and public service, but that service garnered enmity as well as accolades. His primary allegiance was to the law as he interpreted it, and if sometimes his opinions or demeanor rendered him unpopular, he did not waver.

Law and order was in Miller's DNA—his father, William B. Miller, was an attorney who, as a young deputy prosecutor, helped obtain a murder conviction against infamous Ku Klux Klan Grand Dragon D. C. Stephenson in 1925. Although Stanley died at the relatively young age of sixty-five, he lived long enough to see one of his sons, Gary, become a trial court judge. Introducing Gary at his son's swearing-in ceremony in January 1991, Stanley alluded to his own lack of popularity, noting that Gary had received a higher rating from the Indianapolis Bar Association: "I cannot tell you how pleased I was to have my son rated higher than I was." Miller kept his sense of humor intact throughout his sixteen-year tenure on the bench. His former law clerk, Frank C. Capozza, praised the judge's good humor in his obituary and said that "When you nailed him (with a joke), he'd just get this big grin."

Born on April 23, 1929, in Indianapolis, Miller graduated from Butler University in 1949 and from Indiana University School of Law in Indianapolis in 1953. He gained admission to the bar that same year. A veteran of the Korean Conflict, Miller served in the U.S. Army Counter Intelligence Corps. He married Mary Elinor Zendell on January 29, 1956, in Indianapolis. Miller was a joiner: He belonged to organizations ranging from Sigma Alpha Mu and Phi Alpha Delta in college and law school, to the Veterans of Foreign Wars, the Monument Masonic Lodge, the Bureau of Jewish Education, where he served on the board, Congregation Beth-El Zedeck, where he taught religious school, and even the American Right of Way Association, for which he served as vice president.

Miller served the public for much of his professional life, beginning his career as a state deputy attorney general from 1955 to 1965, and then moving to the Marion County Prosecutor's Office, where he worked as both a deputy prosecuting attorney and chief counsel. Acting upon recommendations by Marion County GOP Chairman L. Keith Bulen, Indiana state Republican chair Buena Chaney, and Indiana governor Edgar D. Whitcomb, President Richard M. Nixon nominated Miller to serve as the U.S. Attorney for the Southern District of Indiana in 1969. As the top federal prosecutor for Indianapolis and southern Indiana, Miller's name frequently appeared in the news over the course of his term, which ended on January 1, 1975, when Miller resigned from the court citing a federal pay freeze as his reason.

Miller's timing was fortuitous. In 1970 voters had ratified a new judicial article in the Indiana Constitution that overhauled the state's appellate court. The measure featured merit selection and yes/no retention by voters, and empowered the legislature to create new districts and judgeships for the court as a whole, when warranted by population and caseload. The Indiana General Assembly created three new judgeships in 1978 to help the court resolve a backlog of 800 cases, and Miller applied. The Judicial Nominating Commission sent Miller's name along with those of two sitting Marion County trial court judges for the new spot in the Second Judicial District and Governor Otis R. Bowen announced his selection of Miller June 9, 1978.

Miller began his tenure on August 1, 1978. Only three years later, the *Indianapolis Star* reported attorneys' dissatisfaction with the court of appeals as a whole and with Miller in particular—he scored the lowest ranking of his colleagues. One attorney wondered if Miller's rating was due to the fact that he was the court's only Jewish member. Yet Miller persevered; his rulings made the news occasionally, as did his sparring with the Marion County Prosecutor during oral arguments on an obscenity case. Miller's sense of fairness remained strong and extended to the treatment of others. When a U.S. attorney was anonymously criticized in the *Star*, he and two other jurists wrote a letter to the editor defending him.

After Miller's untimely passing in 1994 Chief Justice Randall T. Shepard remarked that his colleagues were "very much sad of heart" upon learning the news. Miller never retired—he worked until the end of his life and died a public servant. He produced nearly 800 opinions during his tenure on the court, the last as forthright and lucid as the first.

Selected Bibliography

Barker, Sarah Evans, Stanley B. Miller, and James E. Young, letter to the editor. *Indianapolis Star*, June 7, 1984.

Farmer, James E. "Indiana Modernizes Its Courts," *Judicature* 54, no. 8 (March 1971): 327–30.

Pulliam, Myrta. "Inconsistency is main criticism of state's appeals court judges." *Indianapolis Star*, May 18, 1981.

"Stanley B. Miller was an appeals judge and a former prosecutor." *Indianapolis Star*, June 21, 1994.

Traub, Patrick J. "Judges get their turn to swear." *Indianapolis Star*, January 1, 1991.

"U.S. Attorney Stanley B. Miller Quits, Citing Federal Pay Freeze." *Indianapolis Star*, January 1, 1975.

INDIANA SUPREME COURT

JAMES B. YOUNG

August 1, 1978–August 31, 1988

FRANK SULLIVAN JR.

James B. Young achieved success and won acclaim as a courtroom lawyer, state legislator, federal prosecutor, and appellate judge. He was independent and outspoken, he suffered from serious health problems, and his career ended in misfortune.

Born in Kankakee, Illinois, in 1928, Young graduated from Franklin College, served in the U.S. Army Counter Intelligence Corps during the Korean War, and earned his law degree from the Indiana University Maurer School of Law. He practiced law in Johnson County beginning in 1955 along with highly capable partners, including Richard W. Vandivier and Stephen L. Huddleston. Young was a venue lawyer of preference, handling highly publicized cases, including that of an Indianapolis Motor Speedway security guard run over by the pace car during the 1971 Indianapolis 500.

Young was elected to the state senate in 1966 from Johnson and Bartholomew Counties after defeating incumbent Republican senator John R. Rees in the primary. He was described as "fast and smart," handling a wide variety of legislative measures and was voted best freshman senator in 1967. Of enduring importance, Young was the Senate Republican sponsor of the constitutional amendment that provided for merit selection of Indiana's appellate judiciary and restructuring the state's judicial discipline process.

Young supported the plan of Republican House Speaker Otis R. Bowen to raise state taxes in 1969 to produce revenue for property tax relief. To Republican governor Edgar D. Whitcomb, any tax increase was anathema. Property tax relief was defeated in the 1969 legislature and Young was defeated at Whitcomb's behest in the 1970 Republican primary by Robert D. Garton.

Bowen was elected governor in 1972 and he hired Young to be his principal lobbyist in the Indiana Senate. Their plan of comprehensive property tax relief and school finance restructuring that passed in 1973 would remain the state's basic fiscal structure for thirty-five years.

From 1975 until 1977, Young served as U.S. Attorney for the Southern District of Indiana. He embraced the position with relish and enthusiasm, and he gave the office strength and stability at the top by promoting Sarah Evans Barker, a junior lawyer in the office, to be his first assistant. For Barker it was a critical step to her later being appointed U.S. attorney in 1981 and Federal District Court Judge in 1984.

In 1978 the general assembly expanded the Court of Appeals of Indiana from nine to twelve judges and Bowen appointed Young to the court effective August 1. He was retained in office by the voters in 1980.

As a judge, the former federal prosecutor appears to have had no reluctance to reverse a criminal conviction when the circumstances required. Ruling on how a judge is to handle a deadlocked jury in *Lewis v. State*, Young deployed a Model Jury Instruction developed by the American Bar Association. In *Allen v. Review Board of Indiana Employment Secretary,* he authored a noteworthy decision awarding unemployment compensation to strikers who unconditionally offered to return to work but had been replaced. Young's opinion in *Public Service Indiana, Inc. v. Nichols* awarded substantial damages to farmers whose dairy herd had been ruined by leakage from high-voltage power lines. His independence showed itself, too, when he defied Chief Justice Randall T. Shepard and the legal establishment in opposing a constitutional amendment to reduce the Indiana Supreme Court's criminal caseload.

Young's most notable opinion on the Court was *4447 Corp. v. Goldsmith*, holding that enjoining the operation of two adult bookstores without any determination as to the obscenity of their merchandise was an unconstitutional prior restraint in violation of the First Amendment. Young wrote: "[W]e are mindful of the current climate of opinion and of political pressures to close adult bookstores and similar establishments. It is the function of this and other courts, however, to insulate basic constitutional guarantees from the temporary vagaries of political expediency and from the vicissitudes of public opinion." While Young's opinion was reversed by the Indiana Supreme Court, his holding as to prior restraint was affirmed by the U.S. Supreme Court.

Young's career came to an end in an unimaginable way. He had been the victim of poor health for many years, including suffering a major heart attack in 1972 and having had open-heart surgery in 1983. Five weeks after major abdominal surgery in August 1987, he was charged with indecent exposure at an adult bookstore. While the charge was dismissed, in return for the dismissal Young completed the term of a first offender program. The Commission on Judicial Qualifications, however, sought to remove him from the bench and he resigned. He later moved to Florida, where he resumed law practice but was stricken by another heart attack and died on August 28, 1998, at the age of seventy.

Described as a "strong-minded, independent stickler for the law," Young made major contributions to Indiana law in all three branches of government and as a private practitioner.

Selected Bibliography

Indianapolis News, February 13, 1967, January 1, 1969, June 26, 1975, February 7, 1975, April 26, 1977, September 24, 1981, March 31, 1984, February 17, August 8, November 12, 1988

Indianapolis Star, March 5, November 10, 1966, February 22, September 23, 1967, February 11, 1968, March 10, 11, 1969, November 26, 1972, April 11, 1973, February 17, 1974, February 9, 1975, March 3, 27, September 26, October 3, 1987, July 9, 1988, September 22, 1991, September 2, 1998.

Staton, Robert H., and Hicklin, Gina M. "The History of the Court of Appeals of Indiana." *Indiana Law Review* 30 (1997): 203, 219–20.

CASES CITED

4447 Corp. v. Goldsmith, 479 N.E.2d 578 (Ind. Ct. App. 1985), rev'd 504 N.E.2d 559 (Ind. 1987).

Allen v. Review Board of Indiana Employment Security Division, 494 N.E.2d 978 (Ind. Ct. App. 1986).

Lewis v. State, 409 N.E.2d 1276 (Ind. Ct. App. 1980), vacated, 424 N.E.2d 107 (Ind. 1981).

Public Service Indiana, Inc. v. Nichols, 494 N.E.2d 349 (Ind. Ct. App. 1986).

INDIANA SUPREME COURT

ROBERT W. NEAL

October 1, 1979–May 27, 1989

ANDREW P. SEIWERT

Robert W. Neal never forgot where he came from, because he never really left. He maintained traditional values and a strong belief in commonsense justice throughout his career. Neal believed that judges and other public officials should never lose their "common touch," that is, the empathy to relate to the everyday concerns of the citizens they served.

Born on a farm in rural Clay County, Indiana on May 14, 1924, he attended local schools, graduating from Clay City High School in 1941. He joined the army in 1942, rising to the rank of staff sergeant. He was wounded during the Battle of the Bulge when shrapnel from a grenade tore a hole in his cheek. He received a Purple Heart and a scar he would bear the rest of his life.

After being discharged from the army, he entered Indiana University in 1946, earning a bachelor's degree followed by a law degree from IU in

1951. While at IU, Neal met and married his wife, Margaret. They had three children, two daughters and a son.

After admission to the bar Neal joined the legal department of a Chicago insurance company but chafed under the strict office environment. Returning to Clay County, he opened a law office in Brazil in July of 1953. Neal also served on the school board and as a deputy prosecutor and, occasionally, as a judge pro tem. The highlight of his private-practice career occurred in 1966 when he obtained a $4 million jury verdict following a three-month trial, representing the plaintiff in a gas explosion. The framed jury verdict was displayed in his offices the rest of his career.

On August 31, 1970, Neal was appointed judge of the Clay Circuit Court by Governor Edgar D. Whitcomb when the prior judge died in office. Although the previous judge's term had not ended, Neal was required to run in the next general election to continue serving. He ran unopposed and began his six-year term on January 1, 1971. He was reelected in 1976. He once observed that a major issue with courts is their "seeming inability to dispense justice with dispatch." That was not an issue as long as he was a judge. A firm believer in the adage that "justice delayed is justice denied," Neal never forgot that a judge's decisions have a direct impact on people's lives. He also took a dim view of judicial activism when judges depart from following precedent in favor of progressive social policies.

Neal was appointed to the Court of Appeals of Indiana in 1979 by Governor Otis R. Bowen, to replace the retired Robert B. Lybrook in the First District. His appellate tenure coincided with his fellow judges of the First District, Wesley W. Ratliff and Jonathan J. Robertson. They enjoyed each other's company, lunching together whenever possible. The judges placed a premium on achieving unanimity in their decisions; it was not uncommon for them to visit one another's office to personally discuss an issue or particular language in an opinion. As a result dissents were extremely rare.

In his nine-year, eight-month tenure he wrote 923 majority opinions, an average of almost two a week, not counting the occasional concurring and dissenting opinion, and this was before computers. Opinions were written in longhand and later typewritten.

Neal's opinions reflected his directness. In *Shatto v. McNulty*, a couple built a house next to a long-standing pig farm and later sued to have the operation declared a nuisance, Neal affirmed the denial. "Pork production generates odors" he said, "which cannot be prevented, and so long as the human race consumes pork, someone must tolerate the smell."

In *Conn v. Conn* Neal expressed his view of judicial activism. In that case a wife sought an abortion without the consent of her husband. The husband obtained a temporary restraining order from a trial court, but the order was certified for an immediate appeal. Reversing the trial court, Neal cited the landmark abortion-rights case of *Roe v. Wade*, but noted "the moral concepts of abortion, as well as the assumption by the Supreme Court of the right to establish social policy, a function ordinarily reserved to legislative bodies, are troublesome to some members of this court, [but] . . . [o]ur duty consists only of applying the law."

Neal retired in 1989. He died on November 12, 2000, and was buried in Clay County.

Selected bibliography

Brazil Daily Times, June 5, 1971, April 12, 1974.
Annual Reports of the Indiana Court of Appeals, 1979–1989.
In Memoriam Resolution. Indiana Court of Appeals, January 8, 2001.

CASES CITED

Shatto v. McNulty, 509 N.E.2d 897, 900 (Ind. App. 1987).
Conn v. Conn, 525 N.E.2d 612, 616 (Ind. App. 1988)
Roe v. Wade, 410 U.S. 113 (1973).

WESLEY W. RATLIFF JR.

January 1, 1980–November 3, 1992 • Senior Judge: November 4, 1992–August 30, 2006

JOHN L. KELLAM

Wesley W. Ratliff Jr. led a life of dedication and service. He was born in Knightstown, Indiana, on September 21, 1925. His parents, Wesley Ratliff Sr. and Ruth Sherwood Ratliff, were both attorneys. Ratliff Jr. graduated from Knightstown High School and in 1943 joined the U.S. Navy, serving in the Pacific theater during World War II from 1943 to1946.

After finishing military service Ratliff earned his college degree from Ball State University and in 1950 his law degree from Valparaiso School of Law. He then joined his parents in their law practice in Knightstown for thirteen years. In 1953 he was appointed deputy prosecutor in Henry County.

His father was judge of the Henry Circuit Court from 1955 until his death in October 1961. In November 1962, Ratliff. was elected judge of the Henry Circuit Court and began his term on January 1, 1963. He served for seventeen years, not only as circuit judge, but also as a teacher and mentor for lawyers and fellow jurists. He was respected by the public. An editorial in the *New Castle Courier Times* in December 1979 said: "Judge Ratliff is first of all, a good lawyer. He knows the law, a fact which other lawyers recognized and consequently came to his court knowing what to count on. He is an outstanding jurist because of his knowledge of the law and the consequent ability to apply it to the circumstances at hand, but any observation of his court makes evident also that he has handled cases in a judicious manner."

In 1966 the Henry County Commissioners, acting upon a 110-signature petition filed by resident freeholders, increased Ratliff's annual salary from $14,500 to $18,500.

Ratliff was a proponent of courtroom decorum. He recessed a hearing in which this author was a participant and directed him to his chambers for a lecture regarding the evils of chewing gum in the courtroom. He knew he could be held in contempt, however, after learning that the judge himself chewed gum, but only in his office, he stocked his desk with Juicy Fruit gum.

Ratliff was appointed to the Court of Appeals of Indiana by Governor Otis R. Bowen and began his term January 1, 1980, upon the retirement of Joseph W. Lowdermilk. While serving on the court of appeals, Ratliff was presiding judge of the First District from 1982 to 1986. On January 1, 1987, he was elected by members of the court to serve as chief judge of the court for a term of three years, replacing Judge Paul H. Buchanan Jr. Ratliff retained the position of chief judge until his retirement in 1992. He was then a senior judge until his death.

In a personal assessment of his tenure on the court of appeals, Ratliff said in a 1985 interview in the *Courier Times* "There are lawyers out there making a 'helluva' lot more money than I am here, but I'm alright. I enjoy this work very much. I enjoyed my work on the circuit bench too but I enjoy this even more. I am using my legal training and experience at the very highest level where I am able to have some input and effect on the legal system." One of his decisions had a definite impact on Indiana law. That case involved a drunk driver who visited an Evansville bar and upon leaving, was involved in an automobile accident. Ratliff decided that the bartender who had served the driver too much alcohol could be held liable to the driver's victims.

Ratliff held many leadership roles related to the realm of Indiana law. Those included president, Henry County Bar Association; president, Indiana Judges Association; vice chair, Indiana Supreme Court Disciplinary Commission; executive board, Judicial Conference of Indiana; and chair, Indiana Judicial Study Commission.

He and his wife Mildred moved to Bloomington from Knightstown in 1987. While living in Bloomington and still sitting on the court of appeals, Ratliff served as an interim professor at Valparaiso School of Law.

Ratliff died August 30, 2006. He was survived by Mildred, his wife of fifty-nine years, by his daughters, Marilyn Ratliff Crum, an attorney in Evansville, Kathy Forbes, an attorney in Valparaiso, and his son, Doctor Wesley Ratliff III of Bloomington.

Selected Bibliography

Interview of Judge Wesley Ratliff, May 13, 1985.
Kellam, John. Personal recollections of Wesley Ratliff.
New Castle Courier Times, December 20, 1966, December 14, 1979.

GIVAN FAMILY COLLECTION

WILLIAM G. CONOVER

October 26, 1981–December 31, 1993 • Senior Judge: January 1, 1994–December 31, 1995

MARK A. BATES

Part of the "Valparaiso Invasion" of appellate judges in the early 1980s, Judge William G. Conover epitomized the conservative "establishment lawyer": military veteran, American Legion, Rotary Club, county prosecutor, GOP county chairman, and county bar association president. Conover called his appointment to the bench "the capstone of his legal career." As the fourth person appointed to the recently created Fourth District Court of Appeals of Indiana, Conover served the citizens of the state well.

Born April 26, 1925, in Valparaiso, Indiana, Conover was the only child of Doctor Garrett D. and Sadye Tapson Conover. After graduating from Valparaiso High School in 1943, Conover served during World War II with the U.S. Navy Seabees, the construction battalion, in the Pacific theater. He worked on projects on the islands of Tinian and Saipan, including building airfields on Tinian. These islands, lying approximately 1,500 miles from Japan, were captured from the Japanese in June and July of 1944. This put the B-29 bombers within striking distance of Japan. It was from Tinian that two bombers departed, carrying Little Boy and Fat Man, the atomic bombs that were dropped on Hiroshima and Nagasaki.

After receiving the navy's Good Conduct Medal, Conover was honorably discharged in 1946. He enrolled in Valparaiso University, graduating with a bachelor of arts degree in 1949 and a law degree from Valparaiso Law School in 1951. Conover started a law practice in the back room of his father's dental office and it flourished. Maintaining his private practice, Conover was appointed to the Valparaiso city court in 1952, worked as the Porter County Planning Commission attorney from 1961 to 1964, and was the Porter County prosecutor from 1964 to 1972.

While enjoying both his private practice and public service, Conover also served on the board of directors for the Junior Chamber of Commerce (1953–58), chaired the Porter County Young Republicans (1956–58) and the Porter County Republican Party (1958–63), served as a delegate to the Republican state convention (1958–76), and a delegate to the Republican National Conventions in 1972 and 1976.

Conover, who had a pilot's license and flew his own plane, belonged to the Experimental Aircraft Association. He also belonged to the Porter County Bar Association, the Indiana State Bar Association, the Institute for Judicial Administration, the American Judicature Society, the American Legion, the Potawatomi Council of Boy Scouts, the Saturday Evening Club, Kappa Iota Pi social fraternity, Phi Alpha Delta legal fraternity, and the Valparaiso Rotary Club. As if that was not enough, Conover and his wife had seven children.

In 1981 Governor Robert D. Orr appointed Conover to fill the opening created by the unexpected departure of Eugene N. Chipman. Conover was considered a member of the "Valparaiso Invasion" by then Chief Justice Richard M. Givan, because appellate judges Wesley W. Ratliff and George B. Hoffman and Supreme Court Justice Alfred J. Pivarnik were all Valparaiso University Law School graduates.

According to a clerk who straddled the transition from Chipman to Conover, the judge came up to speed quickly, but this meant long nights and very hard work. Conover often slept in his office and asked a lot of questions, but, relying on his legal experience, he did just fine.

During the fourteen years he served, Conover wrote 770 published majority opinions, as well as twenty-one concurring opinions and fifty-eight dissents. He averaged at least one published opinion each week, a pace he maintained while also writing unpublished memorandum decisions and voting on the decisions by his fellow judges.

Conover's opinions reflected not only his gentleness and common sense but also his confidence in the integrity of the judicial system. For example, he believed one could not presume judges would act improperly by appointing public defenders in their courtrooms, absent any proof that the appointments adversely affected the quality of their representation. Conover was a good person and he believed others were just as good, at least until he was proved wrong.

Conover retired as senior judge in 1995 and returned to Valparaiso, where he died on January 9, 2012. His death meant that America had lost another member of the Greatest Generation, but his legacy of hard work, honor, and commitment to the law lives on.

Selected Bibliography

Dilts, Jon P. Interview with the author, May 29, 2019.
Indiana Lawyer, January 10, 2012.
In Re Adoption of Resolution of Court of Appeals of Indiana in Memory of the Late William Conover. 980 N.E.2d 362 (Ind. Ct. App. 2012).
Prefer, Nathan N. *The Battle for Tinian: Vital Stepping Stone in America's War against Japan*. Chapter Twelve. Kindle Version.
South Bend Tribune, November 13, 1981.
Valparaiso Vidette-Messenger of Porter County, January 11, 1946.

CASES CITED

Wright v. State, 436 N.E.2d 335 (Ind. Ct. App. 1982).

INDIANA SUPREME COURT

LINDA L. CHEZEM

November 21, 1988–December 31, 1997

JENNIFER A. BAUER

Linda Lucille Chezem is known as a trailblazer. Her appointment to the Lawrence County Court in 1976 made her the first woman in the state to serve as judge of a county court. She was the third woman to serve as a trial judge in Indiana, following Vivian Sue Shields in 1964 and Betty S. Barteau in 1975. In 1982 Chezem became the first woman to serve as a circuit court judge. When Governor Robert D. Orr appointed her as the second woman to the Court of Appeals of Indiana in 1988, she said the message was "if you do a good job, the opportunities are there for you."

Born in Brazil, Indiana, on September 26, 1946, Chezem grew up on her family's Clay County farm where she was active in 4-H and dreamed of writing the "Great American Novel." She graduated from Brazil High School and attended Indiana State University to become a teacher. After graduating from ISU with an English degree, Chezem opted for law school instead of teaching. She graduated from Indiana University School of Law in Bloomington in 1971, beginning her legal career as the first woman to practice in Orange County.

On the bench in Lawrence County, Chezem did more than a good job. She was well respected, earning a reputation as tough and compassionate. She addressed growing caseloads with innovative programs for repeat alcohol offenders and at-risk youth. Her expertise in substance use issues was tapped with appointments to Indiana's Addiction Services Advisory Council, the Governor's Task Force to Reduce Drunk Driving, and the White House Conference for a Drug Free America. The community revered her for outreach with children and local groups. Chezem had a banner year in 1988 when she was named juvenile judge of the year, received a governor's exemplary program award and a Sagamore of the Wabash, and was appointed to the court of appeals.

Chezem's arrival at the court of appeals coincided with the passage of Proposition Two, which amended the Indiana Constitution to reduce the Supreme Court's mandatory criminal docket. This resulted in a dramatic increase in the court of appeals' caseload. She welcomed the opportunity to thoroughly study cases, authoring over one thousand majority opinions in nine years. Her landmark decision in *Cowe v. Forum Group* made Indiana just the fourth state to recognize an action for "wrongful life." Although the Indiana Supreme Court reversed the decision, the Court acknowledged it as "thoughtful and concerned," and debated the issue for several more years.

Her decision in *Snyder v. State* also garnered headlines as it concluded state police did not violate the Fourth Amendment by stopping a man who attempted to avoid a drunk-driving roadblock. In addition to the traditional duties of an appellate judge, Chezem helped modernize the court with computerized transcripts, advised the nation's drug czar, and worked on the National Drug Control Strategy. Influenced by the writings of Robert K. Greenleaf, founder of the modern servant-leadership movement, she joined the board of the Greenleaf Center for Servant Leadership. In 1992 Chezem successfully stood for retention with 65 percent of the statewide vote.

Chezem retired from the court of appeals in 1997 to head the Department of 4-H Youth at Purdue University, another first for a women. This career move surprised many, but Chezem saw it as an opportunity to use her judicial experience to help children and families. Her roots in 4-H convinced her it could be an effective delinquency prevention tool, as well as a healthy way to develop children. She focused her scholarship on alcohol abuse and underage drinking, rural health issues, and judicial system education. Chezem also consulted with the National Institute on Alcohol Abuse and Alcoholism, the Office of Juvenile Justice and Delinquency Prevention, and the National Highway Traffic Safety Administration. Her teaching and research efforts were honored with the Fairbanks Circle of Hope Award in 2008 and NHTSA's Public Service Award in 2009. She has held appointments as Professor Emerita of Youth Development and Agriculture Education at Purdue and adjunct professor at Indiana University School of Medicine's Alcohol Research Center. Staying true to her agricultural upbringing, Chezem continued to own and opperate the family farm from her youth. In addition to her duties at Purdue, Chezem began serving as the Monrovia, Indiana, town attorney.

Chief Justice Randall T. Shepard described Chezem as a "bright light . . . energetic and ingenious . . . and especially innovative about working with youth," and the *Bedford Times-Mail* described her as "one of the most able, capable jurists who has ever sat on the bench." Her distinguished careers as judge and educator are historic, defined by big ideas and tireless effort.

Selected Bibliography

Barteau, Betty. "Thirty Years of the Journey of Indiana's Women Judges 1964–1994." *Indiana Law Review* 30 (1997): 43.

Bedford Times-Mail, November 8, 1981, January 21, 1982, November 5, 12, 17, 18, 1988, August 3, 1989, November 14, 19, 1997.

Brazil Times, June 2, 1992.

Indianapolis Star, October 4, 1981, November 12, 1988, May 24, 1989, August 3, 1989, November 4, 1992, December 27, 1996, November 16, 1997, April 19, 1998.

Indiana Court Times, March/April 2008.

Indiana Court of Appeals Annual Reports, 1989–1997.

Shepard, Randall T., State of the Judiciary Address, January 17, 1990.

Staton, Robert H., and Gina M. Hicklin. "The History of the Court of Appeals of Indiana." *Indiana Law Review*, 30 (1997): 203–231.

Sullivan, Frank, Jr. "A Look Back: Developing Indiana Law: Post Bench Reflections of an Indiana Supreme Court Justice." *Indiana Law Review* 50 (2017): 1493.

CASES CITED

Cowe v. Forum Group, 541 N.E.2d 962 (Ind. App. 1989), affirmed in part, reversed in part, 575 N.E.2d 630 (Ind. 1991).

Snyder v. State, 538 N.E.2d 963 (Ind. App. 1989).

INDIANA SUPREME COURT

JOHN G. BAKER

June 2, 1989–July 31, 2020 • Senior Judge: July 31, 2020, to present

RANDALL T. SHEPARD

As we begin to write the story of modern judicial reform in Indiana, there can be little debate that John G. Baker played a central role in transforming the state's courts from isolated individual operations to a statewide collaboration of innovators bent on improving justice.

As recently as the 1970s, the state's courts existed as a collection of islands, most of them functioning as independent operations with a single judge and separate staffs and budgets. There was little working relationship between counties or between the trial and the appellate courts.

Such was the landscape in 1976 when Baker became judge of a new court in Bloomington at the age of twenty-nine. The legislature had eliminated hundreds of justices of the peace and created fifty-eight new courts. The appointees had to construct these operations essentially from scratch with relatively little assistance from headquarters. Once his own court was up and running, Baker built a remarkable career leading the profession at both the state and national level. Forty-four years later, he retired from full-time service at the Court of Appeals of Indiana. He had authored approximately 5,500 opinions, more than anyone in history.

Stewards inside the legal profession asked him to lead in multiple venues. There was a period in the mid and late 1980s when he was chief judge of the Monroe Superior Court, president of the Indiana Judges Association, a delegate at the National Conference of State Trial Judges and at the Indiana State Bar Association, a director of the Indiana Judicial Conference, and later chief judge of the court of appeals.

Most important in these periods of leadership, Baker believed that success could not be measured simply in moving along a growing volume of cases, but rather that a judge's long-term legacy would lie in what the judge could do to reform the system for better service to citizens and lawyers.

Such reforms often meant making requests to the Indiana General Assembly, and Baker became a face of the judiciary over several decades at the statehouse. From achieving a unification of the disparate courts in Monroe County during his second year as a judge, he continued to play a central role in too many advancements to recount such as building capacity at the Indiana Judicial Center to assist judges who confronted the special tasks for which local help was often insufficient. He knew countless legislators by name, and they knew his and trusted his advice. He was central to the most important judicial pay bill ever in 2005, which provided for substantial raises for judges and prosecutors, who had gone eight years without even a cost-of-living increase.

But Baker worked reform in multiple places that were not as visible. By the time he became the first person to serve two terms as president of the Judges Association, it was far more representative, with a board finally chosen by the members, a refreshed lobbying team, and yearly retreats for officer planning. Sometimes his contributions covered elementary matters that still reached statewide. Today's system of numbering cases is a product of his work.

Born in Aurora on October 4, 1946, Baker built this career after graduating from Culver Military Academy in 1964. He majored in history at Indiana University in Bloomington, graduating in 1968, received a law degree there in 1971, and earned a master's of law in the judicial process at the University of Virginia in 1995. He was an Eagle Scout and a captain in the U.S. Army Reserve.

Baker always saw education as a key to upgrading the profession and the courts. He himself studied at Bloomington, at New York University, and at the University of Virginia. What he learned there and elsewhere, he labored to pass on to the next generation by teaching at the IU School of Public and Environmental Affairs for thirty-three years, at the Maurer School of Law in Bloomington for five, and at the McKinney School of Law in Indianapolis for ten.

Beyond that, he was central to expanding the educational opportunities for sitting judges, including as a founder of the Indiana Graduate Program for Judges, following on his experience at Virginia.

Jurisprudentially, Baker liked to describe his approach as "running to the middle." This is not to say that he did not move beyond the expected when the times demanded it. In *Infant Girl W,* issued in 2006, he wrote for a divided panel that Indiana's statute authorizing adoption petitions by "residents" included a gay couple. As a decision based on statutory interpretation, it could have been overturned by majority votes in the legislature. There were several attempts to do so, but the legislature decided to let the ruling stand. Baker had hardly made the law stand still, but he had reached a decision on a contentious issue that was close enough to the middle that most people accepted it.

Selected Bibliography

Baker, John G. "The History of the Indiana Trial Court System and Attempts at Renovation." *Indiana Law Review* 30 (1997): 233–61.

———. "Indiana Judges: A Portrait of Judicial Evolution." In David Bodenhamer, and Randall Shepard, eds. *The History of Indiana Law,* 303–24. Athens: Ohio University Press, 2006.

———. "Now or Never: Reforming Indiana's Court System." *Indiana Law Review* 41 (2008): 817–35.

CASES CITED

R. K. H. v. Morgan County Office of Family and Children (In re Infant Girl W.) 845 N.E. 2d 229 (Ind. App 2006).

PHOTO BY JOHN GENTRY

BETTY S. BARTEAU

January 1, 1991–April 31, 1998 • Senior Judge: 2004 to present

SUSAN D. HINKLE AND JOSEPH H. MERRICK

Betty Scales Barteau consistently chooses to seek the "unknown territory," as she called it, and the legal profession in Indiana and worldwide has been improved through her fearlessness and ambition.

Barteau was born in rural Warrick County, Indiana, on October 19, 1935, in a home with no running water, no electricity, and no heat. She graduated from Boonville High School in 1952. After graduation, she worked for Standard Oil Company, married, had four children, and moved to Indianapolis. In 1956 she took classes at Indiana University Extension while working part time.

Barteau learned of a special examination to be admitted to Indiana University School of Law-Indianapolis without an undergraduate degree. With encouragement from her brother John Burley Scales, who was a law student, she passed the exam and was admitted in 1961. Barteau graduated with honors in 1965 as only one of two women in her class. She gave birth to her fifth child months after graduation.

Barteau returned to Boonville to practice law, sharing an office with her brother. She was one of only two or three practicing female lawyers in southwest Indiana. She worked part time as a deputy prosecutor from 1965 to 1967 in Warrick and Spencer Counties, and, in a move that presaged her eventual career, served as Boonville City Court Judge from 1967 to 1969.

In 1969 Barteau returned to Indianapolis. From 1970 to 1972 she served on the Employment Security Review Board, reviewing unemployment appeals. Later, she became a partner in Runnels, Barteau, and Pontius. During this time, she advocated for the passage of the Equal Rights Amendment.

In 1974 Barteau ran for a superior court judgeship in Marion County. She won, and on January 1, 1975, she took office as the first elected female judge in Marion County, and only the second woman elected to a judgeship in Indiana.

Barteau was assigned to hear major civil litigation and family law cases, including about "1,000 divorces a year." She was one of the first Indiana judges to grant full child custody to an LGBTQ parent, Van Kirby. Barteau later stated, "I don't know whether I was totally discounting that there was any homosexuality involved, or whether I was just looking at [the parents] as people. As parents. I think it had to be that."

While she was a trial judge and raising five children, Barteau joined and later led the Association of Family and Conciliation Courts, an international organization that presented programs to address the trauma involved in divorce. She spoke and taught around the world. Barteau also helped to set uniform child-support guidelines in Marion County, long before the state established requirements. In addition, she took classes at the National Judicial College in Reno, Nevada, eventually joining the faculty, serving in that capacity from 1978 until 2003, including a term as faculty chair. Barteau was also a founding member of the National Association of Women Judges

In 1991 Barteau applied for a seat on the Court of Appeals of Indiana and was appointed by Governor Evan Bayh to the court's newly created Fifth District. She took office in January 1991 and served until her retirement in April 1998.

During her term on the court of appeals, she authored approximately 280 opinions and hundreds of additional memorandum decisions. Among other opinions, she wrote the much-cited *Young v. Butts*, which addressed litigants' duty of honesty to appellate tribunals.

While an appellate court judge, Barteau enrolled in the University of Virginia School of Law master-of-laws program, graduating in 1995. Her thesis chronicled the journey of Indiana's women attorneys and judges from 1964 to 1994.

In retirement Barteau became Chief of Party for the Russia Judicial Reform Project, a U.S. Agency for International Development project that assisted Russians in reforming their judicial system. During two terms from 1998 to 2003, she lived in Moscow, leading a team of seven to nine people. Barteau traveled across Russia, establishing seminars, presenting lectures, proposing reforms, and meeting officials, including judicial leaders visiting from Europe and the United States.

After a new federal government took power in Russia and rejected international reform groups, Barteau returned home in 2004 and was appointed senior judge to the court of appeals. She remains a senior judge, continuing her lifelong commitment to the law.

Barteau continues to enjoy time with her family and traveling. As she said when leaving her post in Russia, "This adventure is over—I can hardly wait for the next one to begin."

Selected Bibliography

Barteau, Betty. "Thirty Years of the Journey of Indiana's Women Judges 1964–1994." *Indiana Law Review* 30, no. 1 (1997).

———. Interviews with the authors, December 19, 2019, January 30, 2020, February 25, 2020.

Beavers, Addison. *The First 100 Years: A Partial History of the Boonville School System*. Printing Professionals and Publishers, 1997.

Evansville Courier and Press, January 29, 1967.

Kirby, Van, and Hoppe, David. *On the Table by the Window: The Journey of a Gay Dad in Indiana*. Indianapolis: Dog Ear Publishing, 2013.

Indiana Lawyer, April 12–25, September 27–October 10, 2000.

Indianapolis Star, April 3, 1978, December 2, 1990.

The McKinney Lawyer. Winter 2014–15.

The Third Branch. Summer 1999.

CASE CITED

Young v. Butts, 685 N.E.2d 147 (Ind. Ct. App. 1997).

PHOTO BY JOHN GENTRY

ROBERT D. RUCKER

January 1, 1991–November 19, 1999 • Senior Judge; May 15, 2017, to present

RAY E. BOOMHOWER

Born in Canton, Georgia, on January 19, 1947, Robert D. Rucker was the oldest of eleven children. He grew up in Gary, Indiana, raised from the age of fourteen by his stepmother. He attended Indiana University Northwest part time while working at Inland Steel. Before he could finish his studies, Rucker was drafted by the army and sent to Vietnam, where he served as radio operator with the First Calvary Division (Airmobile) and rose to the rank of sergeant. Rucker participated in Operation Pegasus, the relief of besieged marines at Khe Sanh in northwestern Quang Tri Province in South Vietnam. He described the experience as "tough and scary." Twice wounded in action, he received the Purple Heart and Bronze Star for meritorious service but does not dwell on his time in combat. He was inducted into the Indiana Military Veterans Hall of Fame in 2017.

Upon his return home to Indiana, Rucker, who had married before leaving for his army service, had "no plans other than raising a family." He returned to work at Inland Steel, but left soon after for such occupations as bank teller and counselor for a jobs training program. Rucker resumed his studies at IU Northwest with plans of graduating and attending medical school. He was inspired in part by the chairman of the university's chemistry department, who told Rucker a challenging course of studies would be five hours each in chemistry, physics, and German. "That got me started in a pre-med program," Rucker noted. "And that made me really appreciate long, long hours of study, spending a lot of time in the library."

Before Rucker graduated, he met Alton Gill Jr., a Gary attorney, who persuaded him he could make a difference if he pursued a legal career. After receiving his bachelor's degree in sociology in 1974 Rucker, with the help of a Woodrow Wilson/Martin Luther King Jr. Fellowship, entered law school at Valparaiso University. "I was motivated most of the time I was in law school by absolute fear of failure," recalled Rucker, who earned his law degree in December 1976. Rucker passed the bar on his first try and joined the East Chicago law firm of African American attorney W. Henry Walker, for whom he had clerked during his first year of law school. Rucker later earned a master of laws degree in the judicial process from the University of Virginia Law School in 1998.

Rucker ran for state representative in 1978. Although he lost the race, he met Jack Crawford, who was elected Lake County prosecutor and then hired Rucker as a deputy prosecutor. His time with the prosecutor's office included a case that Rucker said gave him the most satisfaction as an attorney. The trial involved the successful prosecution of two men who had defrauded numerous consumers purchasing heating systems. Rucker was also successful in getting liens removed that had been placed on the victims' homes. Rucker, who lost a 1980 election for a Lake County judgeship, left the prosecutor's office to return to private practice. He later served as the deputy city attorney for Gary from 1987 to 1988 before opening his own law practice.

Rucker broke new ground for the state when in 1990 Governor Evan Bayh appointed him to serve as the first African American judge on the Court of Appeals of Indiana. "I think my appointment does mean a lot of things to a lot of different people—male, female, black and white," Rucker said at the time. "And I hope that the appointment can serve as a beacon of inspiration to our children, certainly to other African-American lawyers, and to the legal community in general." In one precedent-setting decision he made while on the appeals court, Rucker wrote the majority decision in a 1998 case from Fort Wayne involving a passenger who left a car halted by police during a traffic stop in a high-crime neighborhood. In his opinion, Rucker wrote that the police officer who detained the passenger was not justified in his action. "The fact that one turns away from the police in a high-crime neighborhood is not sufficient to establish reasonable suspicion of criminal activity," Rucker noted.

In 1999 Governor Frank O'Bannon, filling the vacancy left by Justice Myra C. Selby's resignation, appointed Rucker to the Indiana Supreme Court. O'Bannon noted that Rucker had proven his ability while on the appeals court and praised him for being a "careful, thoughtful, thorough and independent judge."

After serving nearly eighteen years on the Supreme Court, Rucker retired in 2017 and began service as a senior judge on the appellate court.

Selected Bibliography

Fort Wayne Journal-Gazette, December 20, 2004.
Indianapolis Star, December 2, 1990, August 21, October 26, November 20, 1999, July 26, 2000, April 23, 2002, November 11, 2004.
Kaelble, Steve. "Finally Convinced to Pursue Legal Career, Rucker Climbs to Supreme Heights." *Indiana Alumni Magazine* (July/August, 2001).

PHOTO BY JOHN GENTRY

JOHN T. SHARPNACK

January 1, 1991–May 2, 2008 • Senior Judge: May 3, 2008–
December 31, 2021

EDWARD W. NAJAM JR.

Governor Evan Bayh's appointment of John T. Sharpnack to the Court of Appeals of Indiana enjoyed widespread approval in the legal community. A third-generation lawyer and partner in the Columbus firm of Sharpnack, Bigley, David and Rumple, Sharpnack was recognized beyond his native Bartholomew County as a first-rate litigator. As a distinguished practitioner, Sharpnack was well prepared to serve on the court.

Like his father, Sharpnack was a Fellow of the American College of Trial Lawyers. ACTL membership is conferred only by invitation and offered only "to those experienced trial lawyers who have mastered the art of advocacy and whose professional careers have been marked by the highest standards of ethical conduct, professionalism, civility and collegiality." Sharpnack's invitation to Fellowship in the College exemplified his exceptional standing in the legal profession.

Sharpnack was born in Columbus on May 7, 1933. He attended high school in Cincinnati, where he lived with his mother and stepfather. He entered the University of Cincinnati in 1951 and earned a bachelor of arts in English in 1955.

Sharpnack volunteered for the draft and served in the U.S. Army for two years. He was an ammunition storage specialist when the captain of his ordnance battalion learned he enjoyed writing and ordered him to take a typing course. Thus, while in the army Sharpnack both learned to type and was first introduced to the law as a reporter for Special Courts Martial.

In 1957 Sharpnack entered the University of Cincinnati College of Law and found his calling. He "really liked" and thrived in law school. He was a member of the editorial board and editor in chief of the *Cincinnati Law Review* and was elected to Order of the Coif. In 1960 he graduated with an LLB, third in his class.

Sharpnack began his legal career as a trial attorney with the Antitrust Division of the Department of Justice. He had been recruited by the Attorney General's Honors Program for high-caliber entry-level attorneys. He was employed in Washington, DC, for three years.

In 1963 Sharpnack returned to Columbus, was admitted to the Indiana Bar, and joined the family firm of Sharpnack and Bigley. His grandfather, Julian, had once served as Bartholomew Circuit Court Judge. His father, Lew, was a well-known and highly respected trial lawyer. The firm traced its origins to 1824, and in 2001 received the Governor's Century Award, having been in business for more than one hundred years.

Future congressman Lee H. Hamilton was also a member of the firm. Hamilton greatly admired Sharpnack's ability and recalls that Sharpnack invigorated the firm and "quickly earned a good reputation" and was a capable lawyer, "a natural." Sharpnack maintained a general practice concentrated in civil litigation and eventually focused on insurance and personal injury defense.

While in private practice Sharpnack served as chair of the Indiana State Bar Association Trial Section and House of Delegates, as president of the Indiana Defense Lawyers Association, on the Supreme Court Committee on Rules of Practice and Procedure, and on the faculty of the National Institute for Trial Advocacy. After joining the court, he continued to serve on the Supreme Court Rules Committee and the NITA faculty. He also became a member and chair of the Supreme Court's Commission on Continuing Legal

Education and a founding member of the Judges and Lawyers Assistance Program.

On January 1, 1991, after twenty-seven years in private practice, Sharpnack became a judge of the newly created Fifth District of the Court of Appeals of Indiana. He had previously applied three times for vacancies on the court, and his appointment to the bench fulfilled a longstanding career goal. At Sharpnack's robing ceremony, Chief Judge Wesley W. Ratliff called his appointment "long overdue."

In recommending Sharpnack's appointment, Evansville attorney F. Wesley Bowers wrote the governor that, "There are not enough superlatives to describe the qualifications of Mr. Sharpnack," and Jefferson Circuit Court Judge Ted R. Todd noted his "reputation for integrity and legal ability" and that "although his trial experience has been largely representing insurance carriers in civil litigation, the plaintiffs' trial bar holds him in high esteem." Chief Justice of Indiana Randall T. Shepard concluded his certification of Sharpnack's nomination with the following words: "He enjoys an exceptional reputation in the legal profession for his skills as an advocate, and for his intelligence, fairness, and professionalism."

Sharpnack's colleagues elected him to three terms as chief judge. He served in that capacity for nine years and three months, the longest term of any chief judge in the court's history. He was returned to the court by retention elections in 1994 and 2004. Sharpnack's reputation was justified by his thoroughly researched and carefully written opinions during his more than seventeen years on the court. Upon his retirement on May 2, 2008, the Indiana Supreme Court appointed him as a senior judge, where he continued his long legal career.

Selected Bibliography

Hamilton, Lee H. Interview with the author. Bloomington, June 13, 2019.
Nixon, William A. Interview with John T. Sharpnack. Indianapolis, April 27, 2001.
Sharpnack, John T. Indiana Judicial Nominating Commission Application for Judicial Position. Indiana Archives and Records Administration.
———. Interview with the author. Indianapolis, March 1, 2018.
Shepard, Randall T. Certification and Evaluations of Nominees for Fifth District, Indiana Court of Appeals, July 30, 1990.

PHOTO BY JOHN GENTRY

EDWARD W. NAJAM JR.

December 30, 1992, to present

JAMES H. MADISON

Judge Edward Najam's career has combined a strong intellectual bent with a passionate love of the law and his home state.

Known as "Ted," Edward W. Najam Jr. was born in North Carolina on August 12, 1947. His family moved to Bloomington in 1954, where his father had accepted a position on the faculty of Indiana University. Najam became an Eagle Scout and graduated from Indiana University High School. He remained in Bloomington to attend Indiana University, where he was elected student body president and received the Herman B Wells Senior Recognition Award as the outstanding student and leader in the class of 1969. He was elected to Phi Beta Kappa, was a Rhodes Scholar finalist, and graduated with highest distinction. Fifty years later, in 2019, IU awarded him its Bicentennial Medal. Following undergraduate school, Najam entered Harvard Law School, graduating in 1972.

As an undergraduate and as a law student Najam took active roles in student protests about the Vietnam War and became a lifelong fan of Bob Dylan. Even in law school he remained close to his home state, writing a paper on public school finance in Indiana that was published in the *Indiana Law Journal* in 1972. His first job out of law school was as assistant to Bloomington mayor Frank McCloskey. From 1974 to 1992 he practiced law in his hometown Both before and after joining the court, he served on various community boards, as president of the Monroe County YMCA, and as chair of the Community Foundation of Bloomington and Monroe County

When Governor Evan Bayh appointed him to the court of appeals in 1992, Najam was, at forty-five, the youngest judge on the court. He had worked as an intern for the governor's father, Senator Birch Bayh, in the summer between undergraduate school and law school. After joining the court Najam continued to live in his hometown, using the time on the commute to and from the statehouse for quiet contemplation and hard thinking.

Najam always had strong cerebral tendencies. He told an interviewer in 2001 that "there is nothing more satisfying than to take on a difficult case and break it down and dissect it and analyze how it should be decided and then to write and edit the opinion." He confessed, too, that he was "something of a perfectionist in opinion writing," including correct and precise use of the English language. Alongside these high standards was a capacity for hard and sustained work, with the goal to write opinions that both "decide the case and articulate the law."

In a 2001 interview Najam emphasized his position as "a strong proponent of individual rights." Among the more than 4,000 majority opinions Najam has authored, several exemplify his judicial perspective. His opinion in *State v Gerschoffer* affirmed the trial court's determination that sobriety checkpoints without probable cause or reasonable suspicion violate Article 1, Section 11 of the Indiana Constitution, although the Indiana Supreme Court ultimately disagreed. His opinion in *Coutar Remainder I, LLC v. State* rejected the state's attempt to condemn property for highway construction without just compensation and sided with the individual property owner.

Najam has also affirmed the constitutional role of the judicial branch. In *Groth v. Pence*, a controversial case regarding Governor Mike Pence's categorical claim of executive privilege from disclosure of his public records, Najam asserted the right to judicial review of those records under the Access to

Public Records Act even though he sided with the governor in this instance. The courts, he concluded in the 2017 opinion, had the right to apply APRA to the governor and his staff and that "APRA does not provide for any such absolute privilege, and the separation of powers doctrine does not require it." A unanimous Indiana Supreme Court denied transfer, leaving Najam's opinion intact.

As chair of the Indiana State Bar Association's Appellate Practice Section, Najam initiated the Appellate Rules Project, which revised the rules of appellate procedure. He has shown a commitment to legal education as a longtime member of the Board of Visitors of the Maurer School of Law and, although not a graduate of that school, endowed a scholarship for Maurer students. He has also argued the benefits of merit selection of judges. His article in the *Indiana Law Review* in 2013 concluded that "forty years of experience with merit selection and retention in Indiana have provided appellate decisions rendered without fear or favor by judges who are not controlled by, or accountable to, any political party or interest group but accountable only to justice and the rule of law." Najam stands in a long line of Hoosier judges committed to justice and the rule of law.

Selected Bibliography

"Interview of Judge Edward W. Najam, Jr." by William A. Nixon, Indianapolis, 2001.

Najam, Edward W. Jr. "Public School Finance in Indiana: A Critique." *Indiana Law Journal* 48, no. 1 (1972).

———. "Caught in the Middle: The Role of State Intermediate Appellate Courts." *Indiana Law Review* 35, no. 2 (2002).

———. "Merit Selection in Indiana: The Foundation for a Fair and Impartial Appellate Judiciary." *Indiana Law Review* 46, no. 1 (2013).

CASES CITED

Coutar Remainder I, LLC v. State, 91 N. E. 3d 610 (Ind. Ct. App, 2017).

State v. Gerschoffer, 738 N.E.2d 713 (Ind. Ct. App, 2000).

William Groth v. Mike Pence, 67 N.E.3d 1104 (Ind. Ct. App. 2017).

INDIANA SUPREME COURT

EZRA H. FRIEDLANDER

January 7, 1993–August 31, 2015 • Senior Judge: September 1, 2015, to present

LARRY L. MORRIS

Ezra H. Friedlander, a man of diverse passions, has never been content to sit back and watch others do the work. He has lived a life of getting involved, a life of leading the way and accomplishing desired results. His path to the Indiana appellate judiciary was not a traditional one. A first-generation American whose parents emigrated from Lithuania, Ezra grew up in the racially segregated neighborhoods of Newark, New Jersey, where his father was a painter. Upon the advice of his uncle, Ezra arrived in 1958 as a sixteen-year-old freshman at Indiana University with designs on a career in medicine. That plan changed when he found the study of history and government more to his liking. After receiving his undergraduate degree, he enrolled in the IU School of Law–Bloomington, where he earned a doctor of law in 1965.

He began his legal career working in a private firm and as a part-time deputy prosecutor, first in Gary and later in Indianapolis. His legal practice in Indianapolis focused primarily upon representing small businesses. In time he served on the boards of several privately held and public corporations. After years of successful private practice, he was appointed to the appellate bench by Governor Evan Bayh in 1993. By that time, he had accumulated considerable experience and expertise in business and transactional law.

In more than twenty-two years on the Court of Appeals of Indiana, he authored more than 3,000 opinions and participated in twice that many decisions. A self-described "bottom-line guy," he viewed his judicial task as resolving legal disputes, not taking the opportunity to write law review articles—a philosophy he shared with every law clerk who worked in his chambers. Declining to "make something more than what [was] before" him, his opinions were legally sound and heavily tinged with to-the-point, practical common sense. His accumulated business expertise proved an asset in his time on the court, both in deciding cases and in guiding the operation of the court. For example, to address the court's burgeoning caseload, he spearheaded changes that encouraged law clerks to stay longer than the one- or two-year slots customary when he assumed the bench. By the time he retired from the court, every judge had at least one experienced law clerk and the court was widely recognized as one of the most efficient state appellate courts in the country.

His public contributions went well beyond his service on the court. During his long legal career, he actively championed the cause of gender, ethnic, and racial diversity in Indiana's legal community. While on the court, he served along with former Justice Myra Selby as the first cochairs of the Indiana Supreme Court's Commission on Race and Gender Fairness. He was instrumental in establishing a summer internship program under the auspices of the Indiana Conference for Legal Education Opportunity for qualified minority, low-income, or educationally disadvantage law students.

His many philanthropic activities include leadership in fund drives for a wide range of worthwhile causes, such as the United Fund, the Heart Fund, the Cancer Fund, and the Indianapolis Museum of Art (now Newfields). In 2018 he and his wife, Linda, were awarded the IUPUI Spirit of Philanthropy Award. Perhaps influenced by his involvement as an attorney in a 1980s case, *Autocephalous Greek-Orthodox Church of Cyprus v. Goldburg,* involving the ownership of 1,400-year-old mosaics from Cyprus, he is a devotee of the arts and an art-glass enthusiast, serving as a member of the advisory board of the Herron School of Art and Design. An avid sports fan, he took the lead in sports endeavors at all levels, from helping found the Carmel Youth Soccer Association to serving on local organizing committees for the 1991 PGA Championship at Crooked Stick Golf Club, the 2005 Solheim Cup, and the 2002 World Basketball Championships.

He has maintained an active role at IU, serving in leadership capacities and roles too numerous to list here. Notably, they include serving on the dean's advisory board of the College of Arts and Sciences and the board of directors of the Indiana University Foundation, including its executive committee. He endowed a scholarship for law students at his alma mater. In 1998 he was named a member of the IU's Academy of Law Alumni Fellows, the highest award the law school can confer upon its graduates.

Friedlander's life is truly a mosaic of leadership, service, and accomplishment, both as a member of the court of appeals and as a leader of the larger Indiana community.

Selected Bibliography

IU's Distinguished Alumni Service Award announcement. http://archive.news.indiana.edu/releases/iu/2015/10/distinguished-alumni-service-award.shtml.

Stafford, Dave. "Friedlander Reflects on Half-Century in Law as Retirement Nears." *The Indiana Lawyer.com* (August 12, 2015)

CASE CITED

Autocephalous Greek-Orthodox Church of Cyprus v. Goldburg, 917 F.2d 278 (7th Cir. 1990).

KRAHULIK FAMILY COLLECTION

PATRICIA A. RILEY

January 1, 1994, to present

INGE V. PORTER

After being told by an attorney in her hometown that there was no room for women in the law, Patricia Riley stubbornly refuted her critics and during an impressive legal career, became an outspoken defender of individual rights, justice, and fairness. One of the most significant responsibilities entrusted to Riley as an appellate judge is the development of law within the framework of published opinions and statutes enacted by the legislature with appreciation for exceptions that can be made to existing precedents when the reasoning is flawed or outdated.

In Bonner ex rel. Bonner v. Daniels, Riley authored the majority opinion in a class-action suit that sought a declaration that the Indiana school-funding system implemented by the Indiana State Board of Education failed to comply with the education clause of Indiana's constitution. Mindful of the court's "role as guardian of the Constitution" and guided by case law history Riley declared the education clause subject to judicial enforcement. However, cognizant of the "prerogatives of other branches of government," Riley recognized the limitations of the judicial branch in setting educational policy.

In the case *B.S. v. State,* Riley broke with the majority and argued for the dismissal of the murder charges brought against a mother who ingested rat poison to kill herself and her unborn child. Riley said that "it was never the intention of the legislature that the feticide statute should be used to criminalize prenatal conduct of a pregnant woman."

Riley's decision in *League of Women Voters of Indiana, Inc. v. Rokita*, that Indiana's voter ID law violated the Constitution drew a vigorous response from the then-governor of Indiana, Mitchell E. Daniels, calling the ruling a "preposterous decision" coming from "a judge who's been reversed before."

A native of Rensselaer, Indiana, Riley was named to the Indiana Court of Appeals, representing the Fourth District, by Democratic governor Evan Bayh in January 1994 and has been retained on the appellate bench by Indiana voters ever since. She earned her bachelor's degree in 1971 from Indiana University in Bloomington and her law degree from the Indiana University School of Law-Indianapolis in 1974. She commenced her legal career as a deputy prosecutor in Marion County and as a public defender in Marion and Jasper Counties before entering private practice in her hometown of Rensselaer. She was elected in 1990 to the Jasper County Superior Court, where she served until her appointment to the court of appeals. She is a former associate professor at Saint Joseph College in Rensselaer and an adjunct professor at the McKinney School of Law. Riley is on the McKinney School of Law Board of Visitors and a School Ambassador. Her peers on the McKinney School of Law Board of Visitors elected her as the Alumna of the Year 2019.

Outside the courtroom, Riley serves on the board of Indianapolis Legal Aid Society that provides legal assistance to indigent Hoosiers in civil matters. She is also on the board of directors of RecycleForce, a nonprofit social enterprise that aids in rebuilding the lives of former prison inmates through employment and social services.

At the international level Riley advances her favorite causes. Starting in 2008, she has promoted women's rights internationally by cofounding the Legal Aid Centre of Eldoret, Kenya, which provides legal services for HIV/AIDS patients at the medical center Academic Model Providing Access to

Health Care and serves as an advocate for survivors of sexual, gender-based, and ethnic violence.

In 2011 Riley accompanied the Washington, DC-based International Judicial Academy to The Hague, Netherlands, to observe the International Criminal Court and two International Criminal Tribunals that conducted hearings in the cases against war criminals from Sierra Leone and the former Yugoslavia. The following year, in 2012, Riley participated in the Third Sino-U.S. Law Conference, held in Beijing, at the National Judges College of the People's Republic of China, which monitors all aspects of China's judicial training, placement, and promotion. In 2013 Riley presented a paper on Ethics Rules in the United States at the Justice Academy of Turkey.

In April 2014 Riley was a mission member with NGO Observer Status at Guantanamo Bay Naval Base, Cuba, through the Military Commission Observation Project of the McKinney School of Law's Program in International Human Rights Law. She monitored hearings in the U.S. Military Commission case of five defendants accused of masterminding the attack on the U.S.S. *Cole*, a U.S. ship docked in Yemen in 2000 that killed seventeen sailors and injured over thirty other service personnel.

For Riley, a girl from rural Indiana who became an internationally acclaimed court of appeals judge, the sky is truly the limit.

Selected Bibliography

Advance Indiana. "Disciplinary Commission Gave Gov. Mitch Daniels a Pass when He Publicly Attacked The Integrity of a Judge," https://advanceindiana.blogspot.com/2013/07/disciplinary-commission-gave-gov-mitch.html/.

"Jasper Judge Picked." https://www.nwitimes.com/uncategorized/jasper-judge-picked/article_c8915063-abb4-5271-b7b6-2590fe4bf506.html/.

Riley, P., *A View from Gitmo: Proceedings lack Transparency available in US Courts*, https://www.theindianalawyer.com/articles/34389-a-view-from-gitmo-proceedings-lack-transparency-available-in-us-courts.

———. *A View from Gitmo: An Update on USS Cole Case and Other Proceedings*, https://www.theindianalawyer.com/articles/35589-a-view-from-gitmo-an-update-on-uss-cole-case-and-other-proceedings.

———. Blogposts, at https://lacekenya.wordpress.com/.

CASES CITED

Bonner ex rel. Bonner v. Daniels, 885 N.E.2d 673 (Ind. Ct. App. 2008), trans. granted

B.S. v. State, 966 N.E.2d 619 (Ind. Ct. App. 2012)

League of Women Voters of Indiana, Inc. v. Rokita, 915 N.E.2d 151 (Ind. Ct. App. 2009).

PHOTO BY JOHN GENTRY

JAMES S. KIRSCH

March 4, 1994–September 30, 2021

JANET AND JOHN VARGO

In *Anatomy of a Murder*, author Robert Traver wrote, "Judges, like most people, may be divided roughly into four classes: judges with neither head nor heart. . . . Judges with head but no heart . . . judges with heart but no head . . . [and] judges who possess both head and heart."

James S. Kirsch is one of those rare judges who possesses both head and heart. He has served in Indiana as a judge since 1988, however, his life reflects much more as a result of his multitalented gifts, his innate intelligence, hard work, perseverance, and interpersonal skills. Kirsch excelled at all levels of his education. Born in Indianapolis on December 9, 1946, and a lifelong Indianapolis resident, Kirsch graduated from Cathedral High School, with honors, in 1964; from Butler University with a bachelor of arts with honors in 1968, and cum laude with a doctor of law degree from the Indiana University School of Law-Indianapolis in 1974.

During law school he clerked for the law firm of Kroger, Gardis and Regas and, upon graduation, he was hired as an associate, where he developed his legal skills to become a highly respected attorney in commercial and business litigation. He became a partner in 1978, a managing partner in 1982, and could have remained a successful attorney for the rest of his life. However, he became a judge in 1988 when he was appointed by the Indiana Supreme Court as judge of the Marion Superior Court. He was later elected to this position in 1990 and became the presiding judge of the court in 1992. Governor Evan Bayh appointed him to the Court of Appeals of Indiana in March 1994, and he was the Chief Judge of the Court of Appeals from March 2004 until February 2007. Indiana voters retained Kirsch on the court of appeals in 1996, 2006, and 2016.

Among his many attributes, Kirsch has an exuberant sense of humor that is occasionally reflected in his opinions. For example, in one case he wrote the majority opinion for a contract case, which, in part, involved a disc jockey's services. A portion of his opinion cleverly referenced titles of numerous 1960s rock-and-roll songs woven into an expressive dialogue rejecting a dissenting opinion.

Although Kirsch is widely recognized as a distinguished judge, he has expanded his talents into the world of academia. In 1990 he was appointed as Visiting Professor of Law and Management at the Krannert Graduate School of Management at Purdue University. He teaches the legal section of the IMM Global Executive MBA program that is attended by professionals and executives from all over the world. He almost single handedly developed his section of the program and was named outstanding professor in 2010 and 2011. Through this MBA program Kirsch teaches law in twenty-eight countries on five continents, holding faculty appointments at Tilburg University in the Netherlands and Central European University in Budapest, Hungary.

Amid all his professional duties, Kirsch found more ways to benefit society by serving on many legal boards and associations. He served as president of the Indianapolis Bar Association in 1987 and the Indianapolis Bar Foundation from 1988 to 1989. These two organizations presented Kirsch with their highest award, the Honorable Paul H. Buchanan, Jr. Award of Excellence. Kirsch was also a Distinguished Senior Fellow of the Indianapolis Bar Association in 1984 and chair of the Indiana State Bar Association Appellate Practice Section from 2004 to 2005. He was a member of the board of visitors of Indiana University School of Law–Indianapolis, and a board member of the Legal Aid Society of Indianapolis.

Kirsch's activities spread beyond the legal arena into the broader community, where he served as a board member of Associates of Rose Hulman Institute of Technology, Goodwill Industries Foundation of Central Indiana, Community Centers of Indianapolis, the Indianapolis Urban League, the Stanley K. Lacy Leadership Association, and the Benjamin Harrison Presidential Site. He is also the past president of the United Way/Community Service Council Board of Directors.

In addition, Kirsch speaks and lectures on a variety of topics and programs and has served on the faculty of more than 300 continuing legal education programs. In recognition of his dedicated services, he received a Sagamore of the Wabash four times, from different Indiana governors, both Republican and Democrat.

Judge Kirsch is married to Jan Kirsch (EdD, MSN, Indiana University). They have two adult children, Adam and Alexandra. After her retirement, Jan occasionally traveled with Jim in his busy schedule, and they both religiously attend Butler University basketball games.

CASE CITED

Breeding v Kye's Incorporated, 831 N.E.2d 188, fn1 at 191 (Ind. App. 2005).

CARR L. DARDEN

October 1994–July 21, 2012 • Senior Judge: July 24, 2012, to present

ALI A. TALIB

Judge Carr L. Darden has served his country, state, and community with honor and distinction. Although Darden was born in Tennessee, he has lived in the state most of his life and often says that he considers himself a proud Hoosier by choice. He served in the U.S. Air Force and after receiving an honorable discharge, he and his wife Lundy and family moved to Indianapolis. He worked for the U.S. Postal Service and became a supervisor. After obtaining his bachelor of science degree in business from Indiana University in Bloomington in 1966 and his doctor of law degree from the Robert H. McKinney School of Law in Indianapolis in 1970, Darden was employed as a public defender in Marion County and as Chief Deputy Public Defender for the State of Indiana. He also engaged in the private practice of law with two different law firms. He served as a presiding judge in the Marion County Superior Court and the Marion County Municipal Court systems.

In 1994 Governor Evan Bayh appointed Darden to the Court of Appeals of Indiana. In making the appointment Bayh said Darden has "compiled an impressive and impeccable record of service to the Indiana judiciary" in more than twenty years as a judge, public defender and attorney. Darden became the second African American to serve on the court of appeals following Judge Robert Rucker, and he presently serves as a Court of Appeals Senior Judge.

Perhaps one of the most scholarly and noteworthy opinions in Darden's eighteen-year tenure on the appeals court is the case of *Hilbert, et al. v. Conseco Services*, decided in 2005. Stephen Hilbert, CEO of Conseco Service, and other Conseco executives bought hundreds of millions of dollars in Conseco Stock with money borrowed from banks with payment of the notes deferred over several years. Conseco guaranteed the participants' obligations. Hilbert failed to repay the promissory notes, creating a financial burden for Conseco, and subsequently failed to pay the debt he owed to the company, including nearly $80 million in interest. Conseco filed suit against Hilbert in the Hamilton Circuit Court, and the trial judge in the case issued a summary judgment ordering Hilbert to pay the interest payments in full, and ordered the foreclosure of Hilbert's mansion, estimated to be worth $30 million. Conseco owned a nearly a $19.4 million mortgage on Hilbert's mansion. Hilbert appealed the ruling to the Court of Appeals of Indiana. Darden, writing for the majority, affirmed the trial court's order in favor of Conseco Services and against Hilbert and others for breaching the payment of promissory notes, and the order for foreclosure on Hilbert's Carmel mansion. Darden's opinion withstood Hilbert's subsequent appeals to the Indiana Supreme Court and then the U.S. Supreme Court.

Darden has always been active in his community, church, and the legal community. He is a lifetime member of the National Association for the Advancement of Colored People, the National Bar Association, and the Marion County Bar Association, and a member of the Indianapolis Bar Association, the Indiana State Bar Association and the American Bar Association. He is a senior fellow of the Indianapolis Bar Association and the American Bar Association. He is a member and former vice president of the 100 Black Men–Indianapolis Chapter. Darden has received numerous awards, including: three Sagamore of the Wabash Awards from three different governors, a Distinguished Alumni Award from the McKinney School of Law, and the Paul H. Buchanan Award of Excellence from the Indianapolis Bar Association. He was inducted into the National Bar Association Hall of Fame and received the Rabb Emison Award from the Indiana State Bar Association. He is also a graduate of the Judicial College of Indiana and the Indiana Graduate Program for Judges. At his retirement ceremony on July 25, 2012, the Indiana Legal Education Opportunity Program announced it would rename its summer program the Carr L. Darden CLEO Summer Intern Program in his honor.

Upon his retirement Senator Evan Bayh spoke eloquently of Darden, saying: “On a professional level, Carr has had a career few have equaled. I had the privilege of making him one of my first judicial appointments to the Marion Municipal Court in 1989. Shortly thereafter, I once again was honored to appoint him to the Marion Superior Court in 1990. Finally, in 1994, I had the privilege of appointing Carr to the Indiana Court of Appeals. He was reelected to that important position twice, by margins much larger than any I have enjoyed in my elections!”

Upon becoming a senior judge, he and his wife Lundy established and fully endowed the Judge Carr L. Darden and Mrs. Lundy M. Darden Public Sector Legal Education Scholarship Fund to help fund and enable students of underrepresented populations to attend the McKinney School of Law.

Selected bibliography

Dinner Dance Brochure. Judge Carr L. Darden Celebrating Milestones in Friendship, Professionalism and Mentorship, September 14, 2012.

Indianapolis Star, December 23, 1990, October 19, 1994, January 4, 2018.

CASES CITED

Hilbert, et al v. Conseco Services, L.L.C., 836 N.E. 2d 1001 (Ind. App.2005).

PHOTO BY JOHN GENTRY

L. MARK BAILEY

January 30, 1998, to present

CRYSTAL G. ROWE

A few days after his forty-first birthday, Judge L. Mark Bailey was presiding over a hearing in Decatur Superior Court when his court reporter passed a note indicating that Governor Frank L. O'Bannon was on the phone. During a short recess, Bailey learned that he was O'Bannon's first appointment to the Court of Appeals of Indiana. Though obviously honored and excited, any celebration of the news would have to wait; Bailey returned to the bench and completed the hearing.

Born in Greensburg on January 21, 1957, Bailey was among the sixth generation to "come of age" on the family's Decatur County homestead. Rural life instilled in him a strong work ethic, humility, and a sense of family and community pride.

At a young age, Bailey decided he wanted to become an attorney. He was a natural fit for the law, given his insatiable quest for knowledge, creativity, quick wit, and analytical style. Lacking a legal mentor to guide him, he contacted law firms listed in the Yellow Pages and was eventually hired as a "file sorter" and "court runner," entry-level jobs that earned him valuable insight into the legal process.

After graduating from the University of Indianapolis in 1978, Bailey gained firsthand experience as a law firm investigator before completing his degree at the Indiana University Robert H. McKinney School of Law. After graduation in 1982, he practiced law with an Indianapolis firm until he and his wife returned to Decatur County to raise their family. Bailey was a solo practitioner until his election as judge of the Decatur County Court in November 1990.

Everyone finds their bus stop, according to one of his law professors, and Bailey determined being a judge was his "bus stop," as he enjoyed "resolving legal disputes better than arguing them." As a trial judge he helped institute changes to benefit his community, including converting the county court to a superior court, which provided citizens more access to the judicial system; starting a work-release program for prisoners; and developing a "basic life skills" program for petty offenders.

As an appellate judge Bailey was appointed by then-Chief Justice Randall T. Shepard as first chair of the Indiana Pro Bono Commission, promoting access to legal representation for indigents. In recognition of his service, Bailey was the first recipient of the Randall T. Shepard Award presented by the commission in 2002. The next year Bailey received from O'Bannon a Sagamore of the Wabash, the highest distinction an Indiana governor can bestow. He later received another Sagamore from Governor Joe Kernan.

On the appeals court, Bailey helped create initiatives to aid Hoosiers to better understand the work of the judiciary. One program, "Appeals on Wheels," presented oral arguments in high schools, colleges, and other venues around the state. The public reacted favorably to these initiatives, and for their efforts Bailey and his First District colleagues on the appeals court received the Law-Related Education Award from the Indiana Bar Foundation.

Bailey has also chaired the Local Coordinating Council of the Governor's Task Force for a Drug-Free Indiana, the Judicial Conference Alternative Dispute Resolution Committee, and the Indiana State Bar Association Appellate Practice Section. Since 2008 Bailey has served on the Supreme Court

Committee on Rules of Practice and Procedure, a committee that critically analyzes court rules to promote simplicity, justice, and efficiency.

Despite his heavy judicial workload, authoring, on average, approximately 160 opinions a year, he earned his master of business administration degree from Indiana Wesleyan University in 1999 and served as the Distinguished Jurist in Residence at Stetson University College of Law in 2006. Bailey was designated a Fellow in 2009 of A*STAR (Agency for Science, Technology and Research), which focuses on scientific discovery and technological innovation. He has also served as an adjunct professor at the University of Indianapolis and has presented at numerous educational seminars.

Bailey's dedication to teaching extends beyond the classroom to his mentoring of his judicial clerks and interns, spending countless hours teaching clerks about legal doctrine, nuanced judicial procedures, and the practice of law in general. In Bailey's chambers is a handmade "scrapbook" assembled by his law clerks in appreciation for his mentorship. Bailey attributes his "paying it forward" philosophy to his own mentor, Harry A. Wilson Jr., a noted Indianapolis trial attorney, who embodied the concept.

As apparent from photos adorning his chambers, Bailey's family remains his greatest success. The most meaningful letters supporting his appellate court nomination came from his young children, with one writing that "my daddy would make a good Court of Appeals guy because he makes the right decisions."

Selected Bibliography

Bailey, L. Mark. "Pro Bono Participation Preserves Justice." *Indiana Pro Bono Commission*, 7B (August 13, 2003).

Fuller, A. James, and Rebecca Blair, "Finding the Bus Stop: L. Mark Bailey." *University of Indianapolis Archives* (April 12, 2006).

"Leadership in Law 2013: Hon. Lloyd Mark Bailey." *The Indiana Lawyer* (April 24, 2013).

Witte, G. Michael, and L. Mark Bailey. "Pre-Adjudication Intervention in Alcohol-Related Cases." *The Judge's Journal* (Summer 1998).

PHOTO BY JOHN GENTRY

MELISSA S. MAY

April 9, 1998, to present

JENNIFER D. WARRINER

On April 9, 1998, Melissa S. May became the fifth woman appointed to the Court of Appeals of Indiana. During her time on the court, May has been fiercely dedicated to educating Hoosiers about the law. Whether serving as a member of the Indiana Judicial Conference's Civil Instruction Committee (1999–2004), on the American Bar Association's Standing Committee on Specialization of attorneys (2003–present), or as an advocate for civility in the bar through the American Board of Trial Advocates Civility Matters program, May has been passionate about improving the law and the legal profession.

May was born Melissa Sue Moller on April 29, 1957, in Elkhart, Indiana. After obtaining a bachelor of science in criminal justice at the South Bend campus of Indiana University in 1980, May attended Indiana University School of Law, Indianapolis, where she was a member of Phi Delta Phi, was vice president of the Student Bar Association, and was a member of and then coach of the International Moot Court Team. She received her doctor of jurisprudence in 1984 and moved to Evansville, Indiana, to practice law as a civil trial lawyer specializing in insurance defense and personal injury. During this time, May married and became Melissa S. Mattingly, the name under which she published opinions when first appointed to the court. After two years on the court, May remarried and released her opinions under the hyphenated "Mattingly-May" until 2003, when she began using simply "May."

Even prior to her appointment to the court, May was a member of the Board of Directors of the Indiana Continuing Legal Education Forum, serving from 1994 to 1999. Over the past twenty years, May has also served ICLEF as a program chairperson and as a program faculty member. From 2001 to date, May has been cochair of ICLEF's Indiana Trial Advocacy College, a yearly four-day workshop to improve the trial skills of practicing lawyers. In 2013 May became program chair of ICLEF's yearly, two-day Robert H. Stanton Indiana Law Update, a position in which she continues to serve. Because of her long-standing dedication to ICLEF's mission, in 2014, ICLEF honored May with its highest award—Excellence in Continuing Legal Education Award.

The Indiana Supreme Court appointed May to the Indiana Pro Bono Commission in 2005, and in 2008, named her chair of that commission. As the 2008 financial crisis unfolded, Chief Justice Randall T. Shepard asked May and the commission to spearhead an initiative to train lawyers all over Indiana to assist homeowners facing foreclosure. With assistance from ICLEF, the Indiana Attorney General's office, law school professors, and practicing attorneys, a three-hour seminar was developed and video recorded. That video was then played at forty locations all over Indiana to educate more than 1,000 lawyers, mediators, and judges on foreclosure law. As a result, during 2009, each of Indiana's fourteen Pro Bono Districts assisted more people than ever before, even as the economic crisis decreased the funding available to assist with legal needs in each district. May's tenure on the Pro Bono Commission ended in 2012, and in 2018 the Indiana Supreme Court appointed May to the Coalition for Court Access, an alliance of interested organizations that is tasked with creating a comprehensive structure to coordinate civil legal-aid programs in Indiana.

In the spring of 2004 May began teaching trial advocacy as an adjunct faculty member at the IU School of Law, Indianapolis, and in 2018 she became head professor of that class. Each year May helps educate citizens around the state about the judicial branch of government by participating in numerous traveling oral arguments for the court of appeals. Recently May joined the steering committee for the 2020 National High School Mock Trial Championship, which is designed to help students develop advocacy and argument skills.

Because of her dedication to educating Hoosiers by bringing one of the court's oral arguments to the university each year since 1998 and her dedication to improving the law and legal profession, the University of Southern Indiana bestowed upon May an honorary doctor of civil law in 2004. In October 2011 the Indiana State Bar Association honored May with the Women in the Law Recognition Award for her dedication to helping women advance in the legal community. May's twenty-one years on the court suggest that, regardless what the future brings, May will continue to use her skills, knowledge, and passion for the law to benefit Indiana's citizens and the legal community.

Selected Bibliography

"Indiana Pro Bono Commission: Bridging the Gap to Justice/Helping Hoosiers through the Economic Crisis." Promotional supplement to *Indiana Lawyer* (May 17, 2010), https://www.inbf.org/Portals/0/Uploads/33/Files/8605ilprobono20100317.pdf.

"Indiana Court of Appeals Judge Melissa S. May Receives ISBA Women in the Law Recognition Award." *Indiana Court Times* (February 6, 2012), http://indianacourts.us/times/2012/02/court-of-appeals-judge-and-spouse-of-supreme-court-justice-both-honored-state-court-administration-staff-join-national-boards/.

"Leadership in Law 2015: Hon. Melissa S. May." *The Indiana Lawyer* (May 5, 2015), https://www.theindianalawyer.com/articles/37008-leadership-in-law-2015-hon-melissa-s-may.

Melissa S. May." History of Attorney Specialization in Indiana." 40 V*alpo University Law Review* 451(2006). https://scholar.valpo.edu/vulr/vol40/iss2/9.

———. "Judicial Retention Elections after 2010." 46 *Indiana Law Review* 59 (2013).

"Mock Trial Steering Committee Announced." *Indiana Court Times* (June 21, 2018), http://indianacourts.us/times/2018/06/mock-trial-steering-committee-announced/.

"Mortgage Foreclosure Attorney Training Update." *Indiana Court Times* (October 31, 2009), http://indianacourts.us/times/2009/10/mortgage-foreclosure attorney-training-update/.

"Supreme Court Opens Three Front Operation on Mortgage Foreclosure. *Indiana Court Times* (April 30, 2009), http://indianacourts.us/times/2009/04/supreme-court-operation-on-foreclosure/.

MARGRET G. ROBB

July 6, 1998, to present

BRIAN KARLE

Margret G. Robb was the first woman, since the court's inception in 1891, to serve as chief judge of the Court of Appeals of Indiana. Born in New York City in 1948, Robb was raised in a family of medical professionals—her father a pathologist and her mother a nurse. She spent her childhood in New York and in northwest Ohio.

In 1966 Robb moved to Indiana and enrolled at Purdue University, graduating in 1970 with a degree in business economics. The following year, she married her husband, Stephen Robb. She returned to Purdue and earned a master's degree in business economics in 1972. After graduation, she began her first job as an Assistant Equal Employment Opportunity Officer for Purdue, ensuring compliance in the university's employment practices.

With the encouragement of her husband, Robb applied to law school and began her first semester at Indiana University's Robert H. McKinney

School of Law in the fall of 1975. She quickly realized a passion and aptitude for the law, finding that the logical approach to analyzing legal issues was a natural fit. Robb received her law degree a semester early, graduating magna cum laude in January of 1978.

After Robb passed the Indiana bar exam, she returned to Lafayette to begin her career as an attorney. She worked at a small firm in Lafayette for six months before transitioning to a position practicing employment law at a firm in Indianapolis. But she had an appetite for variety that a one-topic practice could not satisfy. After two years working in Indianapolis, Robb returned to practice in Lafayette, where she remained until her ascension to the Court of Appeals of Indiana.

Robb found Lafayette to be a welcoming legal community full of attorneys willing to share advice and lend a hand. Over the next two decades she developed a successful practice. A fitting preparation for a seat on the Court of Appeals, her private practice was wide ranging. She litigated matters of divorce, custody, and guardianships, and she held a reputation for expertise in the realm of family law. Robb represented indigent clients as a public defender in Tippecanoe County. She served as a bankruptcy trustee at the Northern District federal courthouse in Lafayette. She litigated civil actions. She acted as a mediator for family law and civil disputes. She also litigated the occasional appeal, including victories in the Indiana Supreme Court in *Stultz v. Stultz* and *Garrod v. Garrod*. In *Stultz*, the court ruled that a child's receipt of Social Security benefits does not per se entitle the parent to a credit against child support. In *Garrod*, the court held that circumstances such as net worth may permit a child support payment higher than the presumptive amount.

In July 1998 Robb was appointed to the Court of Appeals of Indiana by Governor Frank L. O'Bannon. As an appellate judge, Robb viewed her role as that of an advocate, approaching each appeal with the goal of writing an opinion that would convince the reader of the correctness of the outcome and the soundness of the reasoning behind it.

Robb's legacy as a Court of Appeals of Indiana judge extends well beyond her twenty-plus years on the bench or the more than 3,000 majority opinions she has authored. Her tenure on the court has been marked with volunteerism and a commitment to furthering legal education. She was active as a volunteer or member in legal organizations at both the state and national level. Among other things, Robb served as the president of the Council of Chief Judges of the State Courts of Appeal and chair of the National Association of Women Judges' annual conference. She was also a member of the American Law Institute. Robb is the recipient of numerous awards and recognitions, including the Indiana Commission for Women's Trailblazer Award and a 2012 Concurrent Resolution of the Indiana House and Senate.

Robb also served as a member of the American Bar Association Accreditation Committee, evaluating law schools for accreditation. She was chair of the Appellate Judges Education Institute, a leading national conference for appellate education. On the state level, Robb volunteered regularly as an organizer, presenter, or panelist for countless legal education seminars.

Robb also took a more personal role in fostering legal education. Every year, she hired a newly minted attorney to serve as a judicial law clerk in her chambers. She believed that mentoring young lawyers built a better bar in Indiana, and she took pride in doing just that. The walls of her chambers are adorned with dozens of framed court decisions—the first opinion drafted by each clerk who worked in her chambers.

Selected Bibliography

Court of Appeals of Indiana, Annual Reports 2008–2018, https://www.in.gov/judiciary/appeals/2343.htm

Margaret G. Robb. Interview with author. Lafayette, October 8, 2018.

Robb, Margret G. "Running Bases, Winning Cases: Why the Grand Old Game of Baseball Is Like the Legal Profession." *ABA Journal* 80 (August 1996): 140.

Staton, Robert H., and Gina M. Hicklin. "The History of the Court of Appeals of Indiana, *Indiana Law Review* 30, no.1 (1997): 203–31.

CASES CITED

Garrod v. Garrod, 655 N.E.2d 336 (Ind. 1995).

Stultz v. Stultz, 659 N.E.2d 125 (Ind. 1995)

SANFORD M. BROOK

October 5, 1998–February 27, 2004

NANCY HARRIS VAIDIK

Sanford M. "Sandy" Brook is at home in the courtroom. In fact, after spending thirty years in Indiana courtrooms as a trial lawyer and then as a trial and appellate judge, Brook joined a firm with a full-sized, working courtroom in its offices—Colorado-based Judicial Arbiter Group, one of the oldest and most successful private judicial services in the country.

Brook was born on June 23, 1949, in South Bend, Indiana. His father was a taxi driver and a salesman, his mother a homemaker and a clerical worker. A run-in with the law during high school led to an encounter with a helpful lawyer, which set Brook down the path to becoming a lawyer. He worked his way through four years of college at Indiana University, Bloomington—including the graveyard shift as a parking-lot attendant—earning a degree in political science in 1971. Brook stayed in Bloomington for law school and graduated in 1974.

Brook began his legal career in private practice as an assistant city attorney for the city of South Bend. His private practice included work in reproductive rights, and he was eventually named to the national board of the Planned Parenthood Federation of America. His life in the courtroom began in earnest with a 1978 conversation with friend and future court of appeals colleague Michael P. Barnes. Barnes wanted to run for Saint Joseph County prosecutor, but he would first have to take down the Democratic Party's preferred candidate in the primary. With Brook playing a major role in his campaign, Barnes pulled off the upset and then won the general election. Brook then became a deputy prosecutor, a position in which he tried almost a hundred jury trials.

Governor Robert D. Orr appointed Brook to the Saint Joseph Superior Court in 1987. Though he often envied the lawyers practicing before him, Brook still spent plenty of time in the courtroom, presiding over more than four hundred jury and bench trials. It was during his time as a trial-court judge that Brook began teaching trial advocacy, both as an adjunct professor at Notre Dame Law School and with the National Institute for Trial Advocacy. In 1994 the NITA published a book that Brook coauthored, *Indiana Rules of Evidence and Objections*. Brook coached a Notre Dame team that won a national trial competition sponsored by the American Bar Association.

In 1998 Governor Frank L. O'Bannon appointed Brook to fill the Court of Appeals of Indiana vacancy created by the retirement of Judge George Hoffman Jr. Brook moved to Indianapolis, which allowed him to begin teaching trial advocacy at his alma mater in Bloomington. He has also taught advocacy in England, Scotland, Northern Ireland, Thailand, and China. Brook became the chief judge of the court of appeals in 2002. He was inducted into the IU Academy of Law Alumni Fellows in 2003. At the time of his inductions a colleague said of him that he impressed upon his students the responsibility "to act with dignity, professionalism, and the utmost ability when undertaking the awesome trust placed in us by those we represent."

Although Brook said good-bye to Indiana and the court of appeals in 2004, he did not leave courtroom life behind. He joined JAG—an alternative dispute resolution firm composed exclusively of former federal and state court judges—and began his career as an arbitrator, mediator, and private judge. Brook is now co-owner of the firm and maintains an active practice, focusing on professional malpractice, products liability, construction, and catastrophic injury cases. He also serves as a litigation training consultant for a large international law firm. He employs his longtime passion for the stage by performing the one-man show "Darrow" for legal groups around the country. To celebrate his seventieth birthday in June 2019, Brook sailed the Amalfi coast in Italy.

Selected bibliography

Brook, Sanford, coauthor. *Indiana Rules of Evidence and Objections.* National Institute of Trial Attorneys, 1994.
Indiana University Academy of Law Alumni Fellows, 2003. https://www.law.indiana.edu/alumni/awards/academy.
Sanford Brook. Telephone interview by Nancy Vaidik, May 10, 14, 2019.

NANCY H. VAIDIK

February 7, 2000, to present

AMANDA J. BUNTON

Wife. Mother of twins. Nana. Gymnast. Foodie. Yogi. Book Clubber. Knitter. World Traveler. Teacher. Attorney. Prosecutor. Trial-court judge. Author. Court of Appeals of Indiana judge for twenty years, six as chief judge. No one ever said Nancy Harris Vaidik does not keep busy.

Vaidik was born on June 24, 1955, in Lafayette and grew up in Portage in Porter County, Indiana. She was exposed to politics at a young age, when she went door to door campaigning for town council and mayoral candidates. Her involvement in politics continued as a teenager, when she campaigned for Congressman Floyd J. Fithian. But politics was not her only interest. She was also a cheerleader and a champion gymnast.

Vaidik attended Valparaiso University. She worked her way through college by pumping gas at Clark Oil and judging high-school gymnastic competitions. Vaidik became interested in the law when a family friend was incarcerated—unjustly, Vaidik believed—just before he was to finish high school. Vaidik tutored him at the jail so that he could graduate with his class on time, but she was not able to help him with his legal troubles. However, after graduating from Valparaiso with high distinction in 1977 with majors in political science and psychology, Vaidik remained at the university for law school. It was during her second year that she gave birth to twin daughters, Kristin and Kelly. She graduated from law school in 1980.

Her legal career began as a deputy and then chief deputy prosecutor in Porter County, trying over a hundred jury trials. She was the prosecutor in the high-profile case *State v. Richard Kirby*, which involved a trial of a father for the murder of his five-year-old son. He was convicted. Also while a prosecutor, Vaidik developed a passion for helping victims. She started both victims-assistance and domestic-violence programs, including the Porter County Sexual Assault Recovery Project, the first of its kind in the state and still in operation today. Vaidik later went into private practice, specializing in family law, probate, municipal law, and general litigation. While in court one day for a hearing, Vaidik leaned over to her client and whispered, "I should run for judge." Her client quickly responded, "I'm your campaign manager." Vaidik's trial-judge campaign was launched that day.

Vaidik was elected judge of Porter Superior Court Four in 1991 and took office in 1992. As a judge, Vaidik continued her work in domestic violence. She was instrumental in bringing together the police, shelters, the hospital, the jail, churches, and prosecuting and defense attorneys to tackle domestic-violence issues in the community. For these efforts, Vaidik was awarded the Indiana Domestic Violence Coalition Judge of the Year in 1996. Also as a judge, Vaidik was the head of the Indiana Supreme Court's Judicial Education Committee. During this time, the philosophy on educating judges changed from learning by lectures to learning by doing. This change in philosophy culminated in a bench-skills course designed by Vaidik that all new trial-court judges must now take during orientation. She was also actively involved in the Indiana Judges Association, serving as its secretary/treasurer, vice president, and president.

In February 2000 Governor Frank L. O'Bannon appointed Vaidik to fill the Court of Appeals of Indiana vacancy created by the appointment of Robert D. Rucker Jr. to the Indiana Supreme Court, and she was retained by election in 2002 and 2012. Vaidik and her husband, James Stankiewicz, kept their home in Porter County and purchased a second house in Indianapolis, with Vaidik returning to Porter County on the weekends.

During this time, Vaidik explored another one of her passions, teaching trial advocacy and evidence. She has taught at many law schools, including Indiana University Maurer School of Law. She has also taught for several organizations, including the National Institute for Trial Advocacy, which awarded her the Honorable Robert E. Keeton Award for Teaching in 2006. Her teaching has taken her all over the world. She has trained United Nations lawyers involved in prosecuting Rwandan war crimes, Mexican lawyers prosecuting drug lords, and attorneys in Northern Ireland, Ireland, China, England, Scotland, Belgium, Switzerland, France, Austria, Czech Republic, Tanzania, Spain, and Canada. She is also the coauthor of two published works: *Point Well Made: Oral Advocacy in Motions Practice* and *Paul v. Dynamo Sporting Goods, Dillon, and Hanson: A Motion Practice Case Study*.

Vaidik was selected by her colleagues to serve as chief judge for the court of appeals for two terms, from January 1, 2014, to December 31, 2019. Her tenure as chief judge was highlighted by improvements in technology and employee wellness. E-filing was implemented in 2015, transitioning the court of appeals from a paper-based system to an electronic one, and Vaidik also started a court-wide blog, called Appealing News, to keep employees connected. In addition, the court of appeals adopted a long-term plan to make a healthier workplace environment for its employees, including providing standing desks and other ergonomic equipment, oversized computer screens, lighting to reduce eye strain, and employee lounges. As chief judge, Vaidik focused not only on the work of the court but also on fostering greater community and collegiality.

When she is not judging, teaching, and writing, Vaidik spends her time visiting Kristin, a lawyer, and Kelly, a medical doctor, doing yoga, reading books, and knitting sweaters for her grandchildren.

Selected bibliography

Cloud, Morgan, Mary Pat Dooley, Terre Rushton, and Nancy H. Vaidik. *Paul v. Dynamo Sporting Goods, Dillon, and Hanson: A Motion Practice Case Study*. Boulder, CO: National Institute for Trial Advocacy, 2018.

Vaidik, Nancy H., and Rebecca Diaz-Bonilla. *Point Well Made: Oral Advocacy in Motion Practice*. Boulder, CO: National Institute for Trial Advocacy, 2016.

CASE CITED

Kirby v. State, 481 N.E.2d 372 (Ind. 1985).

PAUL D. MATHIAS

March 30, 2000, to present

NANCY E. BOYER

When Judge Paul Devon Mathias began practicing law in 1979, the Internet, smart phones, and other electronic devices did not exist. However, Mathias has been instrumental in the transformation of the Indiana judiciary by leading Indiana from a paper-based court-filing system to an electronic-filing system.

Indiana Supreme Court Justice Steven David said, "Judge Mathias has not only been the technological visionary for Indiana but he has helped to shape and influence the merger of Technology, Case Management Systems, E-Filing, and Court Services throughout the nation. His contributions can never be overstated."

Whether professionally or outside the legal realm, Mathias's life has been rooted in service to others. Born on December 7, 1953, in LaGrange County, Indiana, Mathias moved at the age of two to Fort Wayne where he remained until his appointment to the Court of Appeals of Indiana on

March 30, 2000. The value and power of education was instilled in Mathias at an early age. His parents, Amaryllis and Devon Mathias, were both educators in the Fort Wayne Community School system. His parents encouraged Mathias to strive for a strong education, which he did when he applied to Harvard University. In 1976 Mathias graduated cum laude from Harvard. While at Harvard, Mathias was a member of the glee club and Harvard's original and oldest small acapella group, The Krokodiloes.

Mathias received his law degree from the Indiana University Maurer School of Law in 1979. Upon graduation he entered private practice at the Fort Wayne law firm of Parker, Hoover, Keller and Waterman (now Faegre Baker Daniels) where he concentrated in construction law and appellate practice. In 1985 Mathias was appointed referee of the Allen County Small Claims Court, where he served until he became judge of the Allen Superior Court in 1989. His tenure in small claims court molded his view of the judiciary. Mathias often stated that small claims is "where the rubber meets the road, with regard to how people feel about the judiciary." Small claims court provided Mathias with the opportunity to help self-represented litigants understand how the judicial system works.

Long before his appointment to the Court of Appeals of Indiana in 2000, Mathias became concerned about court intervention regarding the mentally ill. As a member of the court, he wrote many majority opinions and dissents concerning definitions of mental illness, due process for the mentally ill, and the need to determine competency at the time of the commission of a crime, rather than much later for the benefit of counsel. In *Wampler v. State,* Mathias dissented from the court's majority which upheld a thirty-three-year sentence given for two felonies and being a habitual offender. Mathias thought that given the defendant's "serious and obvious mental illness" he should have been given a civil commitment, not incarceration. He said the court's ruling represented the "failure, yet again, of our criminal justice system to adequately address and properly respond to and treat those with mental health issues."

In 2016 Mathias authored an opinion that would eventually cause the incorporation of the Eighth Amendment Excessive Fines Clause to all fifty states. In *State v. Timbs,* Mathias held that civil forfeiture of a $40,000 motor vehicle was punitive and disproportionate to the crime committed in violation of the Excessive Fines Clause. In affirming Mathias, the U.S. Supreme Court ruled that the Excessive Fines Clause is a protected right under the Fourteenth Amendment's Due Process Clause, and therefore applies to state actions.

In addition to his extraordinary legal work, Mathias's community contributions are exemplified by his leadership in the "We the People" program, developed in 1987, to teach students how government works. It culminates with a simulated congressional hearing where the students appear before a panel of "judges," demonstrating their knowledge and understanding of constitutional principles. Mathias said, "[We the People] is the best way to teach students their responsibilities, as well as their rights, under the Constitution." For his strong devotion to "We the People," he received the Indiana Bar Foundation's William G. Baker Civic Education Award in 2010. In addition, Mathias has received the Indiana State Bar Association's Centennial Service Award, and has been named a Sagamore of the Wabash three times.

Whether through music, technology, law, or teaching, Mathias's contributions to the law, the judiciary, and the citizens of Indiana cannot be overemphasized. Mathias said, "I am so honored and fortunate to serve Hoosiers on the Court of Appeals. It has provided me the opportunity to be a part of something greater than myself, and I hope that my service has been for a higher purpose." Indeed, it has.

Selected Bibliography

David, Steven. E-mail message to Nancy E. Boyer, March 20, 2019.

"The Harvard Krokodiloes." Wikipedia, https://en.wikipedia.org/wiki/The_Harvard_Krokodiloes. Last modified March 7, 2019.

Indiana Bar Foundation. "We the People Program." https://inbf.org/Educational-Programs/We-The-People. Accessed May 1, 2019.

Leblanc, Matthew. "High Court Rules on Fines by State." *Fort Wayne Journal Gazette*, February 21, 2019. http://www.journalgazette.net/news/local/courts/20190221/high-court-rules-on-fines-by-state.

Mathias, Carlabeth. Personal Interview by Nancy E. Boyer. Fort Wayne, March 8, 2019.

Paul Mathias's Linkedin page. https://www.linkedin.com/in/paul-mathias-7a6790a/. Accessed May 1, 2019.

Mathias, Paul. Interview by The Lasting Lawyer Legacy Project. Video interview. Fort Wayne, http://genealogycenter.info/LifeStories/lawyerlegacy/video_paulmathias.php.

Mathias, Paul. E-mail message to Nancy E. Boyer, October 9, 2018, April 16, 2019.

CASES CITED

Wampler v. State, 57 N.E.3d 884, 890 (Ind. App. 2016).

Wampler v. State, 67 N.E. 3d 633 (Ind. 2017).

State v. Timbs, 62 N.E. 3d 472 (Ind. App. 2016).

State v. Timbs, 84 N.E. 3d 1179 (Ind. 2017).

Timbs v. Indiana, 139 S.Ct. 682 (2018).

MICHAEL P. BARNES

May 22, 2000–June 15, 2018 • Senior Judge: June 16, 2018–May 22, 2020

TERRY A. CRONE

Michael P. Barnes was born in Peoria, Illinois, on December 12, 1947. He was too young to watch his beloved Cleveland Indians win their most recent World Series pennant in 1948, but he made up for lost time by attending countless games, spring training sessions, and fantasy camps, where he ferried around Hall of Famers Larry Doby and Bob Feller.

Barnes's passion for sports developed during his childhood in rural Bradford, Illinois, population 850. Two nuns at his parochial elementary school taught him the finer points of baseball, and he played on the undefeated conference champion high school football team in 1964. He attended Saint Ambrose College in Davenport, Iowa, where he was student body president and received a bachelor of arts degree in history in 1970. He obtained his law degree from the University of Notre Dame Law School in 1973 and remains a diehard Notre Dame football and basketball fan.

After graduating from law school, Barnes practiced law at the South Bend, Indiana, firm of Voor, Jackson, McMichael and Allen, and served as a part-time deputy prosecutor. In 1978 he was elected as the first full-time Saint Joseph County prosecuting attorney. During his two decades in this office, he spearheaded several innovative initiatives, including a domestic and family violence unit for abused and neglected women and children, as well as a pretrial diversion program for nonviolent misdemeanor offenders that served as the basis for successful statewide legislation. He was instrumental in establishing the Child Abuse Services, Investigation, and Education Center for abused, neglected, and exploited children, which has been upheld as a model nationwide. His office collected more than $100 million in delinquent child support payments and received state and national recognition for those efforts.

While prosecutor, Barnes personally tried more than twenty-five murder and other major felony cases and oversaw a staff of sixty-five. He was elected president of the National District Attorneys Association (1995–96) and served as chairman of the board, Indiana Prosecuting Attorneys Council (1982–83, 1992–93), president of the Saint Joseph County Bar Association (1992–93), and chairman of the board of Regents, National College of District Attorneys (1997–98). He was a member of the National Board of Trial Advocacy (1995–96), National Advisory Council on Violence Against Women (1997), American Prosecutor's Research Institute (1997–98), and served on the boards of various other professional and civic organizations.

In 1984 Barnes campaigned unsuccessfully for a seat in the U.S. House of Representatives. His campaign against nude dancing in Saint Joseph County was more successful, so much so that he was named as a defendant in a federal lawsuit brought by adult entertainment businesses challenging the constitutionality of Indiana's public indecency statute. The case wound its way to the U.S. Supreme Court, which held in *Barnes v. Glen Theatre, Inc.* that the statute did not violate the First Amendment protection of freedom of expression. The transcript of the Court's oral argument, which Barnes attended as a party to the lawsuit, was developed into an off-Broadway multimedia stage production, which he attended as an honored guest.

In 1994, while attending a Cleveland Indians away game against the Chicago White Sox, Barnes played a supporting role in the drama surrounding a corked bat used by Indians slugger Albert Belle. The bat was impounded by the officials, but an Indians player replaced it with another player's bat. The switcheroo was discovered, and controversy ensued. Barnes served as a pro tem lawyer for Indians management and convinced the interested parties that the incident was a baseball administrative matter and not a criminal legal matter.

In May 2000, after a brief stint in private practice, Barnes was appointed to the Court of Appeals of Indiana by Governor Frank L. O'Bannon. In *Ritter v. Stanton*, decided in 2001, he affirmed what was then Indiana's largest jury verdict in a personal-injury case. He wrote more than 2,800 majority opinions during his tenure. Several of his concurring opinions were adopted by the Indiana Supreme Court. In 2008, in *Ind. Family & Soc. Servs. Admin. v. Meyer*, the Court agreed with Barnes's concurring opinion regarding a trial court's discretion to allow the belated filing of an agency record. Also, the Court adopted several of his dissenting opinions. In 2008, in *State v. Washington*, the Court agreed with Barnes's dissent regarding whether an officer may question a motorist about possible criminal activity unrelated to the traffic stop arrest absent reasonable suspicion.

Barnes was retained on the court by election in 2002 and 2012 and served as presiding judge of the Third District from 2009 through 2011. He retired from the court in June 2018 and was appointed by the Indiana Supreme Court to serve as a senior judge for the court of appeals.

Barnes was married to Alberta Edwards Barnes, a retired educator, who taught school to pay for his law school tuition. They had two sons and four grandchildren. Judge Barnes died on May 22, 2020.

Selected Bibliography

Covington, Olivia. "Friends, Colleagues Laugh and Cry during Barnes' Retirement Ceremony." *The Indiana Lawyer* (May 31, 2018), https://www.theindianalawyer.com/articles/47174-friends-colleagues-laugh-and-cry-during-barnes-retirement-ceremony.

———. "Retiring Barnes Reflects on Time as Prosecutor, Judge as 3 COA Finalists Selected." *The Indiana Lawyer* (May 29, 2018), https://www.theindianalawyer.com/articles/47124-retiring-barnes-reflects-on-time-as-prosecutor-judge-as-3-coa-finalists-selected.

Indiana Chapter of National Children's Alliance. "Appellate Judge Michael Barnes talks duty to children, women, and families." (July 26, 2016), https://incacs.org/judge-michael-barnes-talks duty-to-children-women-families/.

Odendahl, Marilyn. "South Bend Nudity Case Goes from Supreme Court to the Stage." *The Indiana Lawyer* (October 22, 2013), https://www.theindianalawyer.com/articles/32637-south-bend-nudity-case-goes-from-supreme-court-to-the-stage.

Stafford, David. "Barnes' Retirement from COA Caps 40 years of Public service." *The Indiana Lawyer* (Jan. 23, 2018), https://www.theindianalawyer.com/articles/45943-barnes-retirement-from-coa-caps-40-years-of-public-service.

CASES CITED

Barnes v. Glen Theatre, Inc. 501 U.S. 560 (1991).
Ind. Family & Soc. Servs. Admin. v. Meyer 927 N.E.2d 367 (Ind. 2010).
Ritter v. Stanton 745 N.E.2d 828 (Ind. Ct. App. 2001).
State v. Washington 898 N.E.2d 1200 (Ind. 2008).

TERRY A. CRONE

March 8, 2004, to present

ROBERT G. ALTICE JR.

Terry A. Crone might just be the fastest judge to ever serve on the Court of Appeals of Indiana, and likely the only one who had a pet monkey. Despite a stern exterior, Crone openly shares riveting and often hilarious accounts of his college, law school, family, and other experiences. Along with his entertaining banter and quick wit, he sprinkles in insightfulness and genuine compassion.

Born on September 28, 1951, and raised in South Bend, Indiana, Crone was valedictorian of Riley High School and a three-time city sprint champion and was inducted into the Riley High School Athletic Hall of Fame in 2002. Crone attended DePauw University, where he graduated cum laude in 1974 with majors in history and political science. His record for the 200-meter dash remains third on the list of all-time top times for DePauw Men's Track and Field. After DePauw, Crone attended Notre Dame Law School, graduating in 1977.

Crone spent the first nine years of his legal career in private practice, which included acting as the Saint Joseph County attorney and serving as President of the Saint Joseph County Bar Association. After a few years as magistrate of the Saint Joseph Circuit Court, he became the judge of that court in 1989 until his appointment to the court of appeals for the third district in 2004. Governor Joseph E. Kernan said of his first and only appellate appointee, "He is a brilliant judge who understands the practical implications of his decisions."

Throughout his career, Crone has focused on improving the system for all citizens, especially the most vulnerable. As a trial judge, he initiated the first Spanish-speaking program for public defenders in Saint Joseph County. In his local community, Crone also helped start a program in South Bend to familiarize minority high school students with the law and related fields and was a founding member of both the South Bend Commission on the Status of African-American Males and the Saint Joseph County Coalition Against Drugs. As an appellate judge, Crone has mentored many interns, including participants in the Indiana Conference for Legal Education Opportunity program. He has also volunteered to participate in numerous continuing legal education programs. When asked in 2014 what one book all appellate judges should read, Crone suggested *Devil in the Grove: Thurgood Marshall, the Groveland Boys, and the Dawn of a New America* by Gilbert King. Regarding his selection, Crone noted the importance of remembering "the abuses that were occurring not so long ago," understanding why we have certain procedural safeguards, and realizing that these safeguards "ought to be adapted to an ever changing society."

Crone's civic mindedness flowed from the examples set by his parents, the late Phil and Beverly Crone, both of whom were named a Sagamore of the Wabash by Governor Evan Bayh and had long and distinguished careers of public service. Crone himself was named a Sagamore of the Wabash by Kernan in 2005. Crone was instrumental in drafting several pieces of legislation to maintain and improve the independence of the judiciary. His background as both a trial attorney and a trial judge provide him with the knowledge and experience to dissect complicated legal issues and explain them in everyday language. Crone is a staunch defender of civil liberties, an enthusiastic inquisitor during oral arguments, and an author of significant opinions in the areas of tort and criminal law. He has not been afraid to question the logic behind existing precedent and has often advocated for changes in legislation and the common law. As of June 2019 Crone had authored over 2,300 majority opinions and eighty dissents, and he led the court in majority opinions issued in 2012, 2013, and 2016.

Crone and his wife Cheryl raised three successful daughters—an attorney, an anesthesiologist and a doctor of psychology—and now have five grandchildren. Crone enjoys time with his family and eagerly embraces challenging cases on the court and lively discussions with colleagues, but that is not to say that you will not occasionally find him on a golf course.

Selected Bibliography

"Beverly Crone, first female St. Joe County commissioner, dies at 85." *South Bend Tribune*, January 2, 2018.

"Interrogatories." *IndyBar* (March 12, 2014). www.theindianalawyer.com/articles/33651-interrogatories-31214.

"Terry Crone '74 Appointed to Indiana Court of Appeals." *DePauw University News*, February 18, 2004. www.depauw.edu/news-media/details/13239/.

CALE J. BRADFORD

August 1, 2007, to present

C. ADDISON BRADFORD

Despite being named after a federal court judge, Cale J. Bradford never thought he would end up becoming a judge—let alone a judge on the Court of Appeals of Indiana. Spending much of his childhood and teenage years on the shores of Lake Tippecanoe, he instead expected his office would likely be on a pontoon boat or at a marina. Although his uncanny ability to weave boat puns into ordinary conversation may have better prepared him for a career on the lake, his kindness and pragmatism ultimately led him to a black robe rather than black swim trunks.

Bradford was elected to the Marion Superior Court in 1996 and was sworn in the next year. He served the first seven years of his trial-court tenure in criminal court and the last three in civil court. Bradford was reelected by county voters in 2002 and on August 1, 2007, Governor Mitchell E.

Daniels appointed Bradford to the court of appeals, filling the seat vacated by Judge Patrick D. Sullivan. Bradford was retained by state voters in 2010.

What led Bradford to prominence among his party, the central Indiana legal community, and his judicial colleagues was unsurprisingly not his interview-format television show "Off the Bench with Judge Cale Bradford," which aired on the governmental access channel and shockingly never broke the top twenty in the Nielson ratings, but his ability to appreciate the scope and nuance of complex legal and policy issues and bring together officials from all political parties and branches of government to craft solutions to those issues. One of those issues was jail overcrowding in Marion County, which had become so significant the county jail had been under federal oversight for almost thirty years. One jail consultant remarked in a federal lawsuit that the "conditions . . . in Marion County were among the worst" the consultant had seen, with some inmates sleeping on the floor, dirty mattresses, and even on picnic tables. Bradford was appointed as the chair of the Marion County Criminal Justice Planning Council, where he brought together officials from all three branches in crafting recommendations to help cure the jail's overcrowding issues. As a result of these recommendations inmate conditions improved, and federal oversight of the county jails concluded.

Bradford continued to use that gift of reconciliation while on the court of appeals. During his first ten years on the court, Bradford authored 1,560 majority opinions, including leading the court in the number of majority opinions in 2017 and otherwise placing among the court's most prolific writers in almost every other year. Many of these opinions were the type of lake-law issues he was around since he was a kid, including cases involving the tort liability and water rights of property owners abutting a lake, as in the cases of *Mohr v. Virginia B. Smith Revocable Trust* and *N. G. Hatton Trust v. Young*, as well as the construction of seawalls next to a lake, addressed in *Indiana Department of Natural Resources v. Prosser*. Bradford further opined on these cases in an article about lake law he coauthored for the *Indiana Law Review* titled "You're Going to Need a Bigger Boat: Navigating the Uncertain Waters of Lake Law."

His ability to bring others together and provide pragmatic solutions to systemic issues was not limited to the courtroom. Concerned with preserving the integrity and independence of Marion County's judicial selection process, Bradford advocated in his personal capacity for the appointment of Marion County's judges through a merit-selection process, rather than through the types of partisan elections that have since come to jeopardize public perception of the judiciary in other parts of the country. Considering Bradford's unique perspective as a judge who served under both partisan and merit selection systems, the Indiana General Assembly adopted a merit-selection process. Bradford later served as the vice chair of this committee.

At a more individual level, Bradford spent much of his time outside the courtroom teaching and mentoring others. Bradford volunteered as a member of the Alumni Association Board of the Robert H. McKinney School of Law and served as an adjunct professor for almost a decade at Indiana University–Purdue University at Indianapolis. And, of course, never losing sight of his childhood, he routinely taught others how to waterski.

Selected Bibliography

Bradford, Cale, J., et al. "You Are Going to Need a Bigger Boat: Navigating the Uncertain Waters of Lake Law. *Indiana Law Review* 51 (2018).

Hoskins, Michael. "Federal Judge Lifts Marion County Jail Oversight." *Indiana Law* (January 1, 2007).

Odendahl, Marilyn. "17 Marion County Judges Begin New Retention Process, 3 Opt to Retire." *Indiana Law* (February 21, 2018).

CASES CITED

Marion County Jail Inmates v. Anderson 270 F. Supp. 2d 1034, 1036 (S.D. Ind. 2003).

Mohr v. Virginia B. Smith Revocable Trust, 2 N.E. 3d 50 (Ind. Ct. App. 2014).

N. G. Hatton Trust v. Young. 97 N.E. 3d 282 (Ind. Ct. App. 2018)

Department of Natural Resources v. Prosser 132 N.E. 3d 397, 401 (Ind. Ct. App. 2019).

ELAINE B. BROWN

May 5, 2008, to present

NANCY HARRIS VAIDIK

"Mom for Judge!" "Elect Elaine!" Those are the refrains that helped make Elaine Becher Brown the first woman judge in Dubois County and the twenty-second woman judge in Indiana.

Brown was born on February 8, 1954, in the small town of Ferdinand, Indiana. Her father served as a waist gunner in the U.S. Army Air Corps during World War II. She has three siblings. After Brown graduated from high school in 1972, she studied at the University of Evansville for a year, before transferring to Indiana University in Bloomington. She graduated in 1976 with a bachelor's degree in fine arts "With Distinction." At the time, there were primarily two career options available to women, either teaching or nursing. Brown could not stand the sight of blood, so she became a teacher and spent three years teaching art in Jasper schools. But wanting something more she decided to pursue law school and was admitted to the

IU Maurer School of Law. Anxious to start practicing she pushed herself to finish law school in two and a half years instead of the usual three. She graduated in 1982 and joined a law firm in Jasper.

At the age of thirty-two, she decided to run for judge against the male incumbent who had been on the bench for ten years. She put her heart, soul, mind, and body into her campaign. She went door-to-door, sponsored a softball team, and used the phrase "Elect Elaine!" to create familiarity. She had a special shirt made for her youngest supporter, her thirteen-month-old daughter, Marissa, that said "Mom for Judge!" Aside from shaking hands with nearly every person in Dubois County, she said a donor gave her $2,500 to make a cookbook to use as a campaign giveaway. The cookbook, "Elaine's 86 Recipes for Success," was filled with her grandma's recipes. On the cover, Brown stands in front of a set of law books, wearing a suit jacket and tie. Her thinking behind the photo was that "the more I looked like a man, the better." Brown won the election, and in 1987 became the first woman judge in the county.

Brown got right to work, initiating a countywide alcohol and drug program, establishing the Dubois County Drug Court, and forming the county's first Community Corrections Advisory Board, while serving as the president of the Dubois County Substance Abuse Council. Her passion for rehabilitative sentencing stems from seeing the negative impact that retributive sentencing had on her community. By using alternative-sentencing options such as work release, home detention, day reporting, and community service, Brown helped shift the focus of drug and alcohol violations from punishment to treatment. The new approach was successful, and Brown's hard work did not go unnoticed. In 1992 she was reelected without opposition. Outside of court, Brown served on the Indiana Supreme Court's Judges and Lawyers Assistance Program Committee, Character and Fitness Committee, and Judicial Administration Committee. She was also part of the Appointed Judicial Officers Task Force of the Indiana Judicial Conference.

In 1998 Brown returned to private practice and worked in insurance defense before opening her own firm and hiring her dad to work for her, partly fulfilling his lifelong dream of becoming a lawyer. Still, Brown's passion for the courtroom could not be contained, and in 2004, she ran for her old seat. Once again, Brown successfully ousted the incumbent in another hotly contested race.

In 2008 the retirement of Judge John T. Sharpnack created a vacancy on the Court of Appeals of Indiana. Brown decided to apply, and became the eighth woman to serve on the court of appeals when she was appointed by Governor Mitchell E. Daniels to fill the opening. When she was appointed, the Indiana Supreme Court had reinvigorated the constitutional review of criminal sentences pursuant to Indiana Appellate Rule 7(B). Using her experience in alternative sentencing, Brown leaned into reviewing sentences under Rule 7(B). After eleven years on the court, Brown is known for her careful review of the appropriateness of a sentence.

Brown is devoted to her alma mater, IU. She is a life member of the IU Alumni Association, serves as a member of the Maurer School of Law Alumni Board, and has taught trial advocacy at Maurer for nine years. Brown's biggest source of joy is her family: her son, Gordon (a physician) her daughter, Marissa (a school principal), her son-in-law (a principal at an engineering firm), her daughter-in-law (an oncologist) and her three granddaughters, Lilly, Maddie, and Belle.

Selected Bibliography

Barteau, Betty. "Thirty Years of the Journey of Indiana's Women Judges." *Indiana Law Review* 30, no. 1, (1997): 152–53.

Brown, Elaine B. Interview by author. Indianapolis, April 24, 2019.

Helmond, Tyler D. "Interrogatories: Candid Q&A with Judge Elaine Brown." *IndyBar Blog*. January 19, 2013. https://www.indybar.org/index.cfm?pg=IndyBarBlog&blAction=showEntry&blogEntry=2936. Accessed June 11, 2019.

RUDOLPH R. PYLE III

August 27, 2012, to present

DENNIS D. CARROLL

"I was not at the movie." Judge Rudolph Pyle's judicial philosophy of appellate review is the concluding sentence of a dissent written by him in 2016 in the case of *Love v. State*.

The *Love* dissent compares appellate review to the limitations of reading only the script of a current blockbuster movie. Pyle says, "If you really want to know whether the script is good, you need to go to the movie." Appellate judges are limited to the trial transcript but they do not review a trial transcript in a vacuum. They bring to bear their own personal history of family and social life, observations as citizens, formal and "street" education, and their prior professional journey. This personal history provides a contextual understanding of the transcript of a trial and of evidence.

Born October 28, 1969, and raised in Rhode Island, Pyle was the middle child of a family of strong faith and big accomplishment. Pyle often played his trumpet in the Sunday worship service. In 1987 the family moved to

Anderson, Indiana, when Pyle's father, an agriculture and family science scholar, accepted a faculty position at Anderson University.

Always a good student, Pyle capped his high school education by enrolling in 1987 at the U.S. Military Academy Prep School. Following prep school and an honorable discharge from the army, Pyle enrolled at Anderson University, completing a degree in history and political science in 1992. During his undergraduate career, Pyle was active in sports and served two terms as student body president. After undergraduate studies, Pyle completed a master's in public policy in 1994 from the College of William and Mary.

His childhood dream of a career in law enforcement was realized in 1994 when Pyle became an Indiana State Trooper, assigned to District 13 in Lowell, Indiana. In 1997 Pyle left the state police to attend law school, graduating from the Indiana University Maurer School of Law in 2000. For the next three years, Pyle clerked for Judge Carr L. Darden at the Court of Appeals of Indiana.

Ready for real courtroom experience, in 2004, Pyle joined the staff of the Madison County Prosecutor as a trial deputy. In 2005 he left the prosecutor's office to open a law practice, but he returned to the prosecutor's office full time the next year, remaining until his appointment in 2009 by Governor Mitchell E. Daniels to the Madison County Circuit Court bench. The citizens of Madison County elected Pyle to a full six-year term in the general election of 2010. Pyle was the first African American jurist to serve in Madison County. Recognizing the significance of his appointment he said, "Here we have the first African American judge in 2009. We, as a community, have come this far."

In 2012 Pyle moved another notch up the judicial ladder when he was appointed by Daniels to serve on the Court of Appeals of Indiana. He won a retention election for the court in 2014 extending his term on the bench for another ten years.

Despite his own education and life of accomplishment, Pyle recalled the burden of historic racism in a concurring opinion in *Middleton v. State* in 2016. Middleton's defense counsel referred to his absent client as a "Negro," failing, unfortunately, to recognize the historic power of that term. While acknowledging that the word "Negro" is not always used derisively, Pyle noted that the term is often cross-referenced in current dictionaries as a vile, racial slur. Thus, for Middleton's advocate to identify his client with a racially offense slur was unacceptable advocacy. History matters.

In the summer of 1996, Pyle experienced an event that likely awakened a Christian and civic duty to be of service. His family was vacationing on the beach in Martha's Vineyard when they noticed a young father and his two children in a rubber raft being pulled by the wind and tide out to sea. The father was clearly losing the battle to return to shore. As luck would have it, Pyle had snorkeling gear with him, and he put on fins and began to swim toward the raft. He reached the raft, grabbed an attached rope, and began the arduous slow swim back to shore against the tide. Later, Pyle reflected, "It needed to be done."

The story of a judge's life shapes and informs his or her character. Some of the most important influences in Pyle's life included being an oceanside hero, a faithful church musician, a student-leader, army vet, adjunct professor, devoted father to Seth, state trooper, trial judge, university trustee, and appellate judge.

Selected Bibliography

"Governor Appoints Pyle to Bench." *Anderson Herald Bulletin*, October 4, 2009.
News Release from the Office of Governor Mitch Daniels. August 7, 2012.
Pyle, Carolyn (Judge Pyle's mother). Interview by the author, February 23, 2019.
Pyle, Rudolph R. Discussions between the author and Judge Pyle, e-mail February 16, 2019, and material provided by Judge Pyle including a current resume (2019).
"Rudolph R. Pyle III, Madison County's First Black Judge." *Indianapolis Recorder*, February 17, 2010.

CASES CITED

Love v. State, 61 N.E.3d 290 (Ind. App. 2016).
Middleton v. State, 64 N.E.3d 895 (Ind. App. 2016).

ROBERT R. ALTICE JR.

September 2, 2015, to present

MARK S. MASSA

Bob Altice spent his childhood and adolescence in several states. Fortunately for Indiana, he met Kris, his Hoosier bride, in college and a decade later found his way to Indianapolis, where he began a remarkable career of public service that led to his appointment to the Court of Appeals of Indiana by Governor Michael R. Pence in 2015.

In every post, "Judge Bob," as he is affectionately known, has brought a natural and informal affability that has made him popular with colleagues, staff, attorneys, and litigants. At his investiture for the Court of Appeals, the Supreme Court courtroom was packed to capacity and an overflow crowd watched streaming video of the proceedings in the House and Senate chambers. But as one speaker noted at that ceremony, "to focus too much on Bob's charm is to overlook his immense talent." He has been a leader and success in every assignment along the way.

Born November 24, 1960, in Norfolk, Virginia, Altice started high school in Ohio, finished in Kansas, and enrolled at Miami (Ohio) University in 1979. Altice went on to earn a master's degree in criminal justice from the University of Central Missouri in 1984 and his law degree from the University of Missouri-Kansas City in 1987. He and Kris wed in 1988, and she earned her law degree from UMKC the following year.

While in law school, Altice worked for the Missouri Attorney General, and as a certified legal intern for the Jackson County, Missouri, prosecutor's office; in the evenings he cooked and tended bar at a tavern in Kansas City, enhancing his people skills and common touch. He became one of the top lawyers in the prosecutor's office, serving as chief deputy prosecutor for the Drug Unit and supervising ten other attorneys.

Altice joined the Kansas City firm of Shugart Thomson and Kilroy in early 1992, defending medical malpractice cases; later that year, Kris accepted a job with an Indiana law firm and the couple moved to Indianapolis. Altice joined Wooden McLaughlin and Sterner, but missed the courtroom and criminal law, and joined the Marion County Prosecutor's Office in 1994. He rapidly rose to courtroom supervisor, chief of the Felony Division, and chief counsel to the prosecutor. He tried more than one hundred jury cases and twenty-five murders, including many in the public spotlight, by specific assignment from Prosecutor Scott Newman, whose trust he had quickly earned. In 2000 Altice was elected to the Marion Superior Court.

During eleven years on the criminal bench, Altice presided over 250 major felony jury trials, including seventy murder trials and seven capital cases. These included many of great public import, including the worst mass murder in modern times in Indianapolis. Yet he still found time to be a leader off the bench, serving as chair of the Marion Superior Court Criminal Term from 2005 to 2007, as a member of the executive committee of the Marion Superior Court from 2007 to 2009, and as presiding judge from 2009 to 2011. Altice also accepted assignments from the Indiana Supreme Court to serve on the Judicial Performance Task Force and the Cameras in the Courtroom Advisory Project.

Altice moved to the civil bench in Marion County in 2013. Two years later, he was appointed to the court of appeals. At a news conference announcing Altice's appointment, Governor Pence read from recommendation letters noting Altice's legal and judicial talents, community involvement, likeability and good-heartedness. "That is what this governor is looking for," he said. "Judge Altice's extensive work in the Marion County judicial system and experience presiding over civil and criminal cases make him a uniquely qualified candidate to serve on the Court of Appeals."

On the court, Altice quickly became popular with his new colleagues for those same traits. "In addition to bringing a wealth of knowledge and experience, he has brought a keen legal mind, quick wit and congenial personality to the court," said Judge Terry E. Crone. In his first four years on the court, Altice authored nearly five hundred opinions.

For two decades, Altice has lectured and taught lawyers and judges in seminars and conferences too numerous to list. His community service has included serving on the board of directors of the Benjamin Harrison Presidential Site, the Indianapolis Police Athletic League, the Martin Luther King Community Development Corporation, and Coburn Place Safe Haven, a transitional housing facility for domestic abuse victims. In 2019 the Indiana State Bar Association's Young Lawyers Section presented Altice with its Outstanding Judge Award. "I hope my legacy is that I've been a great mentor for law students and young lawyers," Altice said.

Selected Bibliography

Altice, Robert. Interview with author, May 31, 2019.
Crone, Terry. Interview with author, June 10, 2019.
Massa, Mark. Remarks at Altice Investiture, September 21, 2015.
"RetroIndy: The Hamilton Avenue Slayings of 2006." *Indianapolis Star,* May 30, 2014.
Stafford, Dave. "Altice Selected to Succeed Freidlander." *Indiana Lawyer* (July 17, 2015).
________. "COA Finalists Await Governor's Selection." *Indiana Lawyer* (June 17, 2015).

ELIZABETH F. TAVITAS

August 6, 2018, to present

ANDREA K. McCORD

Evident to all who meet Judge Elizabeth Tavitas is her love of family, the law, her friends, and the University of Notre Dame. Her resolve to be the best at what she does is apparent in all aspects of her life, but her fervor for service is exemplary. She projects excellence, professionalism, civility, and empathy for others in her legal life. Governor Eric J. Holcomb appointed Tavitas to the Court of Appeals of Indiana in 2018, and, at her investiture ceremony, he said she was "the exact right person, at the exact right time, Indiana needs on the Court of Appeals. This statement is attributed to her keen intellect, her steady temperament and the fact that she 'gets' the public service aspect of leadership."

Born Elizabeth Frances Thoman in 1961, she grew up in Mishawaka, Indiana. Tavitas attributes her heart for serving others to her parents who taught her what was important in life—"family, faith, friends and education. They taught us to treat people the way we wanted to be treated." These instilled principles pushed Tavitas to earn her bachelor of arts, cum laude, from the University of Notre Dame in 1985 and her law degree from Notre Dame Law School in 1990; she was admitted to the Indiana Bar that same year. She graduated in 2007 from the Indiana Judicial College, a program created by the Indiana Office of Court Services to promote judicial education and to offer recognition to judicial personnel including state and court judges. In 2012 she graduated from the Indiana Graduate Program for Judges, a program designed for graduates of the Judicial College who continue to serve on the bench.

Prior to her appointment to the court of appeals, Tavitas served for more than twelve years as the presiding judge of the Lake County Superior Court, Civil Division, after her appointment by Governor Mitchell E. Daniels in 2006. Before her judicial service, she served as a deputy prosecutor in the Lake County Prosecutor's Office from 1990 to 1993. She was a juvenile public defender in the Lake Superior Court, Juvenile Division, and maintained a private law practice from 1993 to 1998. In 1998 Tavitas was appointed as a referee in the Lake Superior Court, Juvenile Division, until 2006. During this time, she presided over nearly 1,200 terminations of parental-rights cases.

Tavitas is lauded for her service outside the courtroom, which has included an excess of committee work and volunteer service for the improvement of the legal profession. As a trial court judge, she expanded services for indigent litigants, including facilitation and low-cost mediation for indigent families. She spearheaded the creation of the cooperative family law rules in Lake County to better serve children involved in domestic relations cases. Tavitas has also hosted several seminars to educate lawyers, judges, and court staff throughout the state of Indiana, including training for Guardian ad Litems to represent children in family law matters. These accomplishments demonstrate why many consider Tavitas to be an influential force in protecting the rights of children and a champion in ensuring all Hoosiers have access to justice.

As a trial court judge, Tavitas served on the Juvenile Bench Book Committee from 2001 to 2006, and as a judicial appointee member of the Indiana Pro Bono Commission from 2007 to 2012. She served as a board member of the North West Indiana Volunteer Lawyers Inc. from 2007 to 2018 and was the organization chair from 2007 to 2012. She was elected a board member of the Notre Dame Law School Association in 2010 and continues to serve as an advisory committee member. She served on the Indiana Supreme Court Domestic Relations Committee from 2012 to 2018 and began her service as a member of the Civil Jury Instructions Committee in 2019.

Tavitas has been an active member in numerous national, state, and local bar associations. She has been a volunteer judge for many statewide middle school, high school, and law school competition programs. She is a champion for the advancement of women in the legal profession and the judiciary and was recognized as the Most Influential Woman of Northwest Indiana in the Law in 2015. She is currently an adjunct professor at the Indiana University McKinney School of Law, sharing her knowledge and experience with students.

In her personal life, Tavitas enjoys time with her son, two daughters, and granddaughter. She enjoys travelling, attending Notre Dame football games, the performing arts, art classes, reading, hiking, rowing, and her rescue dogs. Her friends describe her as collegial, loyal, and having a good sense of humor about herself and life.

Selected Bibliography

Holcomb, Eric. Comments at the Investiture of Elizabeth Frances Tavitas, October 1, 2018.

Tavitas, Elizabeth F. Comments at her investiture, October 1, 2018.

LEANNA K. WEISSMANN

September 14, 2020, to present

LINDA C. GUGIN

Leanna Weissmann was on a trajectory toward becoming an appellate court judge for most of her adult life—from her experiences as an undergraduate at Indiana University Bloomington, to her legal education at the IU McKinney School of Law in Indianapolis, and her twenty-year solo practice of law, "Hoosier Appeals," in Lawrenceburg, Indiana. These experiences prepared her for a career in law and shaped her view of the role of courts, and particularly the importance of appeals in assuring justice for every person regardless of economic status.

Weissmann, was born Leanna Kay Rector on October 12, 1969, in Aurora, Indiana, in Dearborn County. She graduated cum laude from Indiana University Bloomington in 1991 with a dual degree in English and journalism. Following graduation, she attended McKinney law school, graduating in 1994 in the top twelve percent of her class. Prior to her graduation she began a two-year clerkship with Judge Robert D. Rucker on the Court of Appeals of Indiana. Rucker said of her appointment that she "had the right temperament and demeanor to be a judge."

After her admission to the Indiana bar, Weissmann handled both civil and criminal cases, with her most significant work in handling appeals. She drafted and filed briefs in more than 400 cases and presented more than twenty arguments before the court of appeals and the Indiana Supreme Court, becoming the first person appointed to the court in roughly twenty years whose background was in private practice.

Weissmann had an outstanding record of successful appeals. In 2018 she participated successfully in petitioning the U.S. Supreme Court to grant certiorari in *Zanders v. Indiana*, a case involving a complex Fourth Amendment issue. Convicted of robbing Whitey's Liquor Store in Dearborn County, Zanders appealed on the grounds that the state had obtained his historical cell phone records without a search warrant in violation of constitutional protections against unreasonable searches and seizures. The Indiana Supreme Court upheld his conviction. Weissmann sought review of the case by the U.S. Supreme Court and the Court ruled that the search of Zanders's historical cell phone records required a warrant based on probable cause. Weissmann said that the case, which began as a small-town robbery, and wound "its way to the top court in the nation made me proud to be part of the justice system."

Weissmann also considers *Tyler v. State* one of her most significant cases. She represented a client accused of child molestation. Although Tyler's conviction was affirmed, the case was still significant because the Indiana Supreme Court made a new application of the "protected person statute." The issue concerned the question of testimony by protected persons, i.e., those under the age of fourteen. State law treats such testimony differently than testimony by adults.

In Tyler's case the prosecution had introduced video testimony by protected persons as well as courtroom testimony. The Indiana Supreme Court determined that allowing the testimony to be presented twice created a "drumbeat effect" that in essence compounded its significance and affected the defendant's right to a fair trial. The Court ruled that the testimony of a protected person could be "presented in open court or by pre-recorded statement but not both." Weissmann said the significance of the case was "due to its long reaching impact on ensuring fair trials in Indiana."

When Governor Eric J. Holcomb appointed Weissmann to the Court of Appeals of Indiana, he said she "is a dedicated practitioner with a deep commitment to her community and all Hoosiers." Indeed, her record off the court demonstrates Weissmann's strong commitment to community, especially causes devoted to young people and disadvantaged citizens. She was a Girl Scout Troop Leader for thirteen years and served as a Big Sister in the Big Brother/Big Sister program. Through a Christian Ministry she created an outreach program for tween girls. Since 2018 she has been an appellate advocate for Indiana's Juvenile Defense Project that works to improve fairness for juveniles facing incarceration. In 2017 the Indiana Bar Foundation named Weissmann a Fellow for her work for the economically disadvantaged. Somehow, she found time to teach four legal classes each semester at Ivy Tech Community College in Lawrenceburg.

Weissmann, a strong proponent of pro bono work, ran a pro bono program through her website that allowed needy participants to apply for legal representation. She did not charge for wills or powers of attorney. Clients who could afford to pay for the legal service were asked to donate any amount of their choosing to a charity in exchange for legal work.

Commenting on her appointment to the court of appeals, Weissmann said "I have a long history with this Court, and I am excited to continue to serve Hoosiers in my new role."

Selected Bibliography

Covington, Olivia. "New COA Judge Weissmann praised for work on and off the Court." *Indiana Lawyer* (September 2, 2020).

Covington, Olivia. "Coming full circle: Weissmann joins COA after years of appellate practice." *Indiana Lawyer* (September 16, 2020).

"Judge Leanna K. Weissmann." Court of Appeals of Indiana (/judiciary/appeals/index.htm).

"Leanna K. Weissmann." Judicial Nominating Commission. Candidate Applications. in.gov/judiciary/jud-qual/363.1 htm.

"Leanna Weissmann Named to Indiana Court of Appeals." IU Robert H. McKinney School of Law, September 3, 2020. mckinneylaw.iu.edu/news/releasees/2020/09.

CASES CITED

Tyler v. State, 903 N.E. 2d 402 (Indiana, 2009).

Marcus Zanders v. Indiana,138 S. Ct. 2702 (2018).

Contributor Biographies

Robert G. Altice Jr. has been a colleague of Judge Terry A. Crone on the Court of Appeals of Indiana since Altice's appointment on September 2, 2015. Altice was a Marion County prosecutor before being elected in 2000 to the Marion County bench, where he served for fifteen years and presided over both criminal and civil dockets. Author of Terry Crone essay.

Lorenzo Arredondo retired in 2010 after more than three decades as judge of the Lake County Circuit Court. He also served as judge of Lake County Court from 1977 to 1980. He received his bachelor's and master's degrees from Indiana University and his JD from the University of San Francisco. The Lake Superior Court building in East Chicago was renamed the Judge Lorenzo Arredondo Justice Center in his honor. His essay of Floyd S. Draper, which appeared in *Justices of the Indiana Supreme Court*, was revised to account for Draper's service on the Appellate Court of Indiana.

L. Mark Bailey, JD, MBA, a judge on the Court of Appeals of Indiana, was appointed by Governor Frank O'Bannon in 1998 after having served as judge of the Decatur County and Decatur Superior Courts. He was retained on the court of appeals in 2000, 2010, and 2020. His writings include "A New Generation for Pro Bono," "Pro Bono Participation Preserves Justice," and "An Invitation to Become Part of the Solution," all published in the *Indiana Lawyer*. He was a member of the Supreme Court Committee on Rules of Practice and Procedure for approximately twelve years and is an adjunct professor at the University of Indianapolis. Author of Frank E. Gavin essay.

John G. Baker, a judge of the Court of Appeals of Indiana since 1989, retired on July 31, 2020; he served as chief judge of the court of appeals from 2007 to 2010. He is the author of "Now or Never: Reforming Indiana's Court System," *Indiana Law Review* (2008); "Indiana Judge: A Portrait of Judicial Evolution," *The History of Indiana Law* (2008); and "The History of the Indiana Trial Court System and Attempts at Renovation," *Indiana Law Review* (1997). He was a contributing author to *Justices of the Indiana Supreme Court* and *Indiana's 200: The People Who Shaped the Hoosier State*. Author of Jonathan J. Robertson essay.

Douglas B. Bates is a partner with the law firm of Stites & Harbison PLLC, currently serving as office executive member for the firm's Jeffersonville, Indiana, office. He has been practicing since 1992 and handles litigation matters throughout Indiana and Kentucky. Author of Joseph O. Carson essay.

Mark A. Bates, JD, is an attorney in private practice in Schererville, Indiana. He is a former law clerk (1981–84) and assistant administrator (1984–91) for the Indiana Supreme Court. In addition to his private practice, he is supervisor of the Lake County Public Defender Office, Appellate Division. Author of William G. Conover and Eugene N. Chipman essays.

Jennifer A. Bauer is a staff attorney with the Indiana Office of Court Services. She is a former Lawrence County deputy prosecutor and former law clerk to Judge Linda L. Chezem (1992–1994). Author of Chezem essay.

Suzanne S. Bellamy, JD, is a researcher and writer. She is the author of *Hoosier Justice at Nuremberg* (2010), a former editorial assistant of the Papers of Lew and Susan Wallace, and served as assistant general counsel of Anacomp Inc. Contributing author to *Justices of the Indiana Supreme Court* and *Indiana's 200: The People Who Shaped the Hoosier State*. Author of Alonzo L. Nichols essay.

Ray E. Boomhower is senior editor, Indiana Historical Society Press, and editor of *Traces of Indiana and Midwestern History*. He is the author of numerous books of Indiana history and biography, including *Robert F. Kennedy and the 1968 Indiana Primary* (2008) and *John Bartlow Martin: A Voice for the Underdog* (2015). His articles have appeared in *Traces* and the *Indiana Magazine of History*. Contributing author to *Indiana's 200: The People Who Shaped the Hoosier State, Justices of the Indiana Supreme Court*, and *The Governors of Indiana*. Author of Robert D. Rucker essay.

Bradley S. Boswell is an associate attorney at Faegre Baker Daniels LLP in Indianapolis. He is a 2010 graduate of Indiana University in Bloomington, a 2019 graduate of the IU Robert H. McKinney School of Law, and a native Hoosier proudly raised in Scott County. Author of George H. Prime and Joseph H. Shea essays.

Nancy E. Boyer became the first female judge in Allen County when she was appointed judge of the Allen Superior Court Civil Division in 1991, a position she still holds. She served with Judge Paul D. Mathias from 1991 until his appointment to the Court of Appeals of Indiana. Judge Boyer currently oversees the Allen County Mortgage Foreclosure Trial Court Assistance Project, which helps homeowners keep their homes. She is also on the state's Civil Instructions Committee, which rewrote civil instructions for juries. In 2017 Judge Boyer was recognized by the *Indiana Lawyer's* Leadership in the Law project. Author of Mathias essay.

C. Addison Bradford is an attorney at Hall, Render, Killian, Heath and Layman in Indianapolis, and son of Judge Cale J. Bradford. Author of Bradford essay.

Cale J. Bradford is a judge of the Court of Appeals of Indiana, representing the second district. Upon joining the court, Judge Bradford filled the seat left vacant by Judge Patrick D. Sullivan's retirement. Author of Sullivan essay.

Elaine B. Brown was appointed to the Court of Appeals of Indiana in May 2008 by Governor Mitchell E. Daniels and retained in office in 2010 by statewide vote. She served as judge of the Dubois Superior Court in Jasper, Indiana, for more than fifteen years and practiced law for eleven years prior to her appointment. She graduated from Indiana University Maurer School of Law and serves on its alumni board and as an adjunct professor. Author of John S. Gonas essay.

Amanda J. Bunton graduated magna cum laude from Indiana University McKinney School of Law in 2000 and has served as Judge Nancy H. Vaidik's judicial clerk since 2002. Although she may be biased, Bunton cannot imagine working for a better judge. Author of Vaidik essay.

Scott M. Bushnell, who died in 2017, was a writer and editor for the Associated Press and author of five books about Indiana history. He wrote essays for *Justices of the Indiana Supreme Court* and *Indiana's 200: The People Who Shaped the Hoosier State*. His essay on Justice Dan C. Flanagan was revised to account for his service on the Appellate Court of Indiana.

Dennis D. Carroll, Judge Rudolph R. Pyle III's former trial court colleague and longtime friend, served for thirty-five years as the presiding judge of Madison County Circuit Court, Division 6, where Judge Pyle served as deputy prosecutor prior to his appointment to the trial court bench. Carroll is now a senior judge for the Madison Circuit Court. Author of Pyle essay.

Heather Kirkham Coy teaches English, public speaking, and debate in the Randall T. Shepard Leadership and Law Academy, a four-year integrated studies program in leadership, law, and social justice housed at William Henry Harrison High School in Evansville, Indiana. She is also a dual credit instructor and adjunct composition instructor for the University of Southern Indiana. Author of French Clements essay.

Terry A. Crone was raised in South Bend and is a graduate of DePauw University and the University of Notre Dame Law School. He was elected to three terms as judge of the Saint Joseph Circuit Court. He was appointed to the Court of Appeals of Indiana in 2004 by Governor Joseph E. Kernan. Author of Michael P. Barnes essay.

Michael J. DeBoer is associate professor of law, Faulkner University, Thomas Goode Jones School of Law. He served as a law clerk to U.S. District Judge Theresa L. Springmann, 2000 to 2003 and 2008 to 2011, and to Justice Brent E. Dickson, 1998 to 2000. Author of "Justice Brent E. Dickson, State Constitutional Interpretation, and the Religion Provisions of the Indiana Constitution," *Indiana Law Review* (2016), and "Equality as a Fundamental Value in the Indiana Constitution," *Valparaiso University Law Review* (2004). Contributing author to *Justices of the Indiana Supreme Court*. Author of Huber W. DeVoss and Francis M. Thompson essays.

Jeffery A. Duvall is a research associate at Indiana University–Purdue University at Indianapolis's Institute for American Thought and assistant editor of the Frederick Douglass Papers. He holds a PhD in history from Purdue University. Contributing author to *The Governors of Indiana* and *Indiana's 200: The People Who Shaped the Hoosier State*. Author of John W. Pfaff and Andrew A. Adams essays.

Sarah M. Frank died in 2012. She earned her JD from Indiana University in 1977 and practiced family law in Indianapolis. She was also an adjunct faculty member, Department of Mathematics, Indiana University–Purdue University at Indianapolis. Her essay on Justice Donald H. Hunter, published in *Justices of the Indiana Supreme Court*, was revised in part to account for his time on the Appellate Court of Indiana.

Trevor Foughty is associate vice president of state relations for Indiana University. He formerly served as campaign manager for Todd Young, who was elected to the U.S. Senate in 2016. Previously, Foughty was deputy chief of staff and communications director for Young's U.S. House of Representatives office. Before that, Foughty worked in communications for the Indiana Republican Party and the political action committee of then-governor Mitchell E. Daniels. Author of Fred A. Wiecking essay.

A. James Fuller, professor of history, University of Indianapolis, has published seven books, including *Oliver P. Morton and the Politics of the Civil War and Reconstruction* (2017) and is completing "Morton, Marshall, McNutt, and Mitch: Four Governors Who Shaped Indiana and the Midwest." Contributing author to *Indiana's 200: The People Who Shaped the Hoosier State*. Author of Charles H. Bedwell, William H. Bridwell, James J. Moran, and Joseph M. Raab essays.

George W. Geib is professor emeritus of history at Butler University. His books include *Indianapolis: Hoosiers' Circle City* (1981); *Lives Touched by Faith: Second Presbyterian Church, 150 Years* (1987); *Indianapolis First: The Centennial History of the Indianapolis Chamber of Commerce* (1990; Miriam K. Geib, coauthor); and *Federal Justice in Indiana: The History of the United States District Court for the Southern District of Indiana* (2007; Donald B. Kite Sr., coauthor). Geib was awarded the Doctor John Morton Finney Award for Excellence in Legal Education by the Indianapolis Bar Association in 2007. Contributing author to *Justices of the Indiana Supreme Court* and *Indiana's 200: The People Who Shaped the Hoosier State*. Author of Paul E. Laymon essay.

Michelle C. Goodman is a staff attorney at the Indiana Office of Court Services. She was an Indiana Conference for Legal Education Opportunity Fellow 1998 and graduate of the Indiana State Bar Association Leadership Development Academy Class IV. Author of Ralph N. Smith and Russell W. Smith essays.

Linda C. Gugin, PhD, is professor emeritus of political science at Indiana University Southeast. She is coauthor of *Sherman Minton: New Deal Senator, Cold War Justice* (1997) and *Chief Justice Fred M. Vinson: A Political Biography* (2002), as well as coeditor of *The Governors of Indiana* (2006), *Justices of the Indiana Supreme Court* (2010), and *Indiana's 200: The People Who Shaped the Hoosier State* (2015). Gugin is also the author of "Sherman Minton: Restraint against a Tide of Activism," *Vanderbilt Law Review* (2009). Author of John C. McNutt, Posey T. Kime, and Leanna K. Weissmann essays.

William F. Gulde is a retired history teacher at North Central High School in Indianapolis and author of *Irvington in 1910: A Year in the Life of an Indianapolis Neighborhood* (2019) and *Of Hopes, Dreams and Books: The Story of North Central High School 1956–2004* (2004). Contributing author to *Justices of the Indiana Supreme Court* and

Indiana's 200: The People Who Shaped the Hoosier State. Author of William J. Henley Sr., Hubert E. Wickens, Edgar D. Crumpacker, and Harry L. Crumpacker essays.

Roger Hardig, vice president of education for the Benjamin Harrison Presidential Site, is responsible for scope and dissemination of educational services for more than 18,000 school-aged students every year. Author of James B. Black essay.

Susan D. Hinkle is a staff attorney at the Court of Appeals of Indiana. She earned a JD from Indiana University School of Law in Indianapolis and an undergraduate degree at Butler University. Coauthor of the essay on Betty S. Barteau.

Libbe K. Hughes is a local history researcher, writer, and lecturer residing in Hendricks County, Indiana. Contributing author to *Justices of the Indiana Supreme Court* and *Indiana's 200, The People Who Shaped the Hoosier State*. Author of Solon A. Enloe essay.

Richard E. Humphrey is research and instructional services librarian, Ruth Lilly Law Library, Indiana University Robert H. McKinney School of Law, Indianapolis. He is the coauthor of "Biographical Sketches of Indiana Supreme Court Justices," *Indiana Law Review* (1997), and he is the author of *Indiana Practice Materials: A Selective Annotated Bibliography.* Contributing author to *Justices of the Indiana Supreme Court*. Author of Harvey J. Curtis and Frank S. Roby essays.

Brian Karle is an attorney in Indiana, practicing primarily in the areas of civil litigation, personal injury, business and corporate, and appellate. He earned a bachelor's in economics from Purdue University in 2010 and a JD, summa cum laude, from Indiana University Robert H. McKinney School of Law in 2013. He is also an adjunct instructor at Purdue University. He completed a two-year judicial clerkship with Judge Margret G. Robb of the Court of Appeals of Indiana. Author of Robb essay.

John L. Kellam is a retired trial court judge. He has been a consultant to the Indiana Supreme Court, a member of the Indiana Supreme Court Commission on Race and Gender, the CMS Governing Board of the Indiana Supreme Court, the Indiana Supreme Court Judicial Technology and Automation Committee, and past president of the Indiana Judges Association. He is the author of "The Indiana Judicial System: An Analysis of Change," *Indiana Law Review* (1988). Author of Wesley W. Ratliff Jr., essay.

Dina M. Kellams is an associate archivist, Indiana University Office of University Archives and Records Management. Contributing author to *Indiana's 200: The People Who Shaped the Hoosier State*. Author of G. Remy Bierly essay.

Krista Kinslow obtained her PhD in history at Boston University in 2019. She is currently working on the first comprehensive history of the 1876 Centennial Exhibition. Author of Frederick W. Caldwell, Milton B. Hottel, and Joseph G. Ibach essays.

James S. Kirsch has served as judge of the Marion Superior Court from 1988 to 1994 and judge of the Court of Appeals of Indiana since March 1994. He graduated cum laude from Indiana University School of Law at Indianapolis, now the McKinney School of Law, in 1974 and with honors from Butler University in 1968. He practiced law with the firm of Kroger, Gardis & Regas from 1974 to 1988 and was managing partner of the firm. Since 1990 he has held an appointment as visiting professor of law and management at the Krannert Graduate School of Management at Purdue University and has taught law in thirty countries and on five continents. He is a past president of the Indianapolis Bar Association and the Indianapolis Bar Foundation and is a Fellow of the Indiana State Bar Foundation and of the Indianapolis Bar Foundation. Author of Paul H. Buchannan Jr. essay.

Donald B. Kite Sr. is an Indianapolis attorney. He is the author of several biographical sketches that were included in *Indiana's 200: The People Who Shaped the Hoosier State* and *Justices of the Indiana Supreme Court*, and was coauthor of *Federal Justice in Indiana: The History of the United States District Court for the Southern District of Indiana* (2007). He was the recipient of the Defense Trial Counsel of Indiana's Defense Lawyer of the Year Award (2005). Author of Daniel W. Comstock, Orlando J. Lotz, Ira C. Batman, Ulric Z. Wiley, Ethan A. Dausman, Willis C. McMahan, and Donald W. Bowen essays.

Carl E. Kramer is vice president of Kramer Associates Inc., a historical consulting firm in Jeffersonville, Indiana, and a retired adjunct assistant professor of history at Indiana University Southeast. He is the author of thirteen books and many articles, most related to the history of the Louisville metropolitan area. His book, *This Place We Call Home: A History of Clark County, Indiana*, was published by Indiana University Press in 2007. He earned his PhD in American history from the University of Toledo. Contributing author to *The Governors of Indiana* and *Indiana's 200: The People Who Shaped the Hoosier State*. Author of A. Jewell Stevenson and Ward H. Watson essays.

Jason S. Lantzer is a historian interested in the intersection of religion, politics, and law in American society and culture. A native Hoosier, he holds three degrees from Indiana University. He is the author of seven books and numerous articles and book chapters and contributing author to *The Governors of Indiana* and *Indiana's 200: The People Who Shaped the Hoosier State*. He serves as the assistant director of the University Honors Program at Butler University. Author of Alphonso C. Wood essay.

John R. Leal, JD, is an attorney. He is the author of "Five Questions," an article on the end-of-life directives. He was a contributing author to *Justices of the Indiana Supreme Court*. He is past president of the Fort Wayne Estate Planning Council. Author of Harold E. Achor essay.

Doria Lynch is the special projects manager at the U.S. District Court for the Southern District of Indiana. She also serves as the court's historian and oversees the court's educational outreach efforts. She holds a master's in public history from Indiana University and was a contributing author to *Indiana's 200: The People Who Shaped the*

Hoosier State and *Justices of the Indiana Supreme Court*. Author of Vivian Sue Shields and Frank Hamilton essays.

Shelly K. McBride, JD, graduated from Mauer School of Law at Indiana University in Bloomington in 2000. She began her legal career as a deputy prosecutor in the Monroe County prosecutor's office in Bloomington. In 2010 she began work as an attorney for the Indiana Department of Child Services in Daviess County. In 2011 she opened her solo law practice in Washington, Indiana. She is the proud mother of Matthew, Nicholas, and Jesse. Author of Francis L. Wiltrout essay.

Andrea McCord is the bankruptcy judge in the Southern District of the U.S. Seventh Circuit Court of Appeals. Previously, she was Lawrence County Circuit Judge from 2007 to 2019. McCord is a graduate of the Indiana Judicial College and past chair of the Improvements to the Judiciary Committee for the Indiana Bar Association. A graduate of Franklin College, she earned her law degree from the Indiana University McKinney School of Law in 1990. Author of Elizabeth F. Tavitas essay.

Julie C. S. McDonald served as a law clerk to Randall T. Shepard, Chief Justice of Indiana. She also was an adjunct professor of legal writing at the Indiana University Robert H. McKinney School of Law, a litigation and appellate associate at Barnes & Thornburg, and judicial educator, research attorney, and deputy director at the Indiana Office of Court Services. She earned her bachelor's degree from the College of William and Mary and her JD cum laude from the Maurer School of Law at Indiana University. Author of Thomas J. Faulconer, Noel C. Neal, and Woodfin D. Robinson essays.

James H. Madison is the Thomas and Kathryn Miller professor emeritus of history at Indiana University Bloomington. He is the author of *Indiana through Tradition and Change* (1982); *The Indiana Way: A State History* (1986); *Eli Lilly: A Life, 1885–1977* (1989); *Wendell Willkie: Hoosier Internationalist* (1992); *A Lynching in the Heartland: Race and Memory in America* (2001); and *Hoosiers: A New History of Indiana* (2014). He has won numerous awards for distinguished teaching. Contributing author to *Indiana's 200: The People Who Shaped the Hoosier State*. Author of Edward W. Najam Jr. essay.

Mark S. Massa was named to the Indiana Supreme Court in 2012 by Governor Mitchell E. Daniels. Massa is a former state and federal prosecutor, law clerk to Chief Justice Randall T. Shepard, and general counsel to Governor Daniels. Before starting law school, he was an award-winning newspaper reporter for the *Evansville Press* in the early 1980s. Author of John M. Ryan essay.

Paul D. Mathias is honored to have succeeded William I. Garrard as a judge of the Court of Appeals of Indiana on March 30, 2000. Mathias was reelected to the court in 2002 and 2012. He was an attorney from 1979 to 1985 and has been a judicial officer since 1985 when he was appointed Small Claims Referee in Allen County. Author of Garrard essay.

Mary Mellon is the assistant archivist at the Indiana University Libraries University Archives, where she manages archival processing and digital projects. She has master's degrees in information science and history from the University of North Carolina at Chapel Hill. Author of Theodore P. Davis essay.

Joseph H. Merrick is a staff attorney at the Court of Appeals of Indiana. He earned a JD at the Indiana University Maurer School of Law and a bachelor's at Indiana University. He lives in Indianapolis with his wife. Coauthor of the Betty S. Barteau essay.

Larry L. Morris earned a bachelor's from Lincoln Christian University, a master's from the University of Illinois–Springfield, and a JD from the Indiana University Robert H. McKinney School of Law. He served for twenty-two years (1993 to 2015) as senior law clerk in the chambers of the Judge Ezra H. Friedlander of the Court of Appeals of Indiana. In 2015 he became court administrator for the court of appeals. Author of Friedlander essay.

Donald J. "D. J." Mote is judge of the Jefferson Circuit Court. He served as the Jefferson County chief deputy prosecutor from 2007 until his election to the bench in 2018. Judge Mote also served as a deputy prosecutor in Marion County beginning in 2000 until moving to Jefferson County and was a staff attorney at the Indiana Supreme Court Disciplinary Commission from 1998 to 2000. He is the grandson of Judge Donald R. Mote. Judge Mote and his wife Katie live in Madison, Indiana, with their daughter Hunter and son James. Author of Donald R. Mote essay.

Edward W. Najam Jr. JD is a judge of the Court of Appeals of Indiana. He was an attorney in private practice before he joined the Court in December 1992. Najam is the author of "Merit Selection in Indiana: The Foundation for a Fair and Impartial Appellate Judiciary," published in the *Indiana Law Review* (2013). Author of John T. Sharpnack essay.

Elizabeth R. Osborn is the coordinator for court history and civic education and is responsible for the educational outreach programs of the Indiana Supreme Court, including the Indiana Supreme Court Legal History Series and Courts in the Classroom. She is the author of numerous publications about the history and operation of Indiana's courts and a contributor to the *History of Indiana Law* (2008). Contributing author to *Justices of the Indiana Supreme Court* and *Indiana's 200: The People Who Shaped the Hoosier State*. Author of Dewey E. Kelley essay.

Inge V. Porter, a native of Belgium, is an attorney licensed in Europe, where she practiced International Maritime Law in her hometown of Antwerp after pursuing a master of laws in international law from the University of Nottingham in the United Kingdom. She was admitted to the Indiana bar after relocating to the United States. She is the senior law clerk to Judge Patricia A. Riley and has worked in her chambers since 2003. Author of Riley essay.

Ruth D. Reichard is education attorney for the Indiana Office of Court Services. She earned a Ph.D. in history from Indiana University Bloomington. She graduated with honors from Ball State University in 1982 and earned her JD from the Indiana University School of Law in Indianapolis in 1985. A former deputy prosecutor and criminal court judge, she worked as a staff attorney at the Indiana Supreme Court Division of State Court Administration. She is the author of *Blood and Steel: Ryan White, the AIDS Crisis and Deindustrialization in Kokomo, Indiana* (McFarland, 2021). Contributing author to *Indiana's 200: The People Who Shaped the Hoosier State*. Author of Stanley B. Miller essay.

David J. Remondini is a flight instructor, attorney, civil mediator, news consultant, mortgage foreclosure arbitrator for five Marion County civil courts and a part time administrative law judge for the Indiana Department of Workforce Development. He is an adjunct professor at Butler University and has taught courses in poverty law and access to justice and community mediation. Contributing author to *Justices of the Indiana Supreme Court*. Author of Paul F. Dowell, Robert B. Lybrook, Milton S. Robinson, Wilbur A. Royse, and George L. Reinhard essays.

Julian L. Ridlen, who died in 2017, was elected to two terms as judge of the Cass Circuit Court and served as senior judge for ten years until his retirement in 2016. He received his JD degree from the George Washington University Law School and was elected treasurer of Indiana in 1978 and 1982. He also served as chairman of the Indiana Housing Finance Authority. Author of Moses B. Lairy essay.

Margret G. Robb is the first female Chief Judge of the Court of Appeals of Indiana (2011–13) in its 110-year history. Recipient of Indiana University Robert H. McKinney School of law Distinguished Alumni Award, member of American Bar Association Law School Accreditation Committee, and president of Council of Chief Judges of State Courts of Appeal. Contributing author to *Justices of the Indiana Supreme Court*. Author of Robert H. Staton essay.

David A. Root, PhD, JD, LLM, is an assistant professor of political science and prelaw adviser at the University of Indianapolis. He is the author of "Chief Justice Leadership: A Brief Sketch of its Landscape, Structure, and Operation" (2018). Author of Edgar M. Blessing and George B. Hoffman Jr. essays.

Crystal G. Rowe, JD, is a Senior Partner at Kightlinger & Gray, LLP, practicing in the firm's New Albany, Indiana, office. She dedicates her practice of law primarily to appellate matters. Rowe had the great privilege of clerking for Judge L. Mark Bailey from 2003 to 2006 and has benefited greatly from his outstanding mentorship. Author of Bailey essay.

James E. St. Clair is professor emeritus of journalism at Indiana University Southeast. He is coauthor of *Sherman Minton: New Deal Senator, Cold War Justice* (1997) and *Chief Justice Fred M. Vinson: A Political Biography* (2002). He is also coeditor of *The Gov-*

ernors of Indiana (2006), *Justices of the Indiana Supreme Court* (2010), and *Indiana's 200: The People Who Shaped the Hoosier State* (2015). Author of Henry Clay Fox, Warren W. Martin, and Frank M. Powers essays.

Ryan T. Schwier is a law clerk for Christopher M. Goff, Associate Justice of the Indiana Supreme Court. Schwier previously served as a law clerk for Mark S. Massa, Associate Justice of the Indiana Supreme Court. After completing his bachelor's in history and political science in 2001 at Indiana University, Bloomington, Schwier earned a master of library science degree in 2004 and a master of arts in public history in 2011, both from Indiana University–Purdue University at Indianapolis. He is a graduate of the Indiana University Robert H. McKinney School of Law (JD, 2016), where he served as executive editorial director of the *Indiana International and Comparative Law Review* (vol. 25). Author of James C. Cooper, Jeptha D. New, and Willard New essays.

Greta Morris Scodro, JD, worked for the Indiana Supreme Court from 1989 until 2016 as a law clerk, staff attorney in the Court's administration office, and for some twenty years as its deputy administrator. Contributing author to *Justices of the Indiana Supreme Court*. Author of Cassius C. Hadley essay.

Jane A. Seigel, JD, is the retired executive director of the Indiana Office of Court Services. Currently she is serving as a consultant to the Indiana Supreme Court on Race, Equity, and Inclusion initiatives. She is grateful to Jenny Kidwell for her research support. Author of Charles F. Remy essay.

Andrew P. Seiwert is a graduate of Purdue University and the Indiana University Robert H. McKinney School of Law in Indianapolis, and a former corporation counsel of the city of Indianapolis and Marion County. The author was a law clerk to Judge Robert W. Neal from 1986 to 1988 and drew upon his personal reminiscences of the judge in preparing his essay on Neal.

Randall T. Shepard served as Chief Justice of the Indiana Supreme Court for twenty-five years, longer than anyone else in the state's history. He is the former president of the Conference of Chief Justices and has taught periodically at Indiana University, Yale Law School, and the University of Notre Dame. He is the author of "Jesse W. Weik, the Young Indiana Lawyer Who Made Herndon's Lincoln Possible," *Indiana Magazine of History* (2009), coauthor with David Bodenhamer of *The History of Indiana Law* (2006), and coauthor with him of the book's lead essay. He contributed essays for *The Governors of Indiana, The Justices of the Indiana Supreme Court*, and *Indiana's 200: The People Who Shaped the Hosier State*. Author of John G. Baker and Elmer Q. Lockyear essays.

Geoffrey G. Slaughter, the 109th Justice of the Indiana Supreme Court, was a law clerk to Judge Allen Sharp from 1989 to 1991. Slaughter, a native of Lake County, Indiana, received his BA, MBA, and JD from Indiana University in Bloomington. Before his appointment to the Supreme Court by Governor Mike R. Pence, he practiced law in Chicago and Indianapolis and served as special counsel to the attorney general of Indiana. Like his former mentor, Slaughter follows the Chicago Cubs, IU football, and generally "is a patron of lost athletic causes." Author of Sharp essay.

Timothy P. Spahr, JD, is Judge of the Miami Circuit Court in Peru, Indiana. Coincidentally, he first learned about Judge George E. Ross, the subject of his essay, while vacationing in La Jolla, California, on the anniversary of Ross's death there. Author of Ross essay.

Carrie Stiller graduated from the Brandeis School of Law at the University of Louisville in 1999 with her JD, cum laude. She graduated from Indiana University Southeast with a bachelor's in political science, magna cum laude. She has practiced law in Floyd County and surrounding counties for twenty years with her primary area of practice in family law. She is also a certified law mediator. In 2020 she was elected judge of the Floyd Superior Court. Author of Charles W. Cook essay.

Frank Sullivan Jr. is Professor of Practice and Indiana University Bicentennial Professor at the Robert H. McKinney School of Law. He was a Justice of the Indiana Supreme Court from 1993 to 2012. Contributing author to *Justices of the Indiana Supreme Court*. Author of Charles F. White and James D. Young essays.

Ali A. Talib has been a practicing attorney in Indiana since 1980 engaging in the general practice of law. Talib first met Judge Carr L. Darden in 1979 while serving as a law clerk in the State Public Defenders Office, where Judge Darden was Deputy Public Defender. Talib later joined Darden as a partner in the private practice of law. Following Judge Darden's appointment to the Marion Superior Court, Talib served as appellate counsel in the Marion Superior Court, Criminal Division, on the recommendation of Judge Darden. Author of Darden essay.

Scott L. Tyler is a partner with Waters, Tyler, Hofmann & Scott, LLC in New Albany, Indiana. He is a 1991 graduate of Indiana University Mauer School of Law and has been in private practice since 1991 with a focus on civil trial work in Indiana and Kentucky. Author of Joe W. Lowdermilk essay.

Nancy Harris Vaidik has been a judge on the Court of Appeals of Indiana since 2000. She served as the Chief Judge of the Court from 2014 to 2019. She is a native of Portage, Indiana, and was a Superior Court Judge in Porter County before joining the Court of Appeals. Author of Elaine B. Brown and Sanford M. Brook essays.

John Vargo graduated from Indiana University School of Law cum laude and was a professor of law at the IU Law School. From 1976 to 1979 he also taught at Bond University Law School and Deakin University Law School, both in Australia. He is the lead author and editor in chief of Matthew Bender's seven-volume treatise *Products Liability Practice Guide* (2008) and is the author of more than forty articles and book chapters. He has been in the private practice of law for more than forty-five years. Coauthor of James S. Kirsch essay.

Janet Vargo graduated with distinction from Indiana University–Purdue University at Indianapolis with a bachelor's degree and Indiana University Robert H. McKinney School of Law with a JD in May 1985. She was in practice with her husband at Vargo and Vargo PC until 1990. From 1991 to 1995 she taught at Bond University and Deakin University Law School, both in Australia. Currently she is editor of the Indiana Trial Lawyers quarterly journal *Verdict*. Coauthor of James S. Kirsch essay.

Jennifer D. Warriner received a PhD in experimental psychology in 1999 and a JD in 2000, both from Indiana University in Bloomington. She was admitted to the Indiana bar in the fall of 2000. Since August of 2000 Warriner has been a judicial clerk at the Court of Appeals of Indiana and, for the past seventeen years, she has served in the chambers of the Honorable Melissa S. May. Author of May essay.

Thomas E. Wheeler II, JD, is a member of Frost Brown Todd LLC, where he practices with the government services group. He is a former Assistant Attorney General for Civil Rights at the U.S. Department of Justice and a former senior adviser to the U.S. Secretary of Education. He has represented Indiana governors Mitchell E. Daniels and Mike Pence. Contributing author to *Justices of the Indiana Supreme Court*. Author of William F. Dudine and Walter Myers Jr. essays.

James R. Williams is a partner at DeFur Voran, LLP in Muncie, Indiana. He formerly served as Judge of the Union County Circuit Court in Liberty, Indiana, from 1998 to 2004 and as Senior Judge until 2008. Contributing author to *Justices of the Indiana Supreme Court*. Author of John R. Ax, John A. Kendall, and David A. Myers essays.

Index